The Ultimate Guide to Exam Success

UniAdmissions

Published by *RAR Medical Services Limited*
www.uniadmissions.co.uk
info@uniadmissions.co.uk
Tel: 0208 068 0438

The information offered in this book is purely advisory and any advice given should be taken within this context. As such, the publishers and authors accept no liability whatsoever for the outcome of any applicant's exam performance, the outcome of any university applications or for any other loss. Although every precaution has been taken in the preparation of this book, the publisher and author assume no responsibility for errors or omissions of any kind. Neither is any liability assumed for damages resulting from the use of information contained herein. This does not affect your statutory rights.

The suggestions, tools, techniques and opinions described within this publication have all yielded positive results for the author in terms of improving exam performance, reducing stress and achieving 'Exam Success' as defined in the introduction of this publication. The author does not in any way state that the suggestions, tools, techniques and opinions described within this publication are the only way to improve exam performance, reduce stress or achieve 'Exam Success'.

The author and publisher give no guarantee of 'Exam Success', improved exam performance or reduction in stress levels for any reader(s) or any other persons. The author and publisher will not be held responsible for any detrimental effects, if any, that this book has on its reader(s) or other persons. In particular, the author and publisher will not be held responsible for any detrimental effects caused by changes in physical activity and movement habits (Principle 5, Appendix 3), changes in diet and hydration (Principle 6), or changes in sleeping habits (Principle 7) based on the content of this publication.

Every scientific fact, study or research paper referenced by the author has been made accurately and without bias, to the best of the author's knowledge and understanding. The author and publisher will not be held responsible for any mistakes made in this publication.

The Ultimate Guide to Exam Success

Kam Taj

Edited by Dr Rohan Agarwal

UniAdmissions

About the Author

Kam Taj is a performance coach, speaker and author. He graduated from University of Cambridge with an Undergraduate and Master's degree in the Manufacturing Engineering Tripos (2011-2015).

During his studies, he consulted for various engineering firms, taught English at a school in China and started his own small-scale life coaching and fitness business. After graduation, he worked as a management consultant at Roland Berger until July 2016, following which he left to start his own personal & professional development company.

Since 2016, Kam has worked with top UK schools and universities to empower students with the tools to manage their mental well-being and optimise their performance. He has also delivered talks and workshops on stress management, resilience and performance optimisation at multinational accounting (Moore Stephens), engineering (Mace) and law firms (Slaughter & May).

When he's not working, Kam can be found on tennis courts, basketball courts or training on his gymnastic rings. He has backpacked around China, South America and South-East Asia. Kam's intention with this book is to empower students to get the best out of themselves, while dealing with the worst of themselves – just as he had to do when he was younger.

About the Editor

Rohan is the **Director of Operations** at *UniAdmissions* and is responsible for its technical and commercial arms. He graduated from Gonville and Caius College, Cambridge and is a fully qualified doctor. Over the last five years, he has tutored hundreds of successful Oxbridge and Medical applicants. He has also authored thirty books on admissions tests and interviews.

Rohan has taught physiology to undergraduates and interviewed medical school applicants for Cambridge. He has published research on bone physiology and writes education articles for the Independent and Huffington Post. In his spare time, Rohan enjoys playing the piano and table tennis.

Introduction   **8**

1. Principle One: Time-Management   **13**

1.1 Overcoming Procrastination   13
1.2 Increasing Productivity   17
1.3 Effective Prioritisation   25
1.4 Effective Planning   31

2. Principle Two: Study Tools & Techniques   **43**

2.1 How To Study: Mastering Study Tools & Techniques   43
2.2 Where You Study: Creating The Perfect Study Environment   59
2.3 When You Study: Finding The Perfect Study Time   64

3. Principle Three: Mind-Management   **67**

3.1 Problem Area 1: Anxiety   67
3.2 Problem Area 2: Outer & Inner Pressures   68
3.3 Problem Area 3: Low Confidence & Self-Doubt   75
3.4 Problem Area 4: Low Motivation   77

3.5 Tool 1: 'RUDMA' Framework   80
3.6 Tool 2: Owning Our Stress Response   85
3.7 Tool 3: The Motivational Fire Formula   93
3.8 Tool 4: Progress & Quick-Win Tracking   104
3.9 Tool 5: Self-Dialogue Transformation   107
3.10 Tool 6: The Path Of Least Regret   111
3.11 Tool 7: Mindfulness Practices   114
3.12 Tool 8: Visualisations & Affirmations   118

4. Principle Four: On-The-Day Performance   **122**

4.1 The Night Before   122
4.2 The Morning Of The Exam   122
4.3 The Exam   124
4.4 The Aftermath   126

5. Principle Five: Movement & Physical Activity   **129**

    5.1 The Importance of Movement & Physical Activity   129

    5.2 Integrating Movement Into Your Lifestyle   130

    5.3 Kam's 'Efficient Study Training' Routines   131

6. Principle Six: Nutrition & Hydration   **134**

    6.1 Nutrition   134

    6.2 Hydration   139

7. Principle Seven: Sleep   **141**

    7.1 Benefits of Sleep   141

    7.2 Factors Affecting Sleep Quality   141

    7.2 Techniques for Falling Asleep   144

    7.3 The Power of Napping   147

8. Principle Eight: Support Group   **149**

    8.1 Academic Support Group   149

    8.2 Mental & Emotional (ME) Support Group   154

9. Final Words   **165**

10. About Kam: My Story   **166**

    Part 1 – Afraid and Insecure   167

    Part 2 – The Path To 'Owning' Myself   168

    Part 3 – The Cambridge Struggles   171

    Part 4 – The Consulting Chronicles   178

    Part 5 – My Motivation As A Coach   179

11. Appendices
11. Appendices   **182**

Appendix 1: List Of All Activities Outlined In The Book   182

Appendix 2: Motivational Fire - The Intention Sheet   186

Appendix 3: Kam's 'Efficient Study Training' Circuit   189

Appendix 4: Glycaemic Load of Common Foods   194

References   **198**

Acknowledgements   **204**

Your Free Book   **205**

BMAT Online Course   **206**

Medical Interview Course   **207**

UKCAT Online Course   **208**

TSA Online Course   **209**

NSAA Online Course   **210**

ECAA Online Course   **211**

ENGAA Online Course   **212**

LNAT Online Course   **213**

Introduction

Welcome to The Ultimate Guide to Exam Success!

Exam Success means performing at your *optimum* level to give yourself the best chance of achieving your *ideal grades,* in the *least stressful* way possible.

"Wait a minute – why are our grades even important?"

Some time ago it was decided that *standardised exams* would be used as the primary tool to measure *how well* we have learned the content that we are taught in school. This *grade* would then be used as an indicator of our intelligence, employability and future potential.

But the world has changed *significantly* since those times. Innovative, new developments in technology, business, science, art and various other fields have transformed how we learn, communicate and live on a day-to-day basis.

Which begs the question: *why hasn't the education system changed?*

It's a great question. One that I could write a book about...

But not *this* book.

What we need to remember is that, at this moment in time, we're being raised in a society where our exam grades still *matter* – whether we like it or not!

They influence the subjects we can pursue, the university we attend, and, to a large extent, the job options available to us. Simply put, achieving good grades helps us to build a *strong foundation* for our future, allowing us to pursue the career that we want, attain a good level of financially security, and provide for our family.

That's the theory behind it, anyway. But I'm not quite convinced.

I'll be honest here – in my opinion, the current system is completely *flawed* given the world that we're living in today. From the subjects that we're taught in school, through to what our exam grades are supposed to represent, I genuinely believe that this system is simplistic, outdated and actually *harmful* to our development.

A simple Google search will show you alarming statistics about the extent to which mental health problems are being experienced by students *and* adults. These issues develop during our formative adolescent years, and we carry them with us into adulthood as we begin our careers and start our families. Many of us are stressed, anxious, afraid and depressed – and we're not being taught *anything* to help us manage these conditions.

We learn how to solve quadratic equations, but we don't learn how to solve our anxiety issues. We can speak about last year's holiday in a foreign language, but we can't speak about the emotions and insecurities we're experiencing today in *any* language. We know how the Second World War was won, but we don't know how to win the war within ourselves.

The education system *needs* fixing.

However, I'm afraid that at this point, I have no economically viable solutions for fixing the education system and convincing our educators to teach us the skills that we really need.

Instead, I'm going to show you the *next best thing*.

I'm going to show you how to *beat* the system.

As part of the Ultimate Guide to Exam Success, I'm going to introduce you to the 8 Principles which have helped me and countless others achieve Exam Success, so that *you* give *yourselves* the best chance to ace your exams and build the firm foundations that will propel you to greater success in the future.

But more importantly, I'm going to share tools and techniques that enable you to stay mentally and physically healthy during the exam process, and ultimately give you the skills to maintain your optimal state of well-being long after your final exams are completed.

"Wow. That's very deep! Okay, I kind of get it. But to be honest, the future seems so far away! I don't even know what I want to do…"

I completely understand! This is the reality that so many of us face. Most of us simply *don't know* what we want to do in the future. I certainly didn't know at age 16, 18 or 22! And even if we *did* know, what would the chances be of us still wanting that *same* future as we actually grow older?

The bottom line is that we're studying for exams, and we're being told that their results are going to determine our future…but we don't even know what future we want!

This makes us feel *anxious* and *stressed* about the importance of our upcoming exams, but also *unmotivated* because we haven't found a future goal to aim for.

If you feel this way, don't worry – you're not alone!

We need to remember that not knowing what we want in the future is exactly *why* it helps to build these *firm foundations*. They ensure that we keep as many doors open as we possibly can. They give us the *flexibility* to not only choose our ideal career, but even *change* careers further down the line.

So, even though our *present-self* (us at this moment and time) doesn't know what it wants to do when it's older, the firm foundations we build now will allow our *future-self* (the future version of us) to choose the career path *they* desire, when *they* finally decide what *they* want to do.

Please don't misinterpret me – it's *entirely possible* to find your ideal career and become extremely successful *without* good exam grades. Many have done it in the past. Many will do so in the future.

But the *weaker* your foundations, the more difficult, time-consuming and costly a task it can become.

So, why risk it?

It's 100% possible to achieve top grades *without* having to deal with stress, anxiety and demotivation. That's why we have the 8 Principles…

"Alright, I'm intrigued! What are the 8 Principles of Exam Success?"

The 8 Principles focus on what we *aren't* taught at school about exams – namely, how to actually *master* the process of preparing for and performing optimally in our exams, while maintaining a healthy mental and physical state.

The 8 Principles of Exam Success are split into 2 groups:

- **Optimising The Studying Process**

- **Optimising The Studying Lifestyle**

Each of the 2 groups is composed of 4 Principles.

The areas that we need to optimise as part of our **Studying Process** include:

1. **Time-Management** – effective prioritisation and planning techniques to increase productivity and reduce procrastination.

2. **Study Tools & Techniques** – optimising how, where and when we study.

3. **Mindset-Management** – understanding the sources of our anxiety, low motivation and doubt, and using 8 different tools to address, manage and resolve them.

4. **On-The-Day Performance** – tactics to implement immediately before, during and after the exam.

The majority of this book will be spent covering these 4 Studying Process Principles, as these are the attributes which will *directly* translate to improved performance in our exams.

Nevertheless, we can't allow ourselves to become consumed with the Studying Process to the extent where we feel that focusing on it *alone* will allow us to excel in our exams. We must recognise that the overall *effectiveness* of our study process is significantly impacted by the *lifestyle* choices that we make during this time.

The areas that we need to optimise as part of our **Studying Lifestyle** include:

5. **Physical Activity & Movement** – the amount of physical activity and movement in our day.

6. **Nutrition & Hydration** – the quality of our nutrition and the importance of staying well-hydrated.

7. **Sleep** – optimising the quality and quantity of sleep we get per day.

8. **Support Group** – the academic and personal support groups that we have access to.

The 4 Studying Lifestyle Principles will not be covered in as much depth as the 4 Studying Process Principles. The main purpose of these chapters is simply to convey the *importance* of the lifestyle choices we make with respect to exams, and to introduce several *methods* by which we can begin to do so.

There will be references to scientific papers and studies throughout this book. We might even briefly touch on the science behind these Principles – without going into a biology lesson, of course!

Please do *not* be put-off by this.

These are just for the benefit of the *sceptics* who doubt the importance of these Principles, and for the *curious* who want to understand *why* these Principles are important.

After all, every one of us has been told countless times about the importance of getting enough sleep, drinking lots of water and doing exercise. But for some of us, it becomes easier to convince ourselves to actually act on these once we understand the basic science behind them, or appreciate that there is *real evidence* proving their benefits.

If that isn't for you, then just *ignore* the references. This is Exam Success, not a biology lesson or literature review.

"Hmm. Not so sure about the science, but the Principles sound good! Still, I am a little bit scared. Is it even realistic for me to apply these Principles? It sounds like there is *so much to cover* and it's just going to make me realise how much I need to change. Where do I even start?"

To help you in applying the content of the book, there will be various *activities* for you to do as you read through each Principle. These will help you to apply the content from the book in *small, manageable steps*. A list of *all* the activities in the book can be found in Appendix 1.

There are also various case studies of my clients using these tools and techniques. Although the names of these individuals have been changed in the book to protect their privacy, I hope that these case studies will help to clarify how the tools can be applied, as well as providing some anecdotal evidence that the tools have worked for various students.

I want you to read this book knowing that you are fully capable of applying *every one* of the 8 Principles outlined within it. I truly believe this. There is no age requirement or prior knowledge required to apply these Principles. All you need is a *commitment* to your goal and a *willingness* to act. The only thing stopping you is your *mind*.

Yes – this book will make you question your current study habits, mindset and lifestyle. Yes – it will push you out of your comfort zone and expose you to the fears holding you back from succeeding in your exams. And yes – it will challenge you to overcome these in order to get the best out of yourself.

If you feel daunted by this, please know that *you are not alone*. We all feel this way when we're confronted with something that seems new and difficult.

Do yourself a favour and give the book a chance. Give *yourself* a chance.

Instead of letting the book overwhelm you, take it one step at a time, and let it *guide* you to where you can focus on making *small* changes. And instead of letting it intimidate you, let it *inspire* you and give you hope that there is so much you can still do to increase your chances of success.

Read every chapter with this quote by the famous martial artist, Bruce Lee, in mind: *"Adapt what is useful, reject what is useless, and add what is specifically your own."*

In other words, keep an open mind and try out each tool. If it works for you, *adapt* it and apply it within your own life. If it doesn't resonate with you, *reject* it and let it go. And always think about how you can *add* your own unique twist to each tool to make it even more effective for you. After all, no one else in this world shares your exact genetic code or your unique life experiences – only *you* can figure out how to make these tools work for you.

Do not forget – Exam Success doesn't come from *reading* this book; it comes from *applying* the Principles described within it. This book is your *guide*; it will show you the way towards Exam Success, but it isn't going to sit your exams for you!

So, believe in yourself, believe that you have the potential to succeed, and commit wholeheartedly to your desire to achieve your *ideal grades* with *minimal stress*.

Let's begin the journey towards Exam Success.

1. Principle One: Time-Management

Time-management is the ability to use our time in an effective and productive way.

In the context of exams, time-management can be broken down into two key areas: **prioritisation** and **planning**.

However, before we address these, it's important to understand *why* so many of us *struggle* to manage our time. There are two traps that we fall into: **procrastination** and **poor productivity**.

1.1 Overcoming Procrastination

Procrastination is defined as the action of delaying or postponing a task.

What does this mean in the context of our studies? Here's an example that many of us can relate to…

We have an important piece of coursework due in three weeks.

We know that we should begin it *today* to ensure that we produce a good quality piece of work without getting stressed out by the approaching deadline…

But three weeks is still *so* far away – besides, there's so much homework we need to do first. Oh, and we have a tennis lesson tomorrow and a piano lesson on Thursday. Oh, and Alex's birthday party is on Saturday…

Time flies! Now we have *two* weeks until the deadline. We read over our coursework assignment and begin doing research... and suddenly, we feel overwhelmed! Where do we even start? How are we ever going to get this done in two weeks? There's so much to do – oh, look, Netflix has just released a new show! I wonder what it's about…

One and a half weeks until the deadline. We *really* need to get started now! We do a full hour of productive work and reward ourselves with a YouTube break. 6 hours later, it's 3am and we know everything about Illuminati conspiracy theories – but we still haven't done any more coursework!

One week to go. Now *panic* starts to kick in. We ask some of our friends how their coursework is going. Some of them are almost done, which makes us feel guilty, useless and angry at ourselves. Others say they haven't started either, which makes us feel relieved and better about ourselves. If they haven't started, maybe it's absolutely fine that we haven't started either, right? Our brain isn't convinced…

3 days to go. Panic overwhelms us. We *finally* get our introduction done.

Two days to go. Really panicking. We start to structure the main points of our coursework and realise we haven't done some of the research that we should have done weeks ago.

We barely sleep that night because we're so anxious.

One day to go. We frantically do the research. We alternate between states of intense work, eating sugary snacks, and panicking. We pull an all-nighter. We manage to finish the coursework thirty minutes before the deadline.

We collapse in relief.

A few weeks later, we get our grade back. It's a low B-grade. A part of us is so proud! In just 3 days, we pulled off a miracle! We're amazing, we're superhuman, we're unstoppable…

…but a thought keeps nagging at us.

If we achieved a B with 3 days of frantic work, imagine what we could have achieved with 3 weeks of relaxed, consistent work. That high A-grade was well within our grasp…

Anyone with a procrastination habit will be familiar with this pattern of events.

Delaying the task; distracting ourselves; stressing incessantly; bursts of productivity; producing a semi-decent piece of work extremely close to the deadline that doesn't reflect what we're really capable of, but is decent enough such that we don't feel a sense of urgency to break our procrastination habit…

So, why do we procrastinate in the first place?

1. **Avoiding a task that we don't want to do.**

   This could be for various reasons. Sometimes, the task seems too difficult or challenging. Perhaps the task is too vague, and it's hard to figure out where to start. Maybe the task is just really *boring* – we don't even enjoy the subject, and there are so many other activities that we would rather be doing…

   But often, these reasons are just the tip of the iceberg; our real motives for procrastination lay deep below the surface of the ocean.

   We fear failing the task. We fear disappointing ourselves if we do badly. We fear disappointing our parents. We're perfectionists – and we'd rather not do the work at all, than to produce something that would fall below our expectations of what we believe we're capable of.

2. **An excuse for not performing well.**

   There's a difference between getting a C-grade, and getting a C-grade *because* we did all the work the night before the deadline or exam.

   The latter statement gives us a chance to create an excuse that the *only* reason why we didn't get a great grade was because we rushed our work as the deadline was approaching. Had we spent more time on our work or studied for longer, we would *surely* have gotten a higher grade.

   But do we really believe this?

   As much as we wish it were true, our mind doesn't fall for these excuses. We may have fooled ourselves on the surface, but deep down we don't believe the reality that we're trying to convince ourselves of.

   In fact, if we look closely, we will notice that the more we reinforce this fake excuse, the more we lose confidence in ourselves and begin to doubt our own ability.

   This is because our *belief* that we could have done better if we'd started studying earlier or if we'd applied more effort is being undermined by the *real evidence* of the poor grades that we're actually receiving.

3. **No clarity regarding our goals; no direction, no motivation.**

When we're unclear about the goals that we want to achieve and *why* we want to achieve them, we become very susceptible to procrastination.

Without clarity and a firm understanding of *why* we want to achieve our goals, our inner voice which tells us that we *should* be studying isn't loud enough to drown out the voice that tells us that there are so many other things that we would rather be doing.

The more clarity we have about our goals and priorities, the more awareness we have about the direction we *want* to move in. The more clarity we have about *why* we want to achieve our goals, the more motivation we possess to begin moving in that direction.

Until we set time aside to get clear about the direction we want to move in, we will continue to become frustrated at our lack of progress in *any* direction. As a result, we're more likely to try to drown out those negative feelings with the instant gratification that our distractions offer us. Ironically, those same distractions ultimately leave us feeling guilty and angry at ourselves after we become aware of how much time has passed, but we're still stuck in the same situation.

4. **Need to rest.**

Every hill looks steeper when we're tired. Fatigue can transform the smallest hill into the largest mountain. The more daunting the climb looks, the more likely we are to delay taking the first step.

There is nothing wrong with taking a break when we're tired. The problem occurs when we don't consciously identify that fatigue is the root cause of our procrastination. We feel unnecessarily guilty and frustrated, when in fact we should be taking some time to relax and replenish our energy. Unfortunately, the negative emotions we feel about ourselves when we procrastinate just drain us of our energy more rapidly.

Activity 1.1: Think of 3 recent examples of procrastination that you've experienced. For each example, write down: the task you were meant to be doing, how you procrastinated, how you felt after procrastinating, and what the overall outcome of the task was. Which of the reasons for procrastination outlined above applied in each situation?

As you can see, procrastination isn't *just* a time-management problem. The reasons why we procrastinate can be linked to our mindset, which is why <u>Principle 3</u> covers Mind-Management.

Through a combination of time-management tools and mind-management techniques, it's possible to break our procrastination habits.

7 Steps To Overcome Procrastination

1. Having *clarity* about what **motivates** us.

   As mentioned earlier, lack of clarity about *why* we want to achieve our Exam Success goals leads to procrastination. We'll discuss motivational clarity and some powerful tools to ignite our Motivational Fire in Principle 3.

2. Conscious *awareness* of our **long-term priorities.**

   Knowing our long-term priorities helps us to determine the *direction* that we want to move in. Our actions should always be aligned with our priorities; the more consciously aware we are of them, the stronger our drive to move towards them. This will be discussed further in the Long-Term Prioritisation section of this chapter.

3. Knowing how to *prioritise* our **short-term tasks.**

   Once we know what direction we want to move in, we want to take the biggest steps possible in that direction. Seeing progress is motivating, therefore we want to ensure that our actions are having as much impact as possible towards accomplishing our Exam Success goals. We will discuss how to identify these actions in the Short-Term Prioritisation Tools section of this chapter.

4. Breaking *big walls* down into **smaller hurdles**.

   Nothing is more intimidating than gigantic walls between where we are and where we want to be. We need to break down these huge walls into smaller, more manageable hurdles. Not only is it easier to climb over each hurdle with greater ease, but we can always see our goal waiting for us at the end. Effective Planning helps us to achieve this.

5. Minimising *distractions* and entering a state of **flow**.

   The hardest part of doing work is *starting* work. Once we get started, we may still encounter obstacles that prevent us from getting into our optimal state of *flow* – the ideal state where we're fully *focused* on our task and everything that we're doing feels *effortless*. However, by managing distractions around us and concentrating on the task at hand, we can enter a productive and enjoyable state of *flow* where our mind won't *want* to stop working! This is discussed further in the following section on Poor Productivity.

6. Giving ourselves *breaks* to **rest** – and being *committed* in returning to **work!**

   Feeling tired is natural. It's very valuable to take a break and restore our energy. However, we should do our utmost to ensure that short breaks don't lead to crazy cycles of procrastination that ultimately lead to us feeling more stressed and tired. So, take some time to rest and replenish – and *commit* to returning to your work once your break is over. Time-management is about balance – work hard, play hard, and rest hard! Effective Planning can help us to achieve this balance.

7. Giving ourselves time to do the *activities* that we **enjoy**.

There is no need to procrastinate when we know with certainty that we're leaving time to do the activities that we love and enjoy. It helps to remember that we enjoy these activities even *more* when we know that we've fulfilled our commitments to our Exam Success goals. Time-management is about balance and satisfaction, not excess or deprivation. When we don't feel deprived of our satisfaction, we no longer seek instant gratification through activities that cause us to procrastinate. Effective Planning helps us to ensure that we fulfil our study obligations, while also making time to do the activities that we enjoy.

8. **Forgiving ourselves** if we procrastinate.

A 2010 study[1] showed that students who forgave themselves for procrastinating when preparing for their first exam reduced their likelihood of procrastinating for their second exam. Self-forgiveness is carried out with the attitude that we intend to *learn* from our mistakes, and that we have the potential to improve our character. On the other hand, self-punishment creates emotions of guilt and self-loathing towards oneself. These negative emotions perpetuate our procrastination habits; by procrastinating, we would simply be acting in line with the negative self-image that we perceive ourselves to already have. In other words, self-punishment focuses on what is *wrong* with us; self-forgiveness focuses on how we can become *better*.

1.2 Increasing Productivity

Productivity has various definitions. In the context of exams, I'm choosing to define it as being able to "complete the most important tasks effectively and efficiently".

Let's take a closer look at this definition.

'Most important tasks': Important tasks are those which take you closer to your goals. In the context of studying, this could refer to revision notes, past-papers, and so on. The *most* important tasks are those which move you closer towards your goals per unit of time spent on them, in comparison to other tasks.

For example, an hour spent on an A-Level Mathematics Past-Paper would bring you closer towards your goal of getting a good grade compared to an hour reading through a Mathematics textbook, since Past-Papers are considered to be a better method for revising A-Level Mathematics.

'Effectively': This relates to completing a task *well*, such that it takes us closer to the result or outcome that we desire. In the context of exams, it refers to doing the task to a high *quality*, such that we get the most out of the task in line with achieving our ideal exam results.

Using the above example, working *effectively* means retaining the knowledge that we learned from completing the Mathematics Past-Paper so that we can apply it in our final exams. Working *ineffectively* means completing the Past-Paper in a distracted and unfocused state, where we don't retain any of the information after its completion.

'Efficiently': This relates to achieving maximum productivity with minimum wasted effort or resources. In the context of exams, it means getting as much of our important tasks done in the *least* amount of *time* and by expending the *least* amount of *energy*.

Using the example above, working efficiently means finishing the Mathematics Past-Paper in 60 minutes in a relaxed and focused state (which doesn't deplete our energy); whereas working inefficiently would mean taking over 90 minutes to finish that same Past-Paper in a stressed or anxious state (which exhausts us quicker).

So, given this definition of productivity, what constitutes *poor productivity*?

-   **Doing tasks that are *unimportant*** – unimportant tasks don't take us closer to our goals.

-   **Doing important tasks that are not the *most important*** – important tasks may take us a few steps closer towards our goals, but we could be taking even *more* steps forward in the same amount of time if we did the *most* important tasks.

-   **Working ineffectively** – doing low-quality work such that we don't yield the maximum benefits from it. This happens when we're unfocused or distracted by other activities or thoughts, and not fully committed to getting the most out of the task.

-   **Working inefficiently** – expending more time and energy to complete a task than is needed. We waste more time when we're constantly being distracted as it interrupts our state of *flow*. We use up more energy when we're in a stressed, anxious or tired state. We also expend more energy when we force ourselves to do work that we don't *want* to be doing. This state of resistance is very energy-consuming.

-   **Multitasking** – studies have shown that our brain can't effectively or efficiently do two tasks at once, or switch between two tasks (especially when the first task has not been completed). Even brief mental blocks created by shifting between tasks can cost as much as 40% of our productive time.[2] Multitasking costs us time because we take longer to focus on new information, we become more susceptible to making mistakes, and we have a lower retention rate of what we learn when we multitask.[3] This means that we spend more time redoing work, and we may not perform well on subsequent tasks because we've forgotten the information that we've learned.

Understanding Flow

I've used the term *flow* on a few occasions.

But, what exactly is flow?

According to psychologist, Mihaly Csikszentmihalyi (what an awesome name!), flow can be defined as "a state of concentration so focused that it amounts to absolute absorption in an activity". Flow can be described by 8 characteristics: [4]

1. Doing a **challenging** task that requires **skills** – and believing that we *can* complete the task given our own individual capabilities and the time and resources available to us.

2. **Clarity** about the goal we want to achieve through doing the task – and **immediate feedback** that gives us an indication of how close we are to achieving that goal, or what we may need to change to attain it.

3. Complete **concentration** on the task.

4. A sense of **effortlessness** and **ease** in carrying out the task.

5. A feeling of **control** over the task – or rather, lacking the sense of worry about losing control that is so typical in many life situations.

6. A merging of **actions** and **awareness** as we carry out the task – self-conscious thought disappears, and our inner critic is silenced.

7. The passage of time **transforms** as we're doing the task – we may feel that time has slowed-down or sped-up.

8. The experience is **intrinsically rewarding** – being in a state of flow is *enjoyable*, regardless of whether the outcome is achieved at the end.

Reading this, many of you may realise that you've experienced a state of flow in the past. Perhaps you're an athlete, and you've experienced the state of flow when you've found yourself 'in the zone'. Perhaps you're a musician, and you've found yourself completely engrossed by the piece that you're playing. Perhaps you've experienced the state of flow while reading a book, conversing with a good friend, or even – dare I say it – while studying.

Being able to enter a state of flow while studying significantly enhances our productivity, allowing us to perform our tasks effectively and efficiently.

We can understand how flow works in the context of studying by considering the 4 Stages of Study Flow using the 'Study Flow Curve' shown below.

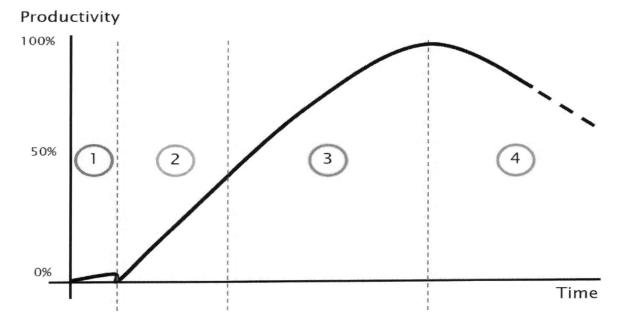

The **X-axis** represents the **time taken** at any stage of the Study Flow Curve. No time units have been written on the graph because the exact time it would take to move between stages differs for all of us; it will also change with practise. However, standard estimates and ranges have been provided in subsequent paragraphs to give you a rough indication of the time taken to move between each stage.

The **Y-axis** represents our **productivity level** as a percentage. At 0% productivity, we haven't begun the task. At 100% productivity, we're in a state of *flow* where we're fully immersed in the task and working in an effective, efficient manner.

Let's take a closer look at each of the 4 stages of the Study Flow Curve.

<u>Stage 1: The Pit of Eternal Procrastination</u>

We spend approximately the first *2 minutes* of any task in the Pit of Eternal Procrastination.

At this stage, our mind is just beginning to process the task ahead of us. It creates thoughts relating to how daunting the task is, how difficult it is, how long it will take, how we would rather be doing *anything* but studying right now, how this is all pointless because we're going to fail our exams anyway, and so on.

This is the stage where we're tempted to succumb to these thoughts. We write a sentence and then gaze out of the window. We leave our desk to get some water from the kitchen. We grab our phone and check social media updates. At this point, we're stuck *in* the Pit of Eternal Procrastination. When we resume our task, we'll be back at time = 0, and we'll have to navigate our way through the dreaded pit once again.

This is why people often say that the hardest part of any task is often just *getting started.*

It's important to remember that while these first 120 seconds are *crucial*, they are *not useful* because our productivity levels are so low. We can take advantage of this by making these first two minutes *enjoyable* and *light-hearted* without much concern for our productivity; for example, by drowning out our thoughts with loud music, reading the textbook aloud in funny accents, or scribbling down messy revision notes!

Once we're safely out of the pit, we can turn our music off and begin implementing our study strategy with focus and determination.

The key action point for Stage 1 can be summarised as "don't think – just do!". We should do *anything* we can to get ourselves beyond the first 2 minutes of the task, without giving our mind any opportunity to talk us out of it.

Once the first 2 minutes are over, we enter Stage 2.

Stage 2: The Yofo-Soco Chasm

Congratulations on getting out of the Pit of Eternal Procrastination. Now, our productivity begins to increase as we immerse ourselves in our task...

But we're still on a slippery slope! If we fall into the Yofo-Soco Chasm, we must return to the beginning of the Study Flow curve and navigate our way through the Pit of Eternal Procrastination again.

This is why this stage is called the 'Yofo-Soco' Chasm. Yofo and Soco aren't two famous scientists. 'Yofo-Soco' is an abbreviation for: "You Fool - you were So Close!" (Bit silly, I'll admit – but at least you'll remember it now!)

The Yofo-Soco Chasm lasts for roughly 8 to 10 minutes. This is aligned with the commonly referenced '10-Minute Rule'. [5]

It's very reasonable to ask ourselves to commit to something for just 10 minutes. An hour may be daunting – but 10 minutes is a piece of cake. More importantly, once we've done a task for ten minutes, we won't *want* to stop doing it because our mind recognises that we've already committed time and energy into starting the task. Our mind accepts that it would be inefficient and undesirable to stop now, especially as we're beginning to enter an enjoyable state of flow.

The key action point for Stage 2 can be summarised as, "whatever you do – don't stop!". This can be accomplished by minimising all external distractions (more on how to accomplish this in Principle 2), avoiding multitasking, making a conscious effort to stay focused on the task, and to keep persisting with the task even if our progress starts to slow down.

Once we have spent approximately 10 to 12 minutes on our task (through the Pit and across the Chasm), our productivity level will have reached around the 40% mark. At this point, we make the transition from the Yofo-Soco Chasm into the Effortless Effort Rise.

Stage 3: Effortless Effort Rise

Once we enter the Effortless Effort Rise, we're beginning to enter the *flow* state where we're fully immersed in our task. This is why it's called Effortless Effort. We're still applying energy to complete the task (Effort), but it feels Effortless as we're working at a steady rhythm and it's much easier to remain focused on the task.

The Effortless Effort Rise takes us from roughly 40% to 100% of our maximum productivity level. In general, it takes between 10 and 20 minutes to reach the 100% mark. The reason for the range in timing is that the more we practise getting into a flow state, the easier it becomes to reach 100% productivity. When we're still beginners, it might take us slightly longer.

Once we're on the Effortless Effort Rise, small interruptions (less than *one minute*) don't affect our productivity levels. We can resume our work in the same state that we left it. This is very different to the Yofo-Soco Chasm, where any distraction could cause us to drop back to 0% productivity levels.

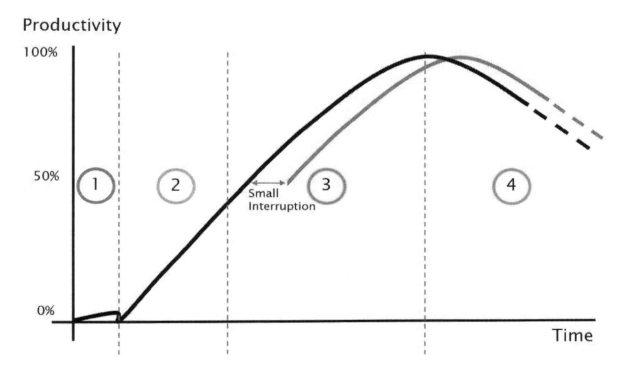

In other words, if your younger sibling randomly comes into your room and you politely let them know that you're busy, you're fine. If your mother asks you what you want for dinner and you reply, you're fine. If your phone vibrates and momentarily grabs your attention, but you ignore it, you're fine.

However, the longer the interruption, the more we risk falling back down the Study Flow Curve when we resume our work. We might find ourselves in the Yofo-Soco Chasm again - or at worst, back in the Pit of Eternal Procrastination.

So, if your phone vibrates and you check the message, reply to it, and then check your Facebook notifications and Instagram stories, you may find that returning to the task becomes much more difficult – and your productivity level will be significantly *lower* when you do.

So, don't risk it. Keep distractions to a minimum. Keep building your state of flow. The key action point for Stage 3 can be summarised as, "enjoy the climb – and stay focused on the peak!"

Stage 4: The Peak of Productivity Mountain

We have made it to the Peak of Productivity Mountain!

When we reach Stage 4, we should first *appreciate the view*. In other words, while we're still working at 100% productivity, we should stay atop the peak of the mountain and continue with our task.

However, as any mountain-climbers among you readers will know, it's very cold at the peak of any mountain. So*, don't freeze to death*. It's unsustainable to stay on the Peak of Productivity Mountain for too long. We'll notice our productivity beginning to drop. This is when we should *get off the mountain* and take a short break.

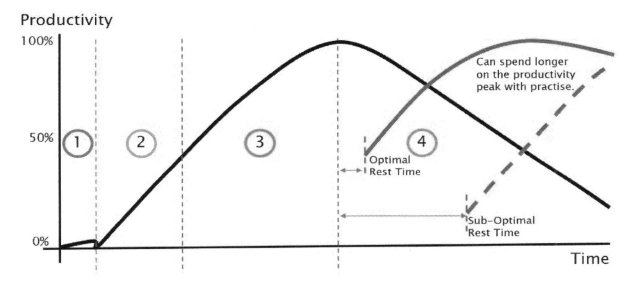

How long we rest for is vitally important. At our *optimal rest time* – no more than 10 minutes, in general – we can resume our task on the Effortless Effort Rise when our break is over. In doing this, we reach the Peak of Productivity Mountain in a shorter period of time, and we can spend longer atop the peak – usually between 10 and 20 minutes.

However, the longer our break, the lower our productivity levels will be when we resume our task. At any *sub-optimal rest time*, we might find ourselves in the Yofo-Soco Chasm again. At worst, we will have to start at the very bottom of the Study Flow Curve – which means getting out of the Pit of Eternal Procrastination again!

Stage 4 can therefore be summarised as, "appreciate the view, don't freeze to death, and don't wait too long before you start climbing again!"

So, how can we bring all of this information together to optimise our productivity?

4 Keys to Optimal Productivity

1. Identifying and completing the **most important tasks** which take us closest to our goal or desired outcome. We can identify these tasks through Short-Term Prioritisation Tools and the 80-20 Rule.

2. Understanding how we can enter a state of **flow** to carry out our tasks *effectively* and *efficiently*. Using the Study Flow Curve as a guide, we may choose a studying pattern which alternates between working up to our *100% productivity level* and taking a short break that corresponds to our *optimal rest time*.

   This will differ for each of us based on how quickly we reach our 100% productivity level, and how long we can maintain it for. Some common practices include a 5-minute break for each 25-35 minutes of work (as in the Pomodoro Technique, discussed further in Principle 2), or a 10-minute break for each 45-60 minutes of work.

3. Approaching tasks with the **right mindset** (Principle 3). This entails making a conscious choice to commit to the task that we're doing without any mental resistance, allowing us to work in a focused manner without depleting our energy reserves.

4. Staying **mentally** and **physically healthy** through physical activity & movement (Principle 5), optimum hydration and nutrition (Principle 6), good sleep habits (Principle 7), and by surrounding ourselves with people who help us, inspire us and empower us (Principle 8).

As you now understand, procrastination and poor productivity aren't *just* resolved using time-management tools. The 8 Principles of Exam Success work *together* to address the root cause of each problem we encounter, allowing us to break out of each trap and continue our Exam Success quest.

Nevertheless, time-management is still vital! Let's take a deeper look at the two time-management tools mentioned at the start of this chapter: **prioritisation** and **planning**.

1.3 Effective Prioritisation

Prioritisation is about being able to recognise the importance of each task or activity that we need to undertake, and using that to guide our decision as to how and when to carry it out.

The first step involved in prioritisation is becoming aware of how we *currently* decide between which activities are most important to us, for example:

- Do we attempt the hardest tasks first, or the most fun tasks first?
- Do we do urgent work as soon as we get it, or delay it until the last minute?
- How much time do we spend in-between tasks on activities like watching YouTube videos, or going through our social media news feeds?

Once we understand how we *currently* use our time, we can *then* use prioritisation tools to manage our time more effectively.

To achieve Exam Success, we must look at prioritisation from two different angles:

- **Long-Term Prioritisation**
- **Short-Term Prioritisation**

Long-Term Prioritisation

This is where we take a *long-term view* with respect to all the things happening in our daily lives in the build-up to our exams. We can then place them within broad categories, for example:

- **Exam preparation and studying** e.g. lectures, revision
- **Job/work commitments** e.g. part-time job
- **Social life** e.g. seeing friends, parties
- **Hobbies and recreational activities** e.g. sports, music, Netflix
- **Home maintenance** e.g. cleaning, cooking etc.
- **Family commitments** e.g. Young Carer

Since you're reading this book, I'm going to assume that achieving Exam Success is something you consider to be important. It may even be your major goal this year!

With that in mind, take a moment and ask yourself where you would place exam preparation on your list of priorities with respect to the other categories listed above…

Don't worry if it's not priority number 1 *at this moment*. Simply becoming aware of the level of commitment you currently have towards your exams is extremely valuable.

The truth is that a lot of us are intimidated about placing exams as our biggest priority.

Some of us feel afraid of the *expectation* that we'll be placing upon ourselves to perform well if we place it at the top of our priority list. We also think that it means sacrificing other aspects of our lives for the sake of a result that *isn't even guaranteed*, which creates feelings of resistance and dissatisfaction towards exams. We must understand that prioritisation isn't about putting pressure on ourselves to achieve an outcome, nor is it about cutting things out of our lives.

It's just about recognising what is most important to us over this *temporary* time period. It's about asking ourselves how we can minimise any chance of regret *regardless* of the outcome that we get, by ensuring that we set aside enough time to prepare for that task and honour our commitment to it.

We're *not* neglecting our friends or stopping tennis lessons while exams are on the horizon, we're simply *deprioritising* them. We're just recognising that our Biology revision notes on osmosis are a **priority** above spontaneously hanging out with our friends at Starbucks or agreeing to fill in a concert slot as soon as someone asks.

It's just a *temporary arrangement!*

And once we have completed our priority tasks, we're absolutely entitled to have fun and address our **deprioritised** tasks, such as social commitments, sports etc.

With this in mind, take a moment to re-evaluate and decide whether you want to change the order of your priorities given your goals regarding exams.

It may be that you realise that exam preparation is going to come above social life and hobbies for this time period, even though it wouldn't ordinarily. That's okay! It's temporary.

For some of you who are also employed during your exams, it may be that your job remains a priority over exam preparation. Again – this is completely understandable.

The key is simply to *know* our priorities and be *fully aware* of them.

Why?

Because we have to **plan in line with our priorities** – which is why planning comes after this section on prioritisation. Failure to identify our long-term priorities will lead to an imbalanced and inefficient plan that may leave us feeling demotivated, stressed, and more prone to procrastination.

Activity 1.2: Write down where you currently prioritise exam preparation with respect to the other categories listed above. Is this something that you want to change in line with your exam goals?

There is one more *powerful* concept for long/mid-term task prioritisation for prioritising our time in terms of the subjects we study and the study techniques we use.

Vilfredo Pareto was an Italian economist who *unintentionally* discovered one of the most useful productivity insights. He recognised that 80% of Italy's wealth was held by 20% of its population, and found that this 80-20 relationship (or similar distribution, such as 70-30 or 90-10) also applied to many other aspects of life.[6] For example:

- 80% of the output is produced by 20% of the input.
- 80% of the results are produced by 20% of the effort.
- 80% of the sales revenue is created by 20% of the customers.

In the context of studying, this is immensely powerful.

It means that roughly 80% of our final grade can be achieved by choosing the *right* way to apply 20% of our effort. However, to get the remaining 20% of our grade, we need to apply roughly 80% more effort!

It's up to us to identify *which* tasks and study methods compose that vital 20% of effort, in order to ensure that we receive *maximum benefits* for *minimal effort*. We then need to **prioritise** this 20% over our other tasks.

These "20% tasks" will differ between individuals, as we all have preferred studying methods that influence our optimum study technique. The tools and techniques discussed in Principle 2 will help you to identify your preferences and find out which methods may work best for you.

For example, I found that for Mathematics, doing Past-Papers was *far more effective* than re-reading my notes. I realised that I gained approximately 80% more value for my time by completing and reviewing a 2-hour past-paper than if I spent the same 2 hours re-reading through my notes.

As such, I *prioritised* doing Past Papers over creating revision notes in my plan. Roughly 80% of my total Maths revision was purely Past Papers and practising questions, and the other 20% was creating and reviewing revision notes.

I used a similar process for allocating study time to different subjects.

My Cambridge offer required an A* in Further Maths – a subject that I was *failing* according to my December mocks (I scored 28%, a U-grade!). However, I only required an A in Physics, which I was on track to attain.

Naturally, Further Maths became a *higher priority* than Physics. I decided that if I spent a total of x hours on Physics and Further Maths, roughly 80% of that time should be dedicated to Further Maths, and only 20% to Physics.

In addition, given that so little relative time was being spent on Physics, I knew that I had to *maximise* the value I would gain from the short amount of time I was spending on it.

In my case, I felt that I would be gaining 80% more value for my time from copying out and memorising Physics past-paper *mark schemes*, rather than if I were to write detailed notes on each topic or complete each individual past paper.

Doing this allowed me to attain my A* in Further Maths and meet my Cambridge offer, while ensuring that I met my A-grade requirement in Physics.

In practise, do not worry too much about keeping rigidly to 80% and 20%. It's just a *guideline* to get you thinking about the most productive way to use your time in order to achieve your goal.

With your long-term priorities firmly in mind, here are two awesome tools that you can use to think about how you prioritise tasks on a daily/weekly basis.

Short-Term Prioritisation Tools

Tool 1: Covey's Quadrants of Time Management

Steven Covey, for those of you who aren't familiar with him, was an absolute *legend*. He authored the bestselling book, The 7 Habits of Highly Effective People, which I honestly recommend.

Covey's Quadrants of Time Management is a simple 2 x 2 matrix that measures **urgency** of a task against the **importance** of the task.

An **urgent task** is one that can't be delayed or put-off any longer, whereas an **important** task is one that can have long-term consequences for your career/lifestyle or accomplishing your goals.

Here is an example of where different kinds of activities and tasks could be entered on the matrix:

	URGENT	*NOT URGENT*
IMPORTANT	**Examples** - Crises - Short-term: Deadline driven projects/examinations - Medical emergencies - Other emergencies **"IMMEDIACY"**	**Examples** - Long-term: Exam preparation or projects - Planning work - Training/ personal development - Recreation for health - Relationship building **"EFFECTIVENESS"**
NOT IMPORTANT	**Examples** - Spontaneous events with friends - Interruptions - Some phone calls, emails and messages - Many issues we consider to be 'pressing' or 'immediate' **"DELUSION"**	**Examples** - Social media news feeds - Some phone calls, emails and messages - Excessive TV - Time-wasting activities - Other 'escape' activities **"WASTE"**

The **first quadrant** is referred to as the *Quadrant of Immediacy*. These are tasks that are *both* urgent and important. There are three kinds of tasks that fill this quadrant:

1. Emergencies or crises that have not been planned for, but need to be dealt with immediately.

2. Last-minute work that needs to be done for impending exams or project deadlines as a result of poor planning.

3. Tasks from Quadrant 2 (Not Urgent + Important) which were not addressed and have now become urgent.

In general, while these are our highest-priority tasks, we shouldn't operate within this quadrant for too long. It can be stressful and fatiguing, and we can quickly find ourselves working at a sub-optimal level.

The **second quadrant** is known as the *Quadrant of Effectiveness*. These are tasks which are important but not urgent. In general, this is the quadrant that we want to be operating in most of the time.

Unfortunately, we often end up *delaying* or *procrastinating* on these tasks (e.g. revision for exams), and they end up moving to Quadrant 1. Other tasks within this quadrant, such as those related to our health, well-being and personal development (e.g. going to the gym, training and self-development courses) will rarely ever move to Quadrant 1, but neglecting them for too long can still be detrimental.

The **third quadrant** is called the *Quadrant of Delusion*. These are tasks which we consider to be urgent, but are *not at all important* in relation to our goals. These are all the tasks which we *think* are adding value, but really aren't! We often feel like we're being productive when doing these tasks (e.g. 'immediate' issues such as cleaning our room, replying to emails), whereas in reality, they are just distracting us from the main issues in the 'Important' quadrants.

The key to managing Quadrant 3 is to assign *set periods of time* to address each task (e.g. replying to emails and missed calls between 2pm and 3pm, room-cleaning between 11am and 12pm). For spontaneous events or meetings, we should get into the habit of questioning whether there are other tasks in the 'Important' quadrants which we would be better-off spending our time on instead. Remember - we don't have to say 'Yes' to everything!

The **fourth quadrant** is called the *Quadrant of Waste*. These are tasks which are not urgent and not important, to the extent where we don't even recognise them as tasks. We often end up doing them when our mind isn't focused – for example, going through our Facebook or Instagram feed (I'm certainly guilty of this one!).

In general, it's recommended to *eliminate* or *avoid* any activity that falls within this quadrant.

However, being honest, this just *isn't realistic*.

The most realistic course of action is to become *aware* of *when* we start to operate within this quadrant, and then ask ourselves *why* we're there.

We may be feeling fatigued, in which case it may be best to take a short break. Or we may be feeling demotivated, in which case we may need to take some time to realign ourselves with our main goals and priorities (after taking a short break, of course!). We will discuss addressing fatigue and demotivation further in Principles 2 and 3.

Activity 1.3: Write down ANY 10 tasks you need to do in the next few days (study-related, leisure-related, home-related, social etc.) and assign them into Covey's 4 Quadrants of Time Management.

Even if you consider it tedious to draw out the matrix for your daily/weekly tasks, just being *familiar* with the quadrant system is a huge benefit. It allows you to assign tasks *mentally* to the quadrants as they come up, helping you to decide on your priority actions.

Alternatively, you can do what my client, Sam, did. He liked this tool so much that he drew a giant 4-quadrant poster on an A3 sheet, stuck it on his wall, and used post-it notes to allocate his tasks (different colours corresponding to different areas of his life e.g. academic, social, health etc.)

Sam found this to be immensely useful. He focused his time on completing his tasks in the Quadrant of **Importance** and the Quadrant of **Effectiveness**. He would remove them from the matrix when they were done. A lot of tasks that he once thought were in the Quadrant of **Importance** turned out to be in the Quadrant of **Delusion** when he was able to visualise the matrix, so he moved them down a column. All the TV shows he wanted to watch ended up in the Quadrant of **Waste**. He could still enjoy them whenever he wanted to – they were great for a short break, following which he'd refocus his attention on his other tasks.

Tool 2: ABCDE Rule

The ABCDE rule is very simple.

We simply write down our tasks, and assign them a letter:

- *A: "Very Important":* There are serious consequences if this task is not completed immediately (e.g. revision for immediate exam, coursework for deadline tomorrow).

- *B: "Important":* Minor negative consequences if not done immediately (e.g. revision for distant exam, paying bills in advance).

- *C: "Nice To Do":* No immediate negative consequences if not done immediately (e.g. gym session, piano practice).

- *D: "Delegate":* Give this task to someone else to do. Examples of this include organising a party or doing groceries. This is more applicable for managers in a working environment who have employees to delegate tasks to – unfortunately, I never figured out a way to 'delegate' someone else to do my exams for me...

- *E: "Eliminate, wherever possible":* Get rid of this activity to free up your time (e.g. watching your girlfriend/boyfriend's favourite Netflix shows!).

Once each task has been assigned a letter, we start by doing the A-tasks. This is followed by the B-tasks and C-tasks. D-tasks are next (good luck finding someone to do your shopping for you...), followed by the E-tasks that we couldn't get out of doing.

When using the ABCDE rule, we should always be aware that that the letter we assign to a task will *change* frequently.

What started off as a C-task can quickly become an A-task if not addressed, for example laundry. No consequences – until we realise that we have no clean underwear left! To account for this, it's best to revisit our to-do list every day.

Activity 1.4: For the same 10 tasks that you wrote down for Activity 1.2, assign each task a letter corresponding to the ABCDE Rule.

Equipped with a view of your long-term priorities, and armed with tools to manage your tasks in the short-term, you are ready to begin the most important process of Exam Success: **PLANNING**...

...but not like any planning you've ever done before!

No more rigid schedules. No more giving-up on overly-ambitious plans. No more time slots to fill in (unless you want there to be!).

1.4 Effective Planning

For so many of us, just hearing the word 'plan' makes us wince. It conjures up thoughts of rigidity and sacrifice. We associate plans with the feeling of frustration, boredom and (inevitably) giving-up.

No longer!

Today, we redefine planning.

And it starts with accepting *one golden rule*:

You will *always* do *more* with a *good* plan than *without* a plan at all.

From now on, if you feel at any point that this rule is not applying to your plan – then it's *not a good plan*! Stop following it, chuck it aside and make a new one.

With this in mind, let me introduce you to the 6 Laws of Study Planning.

The 6 Laws of Study Planning

1. **LONG-TERM :** *I solemnly swear to create long-term plans.*

No more daily plans or weekly plans. Short-term plans are a recipe for disaster – we try to do too much in too little time, only to find out later that we did the *wrong* things due to our short-sightedness.

Feel free to create daily to-do lists in the morning, or to write down the next day's actions the night before – however, these should only be a *supplement* to your primary, long-term plan. For a plan to lead to a successful outcome, we need to be able to *visualise* time beyond a week or two.

In fact, we may even need to start our plan *at the finish.* (More on this later.)

2. **FLEXIBLE :** *I solemnly swear to leave 'slack' in my plans.*

Slack (also known as *float*) is a project management concept that, for the sake of a study plan, just means 'giving myself more time than I think I need to finish a task, and leaving time to catch-up if I fall behind'.

In the context of revision, this may mean adding an extra 30-minutes to finish a 2-hour task, or leaving 3-4 hours free every few days (or roughly one day free a week). This will allow us to catch up on work that was delayed because other tasks took longer than we thought they would. A simple but important step that is very easy to overlook.

3. **ADAPTABLE :** *I solemnly swear to check and update my plan at least twice a day for a minimum of 5 minutes each time.*

Emergency tasks invaded your priorities? Caught a bad cold? Just had a 2-hour lie-in because you didn't hear your alarm? No problem. Just move things around. The days of rigid planning are long gone.

Because we have started our plan with the *end* in mind, we can take tasks off *from the end* (i.e. get rid of the 6th past paper you initially planned the day before the exam, and shift everything else forward a day), or assign time on our nearest *slack day* to catch up on what we missed. Remember – we're still doing *more* than we would have done without a plan.

In addition, spending 5-10 minutes twice a day to adapt our plan is *nothing* compared to the time that we're gaining from being more efficient, and the anxiety that we're preventing because our mind *knows* what it needs to do between today and exam day.

So, make it a *habit.* Know exactly *when* you are going to check and update your plan, and *how long* you are going to do it for – and then *do it!*

4. *REALISTIC :* *I solemnly swear to be realistic in creating and adapting my plan.*

Don't demotivate yourself by creating the most difficult plan ever – maybe 6 hours of revision notes after a 9-5pm day of lectures is slightly over-ambitious. Similarly, don't go too easy on yourself either – splitting one past paper over three days is slightly questionable!

Realistically, when it comes to long-term plans, we *will* deviate from our plan. This is why we have to be diligent in adapting our plans to our ever-changing circumstances.

If you realise at the end of your exams that your plan never needed to be adapted once, you are either incredibly disciplined, or your plan was not challenging enough. To *achieve* our best, we need to *give* our best. No more – but also no less.

5. **PRIORITISE** : *I solemnly swear to plan in line with my priorities and commitments.*

If your Mathematics grade is more important to you than your History grade, your plan should reflect this in terms of the time you spend on each subject. Similarly, if you have school, lectures or work, studying and revision must be planned *around* those commitments.

This also applies to hobbies and other activities. If participating in sport or occasionally seeing friends helps to keep you mentally and physically healthy, plan your studies around it. It's motivating to look at our plan and see that we have enjoyable activities to look forward to. Setting aside small amounts of time to do what we *want* to do makes it easier to spend more time doing what we *have* to do.

If necessary, use your slack time to make up for those urgent, important (Quadrant 1) high-priority tasks that may unexpectedly invade your plan.

6. **TRACK** : *I solemnly swear to track my progress throughout the entire duration of my plan.*

Highlight the days as they are completed. Tick tasks off as you complete them. As well as being a useful guide to gauge whether we're on track or not, it's also immensely motivating to see that we're making progress. Every tick is a small step towards Exam Success!

Not convinced yet? Here are five benefits that you'll gain from following the 6 Laws of Study Planning when creating your study plan:

-   **Increased Motivation:** It's a lot easier to do tasks that we've planned to do in advance, than to spontaneously decide to do a task. It's also a lot more motivating to keep going when we can see that we're making progress every day, no matter how small the step we've taken towards our goal feels. It also makes studying far more bearable when we know that we've set aside time in our plan to do the activities we enjoy.

-   **Decreased Anxiety:** When our mind runs ahead to the date of our exam and conjures up feelings of anxiety and fear, we can gently remind it that we know *everything that we need to do* right up until Exam Day to give ourselves the best chance at success. Simply being able to *visualise* the timeline between today and Exam Day being filled with planned work helps immensely in reducing anxiety – provided that the plan is realistic!

-   **Decreased Guilt:** During the build-up to exams, students often complain about not being able to fully enjoy themselves when they do an activity that they *normally* enjoy. We feel guilty when we're not studying, and anxious that the time spent away from our studies might negatively impact our final grade. Good planning allows us to ensure that we're prioritising our studies and remaining on top of our commitment to achieving good academic grades. This allows us to set aside time for our recreational activities, which we can then enjoy without feeling guilty about doing them.

- **Increased Resilience:** When things don't go according to plan, we become less likely to give up on them completely. Instead, we'll proactively approach the situation and do our utmost to adapt our plan to it. A pretty good lesson for exams (and life!), when things rarely go exactly to plan.

- **Decreased Opportunity for Regret:** No matter how much we must adapt our plan, we're minimising our chances for regret upon receiving our results. In part, this is because we're more likely to succeed in getting the grades we desire! However, in the event of a disappointing outcome, we can also look back on how we have spent our preparation time (Law 6: Track), understand what may need to be changed, and apply those lessons to future exams. There's no room for regret if we're able to learn and grow from our mistakes.

Making The Study Plan

As mentioned in The First Law of Study Planning, we need to plan with the *end* in mind. The beauty of exams is that there's a fixed deadline by which we must have finished our preparation; whether we feel ready or not, we still have to do the exam!

So, given that our exams can be anywhere from one week to one year away, what methods can we use to create a long-term plan?

Broadly speaking, we have three main options, each with advantages and disadvantages:

1. Hand-written A4/A3 sheets of paper (or white-board).

Advantages:

- Always physically in front of us – helps with visualisation.
- Can physically cross tasks off the list when they are completed.
- Can highlight and use different colours to categorise tasks.
- No distractions (unlike with phone apps and laptops).

Disadvantages:

- Can get *very* messy as we adapt the plan.
- Can get time-consuming if we have to keep re-writing new plans on new sheets.
- Easy to run out of space to add new tasks.

2. Apps or calendars e.g. Google Calendar.

Advantages:
- Our phones rarely leave our side, so we can check our plan frequently.
- Apps and calendars have features to assign time, location (etc.) to tasks.
- Apps often include categorisation tools, for example by priority-level or project-name.
- Easy to amend and move tasks around once we get familiar with the app.

Disadvantages:
- Time-consuming to get used to the app – data entry can be very tedious.
- Defined format for how we enter data, harder to tailor to individual preferences.

- Can't *visualise* how tasks are spread over weeks/months due to smaller screens and app limitations.
- Easy to get distracted by social media/Internet.

3. Spreadsheet software e.g. Microsoft Excel, Google Sheets.

Advantages:

- Easy to *visualise* the spread of time over a month-long period.
- Manual entry means that we can describe tasks using the tone or style that suits our individual preferences.
- Can highlight and label with different colours, fonts (etc.) to categorise tasks.
- Easy to copy and paste tasks to different days, and move tasks around between days.
- Often have apps which can be used with smartphones.

Disadvantages:

- Can be a bit intimidating at the start (most of us are as afraid of Excel as we are of exams!)
- Learning to move in and out of 'cells' and entering data can be time-consuming.
- Difficult to enter data on phones or tablets, and laptops or computers are not always convenient or available.
- Easy to get distracted by social media/Internet.

Overall, each method has its advantages and disadvantages – it's completely *up to you* and your individual preferences as to how you approach this.

Once we've decided which platform (hand-written, apps or spreadsheet) we're going to use as the foundation for our study plan, we need to actually *create* our plan.

I recommend setting aside between 30 minutes and 2 hours to create the initial plan, depending on how many weeks/months the plan covers. After that, 5 to 15 minutes a day to adapt and adjust the plan will be more than sufficient.

A **5-step process** can be used to create our initial study plan:

1. Make a physical *list* (or an Excel sheet) of all the subjects or topics you have exams on. In this list, include all the modules you need to cover and Past-Papers available for each subject/exam. Assign *time estimates* for how long it will roughly take to complete revision for each topic in the module (e.g. making revision notes on each specific topic), and time estimates for how long it will take to complete and mark each Past-Paper. An example of my Module Sheet and Past-Paper Sheet will be shown in the <u>next section</u> of this chapter.

2. Identify the ***end-point*** on your planner. If your exams are less than a month away, the end-point may be the *day before your final exam*. If this date is more than a few months away, use an *earlier milestone* – for example, the date of your first mock exam, or the start of your Easter break. Any date between 2-6 weeks away will work as an *end-point* for the plan. Once that date is reached, identify another end-point 2-6 weeks away, and follow the same process outlined below.

3. Populate the ***non-revision*** sections of your planner (e.g. homework plan, lesson plan, tasks and commitments) starting from today's date. A section for tasks and commitments (e.g. sports, music, seeing friends, family occasions, shopping etc.) is highly recommended. Not only does it help you to manage your expectations in terms of how much work you can realistically achieve on a given day, but it's also very motivating to see that you are still giving yourself the time to do the activities that you enjoy.

4. Populate the ***revision*** section of your planner with the content you wrote down in Step 1 (e.g. revision notes on osmosis, review 'Of Mice and Men' Chapter 1, 2014 Maths Past-Paper). Consider the order in which you want to approach your revision tasks. For example, do you need to make revision notes first, or do you want to begin with Past-Papers immediately? Assign a *time estimate* to each task, and make sure to *leave slack* as you continue to fill in your plan. Remember to keep the plan *realistic* - you may not have the energy to do 4-hours of revision notes after a full day of school, homework, and a tennis lesson. Remember your *priorities* – if there is no way to fit the revision that you need to do into your plan, you may choose to replace an event or activity with extra revision.

5. **Revisit** the plan *at least twice daily*, adding in new tasks as necessary and moving things around. Often, revision will have to be shifted as homework is set – this is completely fine! As explained in Law 3, use your slack time to account for this, or take tasks off from the end of your planner. Remember - you will still do *more* with a good plan than without a plan at all.

Don't forget – *motivation* gets us started, but *habit* keeps us going. Use your initial enthusiasm to create your plan, and then create a *habit* as to when and how you adapt it. Applying a tool often (*frequency*) at regular times (*regularity)* for specific tasks *(specificity*) is the key to creating habits that stick regardless of how much (or how little) motivation, energy or confidence we have.

How long it takes to form a new habit or behaviour varies significantly depending on the person, their environment, and the complexity of the behaviour that they're trying to turn into habit. On average, it takes approximately **66 days** (just over two months) to form a new habit to the extent where our new behaviour becomes automatic.[7] At this stage, it's easier to carry out our new habit than to revert to old behaviours.

So, don't be intimidated or disheartened if you're finding it difficult to implement a habit you're trying to create – it's perfectly normal! To paraphrase world-renowned leadership expert, Robin Sharma, "Change may be difficult at the start and messy in the middle, but it's incredibly *rewarding* at the end." Keep your focus on how the habit will enrich your life when it's formed, instead of focusing on how difficult it is to implement at the moment.

Activity 1.5: Decide on the method that you want to use to create your plan. Using the 6 Laws of Study Planning and the 5-step process outlined above, create your own initial plan. If you don't know where to start, read the next section outlined 'Kam's Planning System' before creating your plan.

For those of you who are curious about how I do my planning, here's my technique.

Kam's Planning System

The system that I use (for myself and my clients) utilises spreadsheet software (Microsoft Excel or Google Sheets) as the foundation for long-term planning. I then *supplement* this with a hand-written daily plan which I complete the night before.

I find being able to *visualise* the spread of time (days, weeks, months) on Microsoft Excel immensely useful, not only for organising tasks and working backwards from my exam dates, but also to help reduce anxiety.

It takes a short amount of time to become familiar with Excel basics: how to move between cells, write in cells, merge cells, and so on. We're not using any complicated functions to make this simple plan!

In screenshot format, this is what a portion of my monthly study spreadsheet looks like before adding in the tasks:

MONTH		Academics		Planner
	School Lessons/ Lectures	Work To Do	Revision Plan	Commitments, Tasks & Events
Tuesday 1				
Wednesday 2				
Thursday 3				
Friday 4				
Saturday 5				
Sunday 6				
Monday 7				
Tuesday 8				
Wednesday 9				
Thursday 10				

Here is a written description of how to create the spreadsheet:

1. Create *individual worksheets* for every month.

2. Going down the *first column*, enter the date for every day in the month (so that you can see a spread of 10-20 days at a time on a laptop, including the tasks you will be doing during those days).

3. Along the *top row*, enter the different categories of work you need to do for each day.

- **School Lessons/ Lectures**: Enter your lessons or lectures for the day, including times. If you are in full-time employment, enter your work hours here.

- **Work To Do**: Enter the work that you plan on completing on any particular day in the future (e.g. homework, interview preparation)

- **Revision Plan**: Enter the revision that you intend to do.

- **Commitments, Tasks & Events**: Enter any events you're attending, or non-study related tasks or commitments you have. Examples may include: tennis training, birthday parties, dinner plans, haircut, laundry, and so on.

The '**Commitments, Tasks & Events**' column is the first part of the planner that I fill out. It helps me to plan more *realistically* and manage my *expectations* of what I can get done on a certain day. For example, I won't plan revision on Sunday morning if I am going to a birthday party the night before! (Although if exams are coming up, I may skip the party altogether... priorities, right?)

I also add a **'Quick-Wins/Diary/Journal'** column, in which I write down any progress that I have made towards my study goals, any sports/physical activity I have done during the day, and any other notable events that I would like to recall when I look back on my plan. As revision increases in the build-up to Exam Day, it's very motivating to see just how much *fun* stuff we've done in the past few months. I'd take a moment to enjoy the memories, remind myself of my exam goals and the progress I was making towards them, and then refocus on the task at hand.

If you like the idea of this planning system but really don't want to use spreadsheet software, you can draw the rows and columns by hand on A4 paper. One of my clients, Nikhil, found it easier to create his plan on landscape-oriented A4 paper. He would separate the page into 7 equally-spaced rows - one for each day of the week - and then draw the columns as described above. He would repeat this for subsequent weeks, keeping in mind the 6 Laws of Study Planning as he filled out and updated his plan. This system worked effectively for him, allowing him to balance his Natural Sciences degree at Cambridge University with his social life and commitments to the university tennis team.

For those of you who prefer to create your study plan according to time (as opposed to task), here is an alternative layout which I created for one of my clients:

DATE		Academics		
		Study Plan: Morning - Lunch	Study Plan: Lunch - Dinner	Study Plan: Dinner - Sleep
Thursday	1			
Friday	2			
Saturday	3			
Sunday	4			
Monday	5			
Tuesday	6			
Wednesday	7			
Thursday	8			
Friday	9			
Saturday	10			

Specific times can be manually entered into the cell, along with a description of the task to be completed during that time. For example, under Study Plan: Morning – Lunch for Thursday 1st, you may enter something like:

- 10:00 – 11:30am: Maths Past Paper
- 11:45am – 12:45pm: Chemistry Revision Notes (Covalent Bonds)

You may also choose to include school lessons and extra-curricular activities when using this planning format.

As mentioned in Step 1 of 'Making The Study Plan', I also recommend creating a separate sheet which includes a list of all the subjects and modules that you are being examined on. The following layout can be used for creating and reviewing revision notes (GCSE Physics example given):

Subject	Modules/Chapters	Module/Chapter Breakdown	Time Required	Review Completed
Physics				
	Particles and Radiation			
		Constituents of the Atom	30 mins	2
		Stable and Unstable Nuclei	30 mins	1
		Particles, Antiparticles & Photons	30 mins	0
		Particle Interactions	45 mins	0
		Classification of Particles	30 mins	0
		Quarks and Antiquarks	30 mins	0
	...Module 2			
		2.1	1 hour	0
		2.2	45 mins	0
		2.3	1.5 hours	0
		etc.		0

Along the *top row*, we can use the following categories:

- **Subject:** Name of subject.

- **Modules/Chapters:** Name of module/chapter.

- **Module/Chapter Breakdown:** Breakdown of module/chapter into smaller sections. Highlight the cell when revision notes for the specific section have been completed.

- **Time Required**: Rough approximation of the time needed to complete the first set of revision notes.

- **Review Completed**: Highlight the cell when the notes have been reviewed. Each time the notes are reviewed, write down the total number of times for which that particular set of notes has been reviewed.

A separate sheet can also be created to list out the relevant Past-Papers which need to be completed for each subject (A-Level Mathematics example given):

Subject	Module/ Exam	Past Paper	Relevant Questions	Time Required
Maths				
	C1			
		2016	All	2 hours
		2015	All	2 hours
		2014	All	2 hours
		2013	All	2 hours
		2012	All	1.5 hours
		2011	All, apart from Q7	1.5 hours
	C2			
		2016	All	2 hours
		2015	All	2 hours
		2014	All	2 hours
		2013	All	2 hours
		2012	All	1.5 hours
		2011	Only Q2,3,4 and 6	1 hour

Along the *top row*, we can use the following categories:

- **Subject:** Name of subject.

- **Module/Exam:** Name of specific module or exam related to the subject.

- **Past-Paper:** Name and year of Past-Paper.

- **Relevant Questions**: Note down the questions in the Past-Paper which are relevant to your exam (e.g. not all questions may be relevant if the syllabus has changed).

- **Time Required:** Time needed to complete, mark and review the Past-Paper.

The planning systems described above have been incredibly helpful for me. Please don't misinterpret this as boasting, but in terms of results, planning in this manner helped me to achieve 13A* at GCSE-Level, 3A* (and 1A – I'm not perfect!) at A-Level, and a place to study Engineering at Churchill College, University of Cambridge.

It's a tried-and-tested method which has also led to positive outcomes for many of the clients that I've shared it with.

But I didn't always use this planning system…

In my first and second years at Cambridge, I had very little passion for the subject that I had chosen to study. I didn't feel motivated to create a study plan. I justified it to myself by saying that it would be too much *effort* to maintain a plan on top of my social life and sporting commitments.

But in hindsight, I recognise that I was *creating excuses* and *lying* to myself. In reality, I had *prioritised* my sports and my relationship because of a *fear* that, no matter what I would try, everyone else would be better than me. My pride didn't want to risk the disappointment of finding out that my best wasn't good enough…so instead, it decided *not to try*.

Not the right attitude at all.

I attained the lowest grade in my college in my 1st year course.

I realised afterwards that my *priorities* had been all wrong. I realised that my *fears* were sabotaging my performance. And I realised that I was dangerously close to putting myself in a position which I may regret in the future.

I knew that I had to make a change.

So, in my second year, I *committed* to doing my best. I studied harder – but I still *didn't plan*. Instead, I just did what my peers were doing. It was quite stressful trying to keep up with their pace. I wasn't studying *efficiently*, and I could feel myself struggling under the weight of my own expectations.

But I kept pushing. I gave my all to attain the 2.1 grade I desired…and I missed it by less than 1%. I missed my goal by the *smallest of margins*. It *destroyed* me to have come so close to my goal, but to have fallen just short of the mark. I felt all the disappointment that my pride had previously tried to protect me from. I had given my best, and my best wasn't good enough.

I took time over the summer to process this. I had failed to meet my goals, and I had serious doubts about whether I could ever get beyond a 2.2 grade. On top of this, I was going through some personal challenges related to relationships and my physical and mental health. This chapter of my life is discussed further in My Story.

However, I came through my personal challenges using the mind-management tools I share in Principle 3. I made a promise to myself that I would continue giving my all. I accepted that my best hadn't been good enough up to this point – but also that my best had the potential to get *better* every day.

I realised that my study methods for the past few years hadn't helped me to achieve the results I desired. It would be foolish to use them to form a study strategy for my all-important 3rd year. As the famous physicist, Albert Einstein, remarked, "insanity is doing the same thing over and over again, but expecting different results."

However, I realised that my planning strategy in GCSEs and A-Levels had been successful in helping me get the grades I wanted. As such, for the third and final year of my Cambridge undergraduate degree, I took the old planning system that had helped me during my GCSEs and A-Levels, and adjusted it to the demands of my final year studies.

With exams in May, I created a revision plan starting at the beginning of January (5 months!). There was a lot of plan adaptation between January and May, but I genuinely believed that I was doing far more *with* the plan than I would have done without it. There were many moments when I doubted whether keeping to my plan would help me achieve my Exam Success goals – but I *trusted the process* and kept following through on my actions every single day.

It was completely worth it.

I ended up achieving a 1st class, the grade which I ultimately graduated with.

I also used this planning system while studying for my Master's Degree in Engineering, which I achieved with a Merit. The plan helped me to balance my studies with my sporting commitments as Captain of the Cambridge University Lawn Tennis Club Men's 2nd Team, as well as running my own small-scale fitness and life coaching business.

My journey hasn't always been an easy one (check the My Story section at the end of this book!) – but it's fair to say that I'm immensely grateful for these plans!

They allowed me to manage my time effectively, so that I could successfully apply the other 7 Principles outlined within this book. This is the reason why I chose Time Management as the 1st Principle of Exam Success.

In summary:

- Procrastination and poor productivity are not *purely* time-management challenges – but good time-management skills are still vital in reducing procrastination and improving our productivity.

- Identifying and *explicitly categorising* our *priorities* is essential in enabling us to plan effectively.

- The 6 Laws of Study Planning will help us to create *more effective plans* that we won't feel like giving up on.

- Create a *habit* of frequently checking and updating your plan.

- You will *always* do more with a *good plan* than without a plan at all.

- Kam likes making plans a bit more than the average person!

Congratulations on making it through to the end of the 1st Principle – the journey towards Exam Success has just begun!

2. Principle Two: Study Tools & Techniques

This Principle will introduce you to some tried-and-tested study tools and techniques that can optimise your learning and productivity, revolutionise your revision process and put you firmly on the path towards Exam Success.

There are three components to Principle 2.

- **How** To Study (learning methods and techniques)

- **Where** To Study (location and surrounding environment)

- **When** To Study (time of day)

2.1 How To Study: Mastering Study Tools & Techniques

Task vs Time-Focused

One of the key factors to consider when identifying our optimum studying style is whether we're **task-focused** or **time-focused** when we approach tasks.

Task-focused individuals will work as long as it takes to complete a task, even if it means falling behind schedule. Once they are in the groove, they are hard to stop. However, it can take discipline to get to work in the first place – and sometimes just as much discipline to stop! It's important for them to define *specific start times*, but also to consider the *latest finish time* they can afford for each task. This will enable them to keep to their plan and avoid falling too far behind because they spent too long on a single task.

Time-focused individuals will set a timer for *x* hours to complete a task, and will then try to complete the task in that specific time period. This sounds effective and well-organised, except that they may also get distracted by WhatsApp messages, Snapchat, and other distractions during this time – and *still* consider it as part of the time they spent working on that task! Techniques such as the Pomodoro Technique (coming up!) are often helpful in allowing them to manage their time more effectively. Setting *realistic time-scales* for task completion and *minimising distractions* is essential to their success.

Neither of these two styles is right or wrong, but it's important to be aware of the advantages and potential pitfalls of each.

Think of the two styles as two ends of a spectrum. Even though we might identify with a few aspects of both, we often have a natural tendency to one over the other. Once we're aware of where our tendencies lie, we can work to ensure that our **planning system** has a way of *accounting* for the potential pitfalls that we might face. We can also begin to experiment with our less dominant style in hopes of combining the benefits of both styles to aid us in our studying.

Activity 2.1: Are you more of a time-focused or task-focused worker? What can you do to prevent yourself from falling victim to the pitfalls of your dominant type?

The 'Learning Styles' Myth

Some of you may have been introduced to the idea of 'Learning Styles' in school; if not, it's possible that you may be exposed to it in the future. The Learning Styles theory suggests that we have individual preferences that determine how we learn best, and that we should be taught using our preferred 'style' in order to maximise our learning. However, scientific studies are becoming increasingly *critical* of this idea.[1]

Before we discuss better alternatives to Learning Styles, it's useful to get a basic understanding of what they are. There are many different categories of Learning Styles, but most include some variation of the following:

1. Learning according to **sensory preference**:

For example, a **visual learner** has a preference for images, pictures and spatial understanding. Useful study methods to learn content would include:

- Mind-maps, pictures and other visual system diagrams.
- Using colour pens and highlighters to emphasise words or concepts.

An **auditory learner** has a preference for sound and music. They may benefit from:

- Listening to sound recordings related to the content being studied.
- Reading notes out aloud, for example with dramatic voice intonations.

A **kinaesthetic learner** has a preference for using their body, hands and sense of touch. They may benefit from:

- Using physical objects that can be touched, felt or held, e.g. flash cards, notes.
- Focusing on the sensation of pen on paper when writing notes.

2. Learning according to **thinking style**: 'concrete' and 'abstract' learners.

Concrete learners prefer to use explicit facts, data and examples when solving problems. They think practically and logically before attempting to solve the problem, and then approach the problem using well-established methods. When being introduced to new content, they benefit from knowing even the smallest details to ensure that there are no gaps in their understanding.

Abstract learners prefer to use intuition and imagination when solving problems, and they apply concepts and rules in a more fluid way. They may take ideas or observed patterns from one domain and attempt to apply it to a different problem. They may also be able to draw analogies and relationships between concepts that others may not notice.

3. Learning according to **speed** and **accuracy**: 'impulsive' and 'reflective' learners.

Impulsive learners are characterised by being able to solve problems quickly, but inaccurately. They *believe* that they grasp concepts quickly and skilfully, but often take shortcuts when processing new information and end up overestimating their capabilities. With practice, they learn to solve problems quickly and accurately, though their accuracy may still be less than *reflective* learners.

Reflective learners tend to solve problems slowly, but with greater accuracy. Although they may initially take longer to process new content, they're also more likely to spend time and effort understanding the information in order to apply it competently. Reflective learners have often been linked with possessing perfectionist traits.

Having read through the Learning Styles outlined above, it's likely that some of us can see ourselves being portrayed quite accurately in their descriptions! So, why have Learning Styles gathered such a negative reputation amongst the scientific community?

The biggest criticisms of the Learning Styles model include:

- **No correlation with learning:** The Learning Styles refer to traits and tendencies we have as individuals, but there has been no scientific evidence to support that these significantly influence how we *learn*. While Learning Styles were originally adopted from other theories in human cognition, they are being *incorrectly applied* to learning.[1] For example, though someone may have a kinaesthetic preference for perceiving the world (i.e. they process the world more through their feelings and sense of touch than, for example, what they see or hear), this doesn't mean that they are going to be a 'kinaesthetic learner'.

- **Neglecting skills that come less naturally to us:** By concentrating on just one or two preferred modes of learning, we neglect to improve our other cognitive abilities. Instead of just focusing on our strengths, we should devote time to developing the skills that may come less naturally to us. This helps us to enhance our cognitive abilities as a whole and gives us a wider range of tools to solve the different problems that we will be exposed to throughout our lives.

- **Nature of subject material is more important than individual preferences:** A 2006 study showed that different groups being taught the same material performed better when taught using one specific Learning Style.[2] This led to the conclusion that the nature of the *subject* being taught is *more important* than students' individual learning preferences. This makes sense – for example, Mathematics may be easier to learn through practising example questions as opposed to listening to tapes on how to solve a problem. In contrast, Spanish grammar may be easier to learn through reading and making notes compared to drawing pictures and diagrams.

- **Defined inconsistently, identified inaccurately:** There are too many ways to describe Learning Styles (over 71 different styles according to a review published in 2004). [3] Not only are definitions inconsistent across different Learning Styles models, but there has also been criticism directed towards the questionnaires being used to help students to identify their individual learning preferences. Questions may be phrased vaguely and misunderstood by students, leading to answers that don't reflect their preferences. As a result, the Learning Style recommended by the questionnaire may not be accurate for the student. In addition, any initial bias that a student has towards what they *think* their preferred Learning Style is can influence how they answer questions. As such, the result may simply confirm their initial belief about their Learning Style, even though their performance may prove otherwise.

Given this, what best practices can we draw by integrating the criticisms of the existing Learning Styles model with new developments in learning theory?

1. Multi-Sensory Approach To Learning

Instead of focusing on learning via one sensory mode, we should look over the content we're trying to learn using a *combination* of different sensory modes.[4]

One of the most popular examples of this is *dual coding*, which involves combining verbal materials with visual materials.[5] Presenting the same information both verbally (e.g. written notes) and visually (e.g. diagrams, infographics, charts, timelines) gives our brain two different ways of remembering it.

The more creative we get with the visual materials we design, the more likely we are to remember the information that is being described. Combining this with more-detailed text reinforces the content that we're trying to learn and allows us to recall it with greater ease and accuracy.

During my studies, when I was revising by reviewing the 'dual-coded' notes that I'd created, I found it even more helpful to involve a *third sensory mode* – the *auditory* sense. I would speak the notes aloud, varying my volume and tone as I reviewed them. I found that using this multi-sensory approach allowed me to memorise content more effectively than if I was just re-reading the notes I had written.

2. Subject-Focused Learning

As mentioned, the nature of the *subject* being taught is actually more important than students' individual learning preferences.[2] We should consider what methods of learning may be best-suited to each subject before incorporating our own individual studying preferences. Some examples of subject-specific studying techniques that have worked for me over the years include:

- **Maths:** Answering textbook/Past-Paper questions; explaining each step aloud as if I was tutoring another person.

- **Sciences:** Notes combined with visual diagrams (dual-coding); reading notes aloud when reviewing; self-testing with flashcards for formulae and key definitions; Past-Paper questions; explaining each step aloud as if I was tutoring another person.

- **English:** Constructing essay plans and model essay structure for different types of questions; using dual coding (notes + mind-maps) to memorise key points from books/poems in the syllabus.

- **History:** Constructing essay plans and model essay structure for different types of questions; using dual coding (notes + timeline) to memorise content.

- **Geography:** Dual-coding (notes + images) to memorise content (especially for physical geography processes); drawing out timelines or mind-maps to describe case studies.

- **Languages:** Colour coding and self-testing for grammar and vocabulary, listening to audiotapes (listening exam); reciting sentences aloud when memorising a script (oral exam); drawing a 'visual transcript' of images that tell the story of the set of sentences that I am trying to memorise (written exam)

I recommend that you experiment with applying different revision techniques to different subjects to discover what works best for you.

There will be more information on how to get the most out of revision notes and past-papers in the next section of this chapter (10 Awesome Study Tools & Techniques).

3. Competency-Based Learning

Whether we have a *concrete* or *abstract* 'thinking style' shouldn't be used to inform how we learn. Instead, we should consider how *competent* we are at the subject or module in question. When we're exposed to a completely new and unfamiliar concept, it may benefit us to focus on developing our understanding of the *concrete* facts and methods that form the foundations of that concept. The more familiar we become with the fundamentals, the more capable and competent we become, and we can then begin to experiment with applying our knowledge in an *abstract* way.

In other words, concrete and abstract do not show two distinctive preferences, but instead reflect our level of expertise at a certain point in time. We should begin as 'concrete learners' when we're a novice or beginner, and then shift to 'abstract learners' as our competency reaches an advanced or expert level.[4]

4. Developing *All* Cognitive Abilities

Instead of just focusing on our natural strengths (as the Learning Styles model promotes), we should devote time to developing the skills that may come less naturally to us. As well as having benefits in studying (e.g. multi-sensory approach to learning is more effective than single-sensory learning), it also helps us to enhance our cognitive abilities overall.

This is invaluable as we make the transition from formal education to the 'real world', where having a wider range of well-developed cognitive skills can help us to solve the problems we encounter (whether in the workplace or in everyday life) in a more practical and effective manner.

To take advantage of this, we first need to identify our natural preferences for learning and problem-solving. In doing so, we can then become aware of the areas that need developing. It's then up to us to make a conscious decision to work on improving these abilities.

Activity 2.2: Think about what your natural tendencies are for how you prefer to learn. Which other cognitive abilities should you develop to help you study more effectively? For each subject you study, which learning methods do you want to experiment with?

-----

10 Awesome Study Tools & Techniques

Here is a collection of 10 of the most effective studying techniques and tools that I have personally attempted over my years of studying. Some have been scientifically tested and validated. Others have been recommended by teachers with many years of experience at top UK secondary schools, or by Cambridge/Oxford students who have excelled in their studies. A few are tools which I've devised myself, although it's absolutely possible that other students and teachers around the world have also thought of them and utilised them in the past.

1.   The Ultimate Revision Note Guide

In all honesty, making revision notes can be a boring and time-consuming process. Most of us don't really know *how* to make effective revision notes, and we end up getting *less* out of them relative to the amount of time and effort we put into making them.

Not ideal at all.

But when done correctly, making revision notes can be an incredibly powerful studying tool.

Let's start with the basics.

Hand-Written Notes vs Typed Notes

Studies have shown that hand-written notes are more effective than notes which were typed on a keyboard or touch-screen.[6] The hand movements involved when writing unique letters and forming words is beneficial to learning. The act of writing leaves a 'motor memory' in the sensorimotor part of the brain, which helps a person to recognise letters and strengthen the connection between what is being read and written. This connection doesn't form as strongly when notes are typed, as each letter on the keyboard/touch-screen has the same 'feel' to it.

Most of us associate typing notes as being quicker than writing notes by hand. Although this is good for completing or reviewing topics in a short amount of time, it isn't conducive to learning. Researchers propose that the additional time taken to hand-write notes promotes learning, as more time is being spent on the task and the brain has more time to process the content being written.[7]

Producing large amounts of typed-notes by copying from a textbook or transcribing verbatim from a lecture or lesson has also been shown to be comparatively less beneficial for learning purposes than creating hand-written notes.[7] Even though they may be very detailed, typing notes in this manner can lead to 'mindless transcribing' of information, where more attention is being paid to the typing process than to the content itself.

Finally, if we're doing a written examination, writing notes during our studying preparation can help us train our 'writing muscles' and improve our 'writing stamina'. Great for those two-hour essay papers!

Kam's Note-Making Secrets

I performed best in exams where I had made detailed hand-written notes on the topic. I used dual-coding (written and visual content) to remember the content more effectively. I would use different coloured pens and highlighters as necessary to categorise content (e.g. formulae in red, definitions in blue etc.) or to emphasise specific words.

I would re-read the notes aloud when reviewing them, often varying my tone, volume and pace to link specific content with stronger auditory associations. I would also read notes aloud as if I was *teaching* the content to a class or *explaining* a concept to someone who had never heard of it before.

This is a very effective technique. Convincing our brain that we not only need to recall content, but that we must also be able to teach or explain it in a simple and clear way, forces us to remember it with greater clarity. In addition, if I found myself struggling to explain a concept, it often meant that I didn't understand it fully. I would then add it to my list of 'weaker topics' and set aside time in my plan to focus on it in more detail.

When reviewing notes, I would also have a scrap sheet of paper beside me where I would re-write the key words and concepts as I spoke them. I would not keep this scrap sheet of paper after finishing my review – the writing was often messy and unstructured. The purpose of making scrap notes was simply to reinforce the content being reviewed at that instant. I would repeat this process every time I reviewed my notes.

Occasionally, I would test myself using the *read-write-recite-repeat* technique. I would read through a section, re-write it on a scrap sheet of paper, and then cover *both* of them up with a plain sheet of paper. I would then recite the content I was trying to memorise until I was successful in doing so. This process could then be repeated until the notes were fully reviewed.

I was only able to follow this 'ideal' revision note-making process when I had a *good plan*. The time-consuming nature of hand-written notes meant that I had to set aside enough time to make detailed, dual-coded notes on all the topics.

And there were many occasions when I didn't have the time to do so…

In these scenarios, I would resort to *typing* revision notes on my laptop. I would quickly type notes in the *same* font and colour. This 'First Run-Through' would help me to re-familiarise myself with all the content of the course. I would then scroll to the top of the document and go through the notes again. On this 'Second Run-Through', I would add bold script, italics, underlines, different colours and other formatting changes to the notes. Re-reading the notes and selecting the appropriate words to format ensured that my mind was focused on the content of the words.

I would then print out the formatted revision notes. With a pen in hand, I would re-read them (aloud) and annotate them, drawing diagrams where relevant. Finally, as I approached the date of the exam, I would re-write my notes in a summarised form on scrap paper as I reviewed them.

This 'best of both worlds' approach was not ideal. However, it worked very effectively when I found myself with plenty to learn in a short space of time. It was my preferred tactic during my 4th year Engineering Master's degree at Cambridge, where we were examined on modules on a weekly/fortnightly basis and I didn't always have time to fully assimilate the material.

Notes – The Cure For Mental Recall Issues

Too many students that I've worked with have had a harmful habit of trying to *mentally* recall the content that they're trying to memorise. They don't recall it by speaking aloud. They don't recall it by writing it down. They simply try to recall a fact or answer in their mind…

…and then enter *panic mode* when they can't immediately recall it mentally!

This inability to recall an answer mentally can happen for many reasons. Most often, it's because we're *tired*. We tend to ask ourselves to mentally recall facts late in the day – or even worse, just before bed! When we find that we can't do it, we become stressed and anxious. Either we decide to 'panic study', only to become more stressed because we're not retaining any information, or we struggle to sleep because we feel unprepared, nervous and worried.

One of my clients, Nikki, first approached me because she had been experiencing a 'mental block' for several days. She felt that she hadn't retained anything that she'd been studying – and she was in the *middle* of her exams! The loss of confidence caused by this 'mental block' had rolled-over to her last two exams and caused her to panic when she saw a question for which she couldn't *immediately* remember the correct answer – even though after the exam, she realised that she actually *did* know how to do the question.

We tried to get to the root of the issue. In this case, the source turned out to be an unsuccessful attempt at mental recall 6 days earlier when Nikki was brushing her teeth before bed! She was exhausted and ready to sleep, had tried to recall a fact from her Biology A-Level paper – and had panicked when she couldn't immediately remember it!

Instead of simply checking her notes and reviewing the content, she suffered an anxiety attack!

I'm not telling you all of this to stress you out.

I'm telling you this because the solution is *so simple*.

With the exception of oral examinations, you'll *never* have to mentally recall a fact, answer or solution in an exam! There will *always* be pen, paper and sufficient time for you to process the question, note down your thoughts, and recall the correct answer. Even if you don't recall the answer immediately, writing down a few key words can help to trigger your memory and aid you in remembering the answer.

And if you can't remember the answer during your revision, you can calmly get your textbook/notes, turn to the relevant page, and write down the correct answer. It's much easier to stay calm when you are processing facts externally (on a piece of paper) than trying to process them internally (in your own mind).

So, if you're going to practise mental recall during your revision, *write your thoughts and answers down,* and give yourself *time* to reach the answer. And most importantly, do *not* practise mental recall when you're tired!

Once we got to the root of the issue, Nikki was so relieved. Just confronting the source of the problem helped to alleviate the issue, as well as the knowledge that she always had a pen-and-paper during the exam to help her remember the content.

I'm grateful to share that the rest of her exams went *a lot* better! I'm also grateful to her for allowing me to share her story – she admitted that she was embarrassed about it, but that it would be worth it if it helped other students!

2. Past-Paper Mark-Scheme Tactics

A warning for this tool. It doesn't work for *everyone*. However, it worked extremely well for me during my A-Levels and Cambridge exams.

For subjects that are not assessed by essays (e.g. Maths, Sciences, Engineering etc.), Past-Papers will often be accompanied by detailed Mark-Schemes. These will offer *worked solutions* for problems involving calculations, as well as *perfectly-worded written answers* for questions involving definitions or explanations.

In general, the *ideal* study process for Past-Papers involves completing the paper under exam conditions, checking our answers, and then using the Mark-Scheme to review what we did wrong. It's always worth setting aside time in our revision plans to complete a few Past-Papers (for example, those from the most recent years) in this manner.

However, when time is limited and there are *many* Past-Paper options available, it might not feasible to do every paper in this fashion.

When this was the case, I would print or download *both* the Past-Paper *and* the Mark-Scheme, and *copy* each Mark-Scheme answer out *by hand* on an A4 sheet of paper. This would be an *active, deliberate* process – there was no point during which I was mindlessly copying out words without thinking about them. This allowed me to 'complete' each Past-Paper in *at least* half of the time that it would have taken to do so otherwise.

If you do this, don't just *read* the mark scheme. The benefit comes from *writing* down the answers in a conscious, thoughtful way. This helps to ingrain into our memories both the methods (for calculations) and the precise wording needed for full marks (for written answers) on the question.

As I mentioned, this is not a *substitute* for doing Past-Papers properly – it's just an alternative to consider if you're constrained for time. It works best when you're confident about the content in your module, and are just trying to commit answers to memory and refine your exam technique.

In addition to this, I would keep an Excel spreadsheet (here we go again...) to *track* the questions that came up in Past-Papers. For each Past-Paper, I would write down a brief description of every question within it, and note down whether I found the question *easy, moderate* or *difficult*. This would help me to identify which topics I particularly struggled on, allowing me to specifically target those areas during my revision.

With enough Past-Papers under my belt, I also tried to notice patterns to help with *predicting* some of the topics that might come up in my real exams. I must warn you that this is *not* accurate, and certainly not something to base your *entire* revision strategy on. If you decide to do this, use it to *supplement* your revision – not become the foundation for it. For example, if the same topic or question has come up in 3 of the last 4 past-papers, we don't lose much by spending a bit more time revising it. It may not come up – but if it does, we'll be prepared.

I strongly recommend *against* 'tactically' ignoring topics altogether because you don't think they will come up in this year's exam based on Past-Paper trends. It just isn't worth feeling like an idiot during the exam when the topic *does* come up and you find yourself completely unprepared. Believe me, I've been there – and those probability questions in my 1st year Cambridge Maths paper punished me dearly!

Plan well, study diligently, and you won't even need to consider resorting to 'tactically' neglecting parts of your course.

3. Pomodoro Technique

The Pomodoro Technique[8)] is a simple productivity tool developed by Francisco Pomodoro in the 1980's. The idea is to work in units of *Pomodoros*. Each Pomodoro lasts for 30 minutes, during which you *work* on your task for 25 minutes, and then take a *break* for 5 minutes. After 4 Pomodoros, you can take a longer break (15-30 minutes), before resetting the Pomodoro counter to 0. This technique revolutionised my studying for the following reasons:

- Setting clear time boundaries reduced the impact of internal and external interruptions on my study *flow*. If I continued beyond the 25-minute mark set by the Pomodoro, I would make a note of it, but still adhere to the 5-minute break until the next Pomodoro began.

- Short, intense time intervals are very productive *without* being overly stressful – this is great if you've had a long day of work or school and can't face the thought of two hours of solid revision.

- We can convince ourselves to do *anything* for 'just 25 minutes' - including not checking our phones! Hour-long blocks can be daunting, and we'll often find reasons to procrastinate within them. A 25-minute burst of high productivity and no procrastination is manageable, even for those of us who are most easily distracted.

As mentioned in the <u>Poor Productivity</u> section of Principle 1, you can adapt this technique to your personal Study Flow Curve timings that enable you to reach and maintain your 100% productivity level. Some people find a 5-minute break for each 25-35 minutes of work (as in the Pomodoro Technique) to be effective, whereas others prefer a 10-minute break for each 45-60 minutes of work.

4. Metacognition

Metacognition means 'thinking about how we think'.

In the context of studying for exams, it refers to the idea of strategising *how* we're going to study, instead of simply diving into the first task that we can think of.

Many of us tend to think less about *how* we're studying, and more on *how long* we're studying for. In doing so, we risk expending large amounts of time and effort doing work which doesn't actually translate to better performance in our exams.

By taking time to reflect on *how* we're going to approach our studies – for example, by considering the different study resources available to us and the different revision strategies we can implement – we increase the likelihood of performing better in our exams.

A 2017 study conducted at Stanford University showed that students who practised metacognition out-performed their peers on exams by the equivalent of one-third of a letter grade.[10] These students also reported feeling less stress and a greater sense of control over their performance than their peers.

How was metacognition practised in this study?

The selected students were first asked to consider the grade that they *wanted* to achieve, how *important* it was to them to achieve that grade, and how *likely* they thought they were to achieve it.

They were then asked to consider which types of *questions* the exam may include and the *study resources* they had available to them, such as lecture notes, practise questions, peer discussions, textbook readings and private tutoring. For each resource, they wrote down *why* that resource would be useful, and *how* they planned to utilise it in their exam preparation.

It's important to note that the selected students were chosen to ensure that there were no statistical differences in their performance compared to their peers prior to the exam. The students were also carefully chosen to ensure that there were no significant differences in their high-school GPAs, current motivation levels, and grades that they were hoping to achieve.[9]

So, what does all of this mean for you?

Before jumping into your studies, first think about *how* you are going to study. Be aware of the expectations and goals you have set for yourself. Recall some of your past exam performances and the key learning points you've taken away from them. Consider the study resources you have available to you and which would be most useful. Think about the exam itself and the types of questions you are likely to be asked. And then bring this information together to form a coherent study plan.

If you're still confused about whether you understand metacognition or not – by reading this book, you're already practising it!

Each activity and study tool outlined in this book is designed to make you *think* about how you currently study, whether a new tool or technique can help you to improve your studying process, and how you can implement it into your routine.

The reason why I have chosen to *explicitly* include metacognition as a studying technique is just to emphasise that scientific studies have *proved* that the steps involved in creating a study plan can help you to improve your exam performance.

5. Test-Based Learning

Self-testing has been shown to be more effective in increasing content retention compared with passive forms of studying, such as re-reading notes or re-watching lectures. [10] These 'tests' aren't like exams – they are simply ways for us to quiz ourselves on the content we're learning in a relaxed, low-stakes environment.

Creating flashcards to quiz yourself on, frequently practising past-paper questions and doing Q&A sessions with study partners can all be effective ways of taking advantage of this.

6. Spaced Studying vs Night-Before Cramming

It might sound obvious, but studies have shown that spacing our studying is more effective than cramming when it comes to retaining information over a longer period of time.[11]

It's worth noting here that cramming can be slightly effective in the short-term for a one-off exam – however, as many of you might have experienced, you forget much of the information a week or month later. This is not helpful if you're being examined on similar content in the future.

If that wasn't bad enough, cramming also increases stress in the short-term and significantly decreases productivity *after* the exam – not ideal if you have another exam coming up within the next few days. Cramming is a consequence of poor planning and high anxiety. These can be removed altogether with a well-formed, long-term plan (Principle 1) and an effective studying mindset (Principle 3).

7. Interleaved Practice & Reviewing

Let's say that we have 3 modules to revise for: A, B and C. In this case, our plan is to spend 3 days on A, followed by 3 days on B, finishing with 3 days on C.

And after finishing C, we will realise that we have already forgotten most of the content from A…

Interleaving involves mixing up how we study these modules. In this case, we will study 1 day of A, followed by 1 day of B, followed by 1 day of C. We would then repeat this process until the modules were complete.

In other words, instead of AAABBBCCC, we'll study ABCABCABC.

In doing this, we're forcing our brain to recall the material covered in the past each time we revisit the module. This 'mini-review' strengthens the link between the content we covered previously and the content that we're covering now. It also signals to our brain that we need to be ready to recall information that may have been collected *more than one day ago*, increasing the likelihood of transferring the information from our *working memory* to our *long-term memory*.[12]

I would also incorporate interleaved practice into my daily schedule. Instead of focusing on one subject for an entire day, I would normally dedicate the morning period to one subject and the afternoon to another. I would tactically choose which subjects and modules I covered. For example, I would always do the *hardest subject first.*

In addition, if I had two different exams in one day, I would always cover the first exam subject in the morning, and the second in the afternoon. This would train my mind to begin associating the two subjects together, so that my brain could recall material from both subjects with greater ease on Exam Day.

In general, working backwards from our exam dates is vital when creating a long-term plan that allows us to incorporate interleaved practice into our revision schedule.

Let me share an example with you from one of my clients.

Nathan was studying Mathematics, Further Mathematics, Physics and Economics, and had received an A*AA offer from Cambridge University to study Land Economy.

His offer explicitly required Economics, which made it one of his most *important* subjects. Physics was the subject he had revised *least* so far. Further Maths was the subject he found most *difficult*. Maths was the subject he found *easiest* – he'd already done exams in 4 modules the previous year (C1, C2, S1, S2).

We created a weekly Easter term/study leave schedule that would allow him to study for his 14 examinations using interleaved practise in the morning (before lunch) and afternoon (before dinner) periods. His after-dinner periods were his own to review notes, or catch-up on any work he missed during the day due to other commitments (sports, etc.).

An outline of his schedule is shown below:

Day 1 Morning: Further Maths (FP2 & FP3)
Day 1 Afternoon: Economics (Theme 1)

Day 2 Morning: Physics (Paper 1)
Day 2 Afternoon: Further Maths (D1 & FP1)

Day 3 Morning: Economics (Theme 3)
Day 3 Afternoon: Maths (C3 & C4)

Day 4 Morning: Physics (Paper 2)
Day 4 Afternoon: SLACK – catching up on any work missed.

Day 5 Morning: Further Maths (FP2 & FP3)
Day 5 Afternoon: Economics (Theme 2)

Day 6 Morning: Physics (Paper 3)
Day 6 Afternoon: Further Maths (Mechanics – M1 & M2)

Day 7 Morning: Maths (C3 & C4)
Day 7 Afternoon: SLACK – catching up on any work missed.

This general approach helped him to cover all examinable material a few months before his exams. It considered that he had his Economics Paper 3 & Maths C4 paper on the same day (Day 3). It gave him the opportunity to focus on each of his Economics and Physics papers (Day 1 – 6). It added extra time to cover the more difficult Further Maths modules (FP2, FP3 - Day 1, Day 5) as well as the easier Further Maths Modules (Day 2, Day 6). It gave him enough time to focus on Maths (Day 3, Day 7), his most likely A* grade.

With each passing week, we'd specify the exact notes or Past-Papers that he would complete on any day. As exams approached, his schedule was amended to account for immediate exams – it's not ideal to be revising for an Economics exam next week when your Physics exam is tomorrow!

This technique worked well for him – Nathan met his offer and commenced his studies at Cambridge University.

8. Memory Devices (Mnemonics)

This technique is helpful for *memorising* content from our courses for our exams. There are three key principles behind the use of mnemonics.[13]

The first principle is **association**, which describes the way we connect the *thing* we're trying to remember to a *method* of remembering it (an *association image*). To recall what we're trying to remember, we then only need to recall the association image. Our minds work in different ways, so different associations will be more effective for each of us.

Examples of ways we can associate things include:

- Linking through colour, sound, shape or feeling.
- Merging, combining or wrapping things around each other.
- Imagining the objects crashing into or penetrating each other.
- Placing things on top of each other.

The second principle is **imagination**. Imagination is how we use our minds to create the links and associations that have the most meaning for us. The more strongly we can imagine or visualise an association, the more likely we are to remember it, so make them as creative, vivid, memorable – and even *weird* – as possible!

The final principle is **location**. Assigning a location to a particular mnemonic can strengthen our ability to remember it. Location provides us with a *context* for our information to further strengthen associations, and can also be used to *separate* unrelated mnemonics from each other.

Our associations will be *unique* to each of us based on a combination of the way our mind works and the content that we're trying to memorise. Nevertheless, here's a client example which I hope will clarify the principles of mnemonics:

Anthony was studying for his History A-level exams. He was complaining that there were too many dates and events to remember. I asked him to give me an example of one fact that was particularly tough to recall. His example was:

- The First Continental Congress took place in Philadelphia in September 1774, with Georgia being the only colony that chose not to send delegates.

He said that he had to be able to recall the year (1774) and the specific detail about Georgia for the exam. Any other details would be a bonus. He then asked me how I would remember this fact.

As mentioned, our minds work in different ways, so you might find the upcoming snapshot into my mind a bit surreal! You've been warned…

In my case, I wanted to link the number 74 to Georgia. After a minute of wondering what my mind automatically associated with Georgia, I came up with my *association image* – a 74-year-old grandmother called Georgia!

I then added *imagination* – my 74-year old grandmother called Georgia was incredibly antisocial and would swear angrily at anyone who invited her to anything – *especially* the First Continental Congress! I made her loud, profane and incredibly animated in my mind.

I then added *location* – Philadelphia. The hometown of the cheese steak, the 76ers basketball team and the Fresh Prince of Bel Air.

I then *reinforced* the association – my antisocial 74-year old grandmother, Georgia, eating cheese steaks and angrily swearing at everyone around her. Once the association was firm, I returned to it and added details, for example that Grandma Georgia's birthday was in September.

I made this association so strong that anytime I watch Fresh Prince of Bel Air or a 76ers basketball match, I can't help but recall Grandma Georgia and the First Continental Congress!

Experiment with mnemonics next time you are revising a content-heavy subject and discover what works best for you. Remember - the weirder, the better!

9. Commitment & Accountability

This very simple tool is effective for people who work better when they feel that they will be held *accountable* if they don't produce work within a defined period of time.

A study group is a great example of this. By committing to meet at a certain time to study, we feel an obligation to arrive on time, begin our tasks and continue working while in the presence of our study group. There's more information on forming an ideal study group in <u>Principle 8</u>.

However, study groups aren't always feasible. We might prefer to work alone, or other people may not be available. In this case, there are several actions we can take to create a sense of *accountability*.

For example, we can inform someone else of the tasks we need to complete on a given day, and *commit* to sending them *pictures* of each completed product (e.g. revision notes, past-paper questions) at specific times. We can also send a *time-lapse video* of ourselves studying for a period of time, or create a blog or social media account dedicated to studying where we upload photos of our work at regular times.

The combination of creating a *deadline* for our tasks alongside having people to hold us *accountable* drives us to complete our tasks quicker and with fewer distractions. The other person doesn't even *need* to do anything; just the *impression* of being held accountable if we miss the deadline can be sufficient as an incentive for us to commit to our tasks.

A cool sibling, cousin or parent is ideal for this role – we respect them enough to want to show them that we're working, but know that they won't get extensively involved and start to interrogate us on what we're doing and how much we're doing. The last thing we want is for (uncool) parents to start grilling us on why we only did 12 pages of revision notes instead of the 15 we 'promised' them!

10. Time-Lapse Videos

Here's an awesome trick which can be combined with the Commitment & Accountability technique above. When I was in my 3rd year, I decided to calculate my *productivity ratio* (yes, I know, how cool am I?). This is because I've always found it easier to convince myself to make improvements based on data I can actually *measure*. In this case, I wanted to identify how much of my 'time spent doing work' was *actually* spent doing work.

In other words, if I was working on a task for 2 hours, I wanted to figure out how much of that 2-hour period I spent *actually working* compared to the amount of time I spent staring out of the window, using YouTube on my laptop, going to the fridge (etc.) while I considered myself to be working.

I decided to set up a time-lapse video on my iPhone to record myself over 2 hours, after which I would look through the footage and roughly calculate my productivity ratio. I connected my phone to a charger, loaded the time-lapse function, and got to work…

This experiment was an utter failure.

Why?

Because I worked steadily for *the entire 2 hours!*

Psychologically speaking, I couldn't bear to find out my *true* unproductivity levels. I didn't want to accept any tangible evidence that *proved* that I was inefficient and easily distracted. So, knowing that I was recording myself, I convinced myself to *stay seated* and *continue working* each time I felt the temptation to get up from my desk.

As a result, I managed to do *productive work* for longer than ever before without taking a break!

So, the experiment failed – I didn't figure out a realistic value for my productive work ratio. But in failing, I learned a powerful productivity trick: *we always do more when we're being filmed!*

Set up your time-lapses for about 40-60 minutes and see how it works for you. Even if you don't feel more productive, you'll be able to figure out a realistic representation of your productivity ratio (which you can then focus on improving). And at the very worst, you simply won't be distracted by your phone while studying – it's hard to check messages when there's a time-lapse recording and your phone is out of reach!

Activity 2.3: Of the 10 studying techniques described above, which ones would you like to integrate into your studying process? How can you begin implementing them?

The more we practise applying these techniques, the *easier* they become to apply, and the *better* we become at using them. Once you've decided on the techniques you want to experiment with, use your plan to help you get into a *habit* of applying them. Applying these techniques often (*frequency*) at regular times (*regularity*) for specific tasks (*specificity*) is the key to creating *habits*.

So far, we've discussed key insights from the Learning Styles model, whether you're a time or task-focused worker, and 10 useful study techniques to help you achieve Exam Success.

Enough of the '*how*' – time to move on to the '*where*' and '*when*'.

2.2 Where You Study: Creating The Perfect Study Environment

Our optimal study environment is different for each of us. In identifying yours, there are several factors to take into account.

Social or Solitary Preferences

The first of these is identifying whether you're a social or solitary learner.

Social learners might choose locations where they are not only surrounded by other people, but can also communicate freely with study partners. Nonetheless, if studying in groups, they should be diligent in ensuring that they limit their communication to studying topics. Try to allocate a defined period of time to cover notes individually, followed by time to discuss or quiz each other on the content covered, followed by a few minutes of relaxed chatting.

Ideas of locations for social learners and their study partners or groups include:

- Classrooms or meeting rooms.
- Coffee shops or other public areas.
- Living room or kitchen.

Solitary learners are often quite sensitive about their environment, and as such prefer to study where they feel most *comfortable*. This largely depends on individual preferences. In general, their study locations are selected to minimise interactions with other people and prevent them from being interrupted during studying.

Ideas of locations for solitary learners include:

- Libraries
- Empty classrooms
- Bedroom (or other room where you won't be interrupted)

In my case, I am a solitary learner. However, I dislike working in classrooms and *can't stand* the dreary atmosphere in libraries. I prefer to work in a home/ dormitory environment where I feel comfortable. If I have the option, I prefer not to work in my bedroom, as I like to physically separate my work-area from my sleep-area. In this case, I choose to work in the living room or kitchen. However, 'll take precautions to ensure that I won't be *interrupted* by anyone else (family, housemates, etc.) while I'm working.

The Perfect Personal Workspace

It can be useful to create a personal workspace where we can completely focus our attention on studying. Our workspace should be a well-lit location with minimal distractions. Our desk should be kept tidy and organised, as any clutter creates a *visual* distraction that makes it easier for our *mind* to become distracted by external stimuli.

We must *leave* our personal workspace during our breaks. This helps us to create a mental association between sitting at our workspace and *only* doing productive studying. Creating this physical separation between 'where we work' and 'where we don't work' also allows us to mentally *detach* from our work, which is vital to our mental health and well-being.

Make it a *habit* to sit at your desk and immediately begin studying, and to leave your desk as soon as you finish. Remember – *motivation* is what gets us started when we begin a new routine, but *habit* is what keeps us going even when our motivation falters! If you create a habit to sit at your desk at specific times and *immediately* begin work, you don't give your mind the option to create negative thoughts about whether you want to study, how much you have left to do, and other thoughts that may keep us stuck in the Pit of Eternal Procrastination (as discussed in <u>Principle 1</u>).

Before we begin studying, we should prepare our workspace with all our stationery, necessary textbooks and a glass or bottle of water (see <u>Principle 6</u> for why this is so important).

Activity 2.4: Create your own personal workspace. Where will it be? What will you choose to have on your desk? What can you do to make a habit of only doing productive work at your workspace?

Music & Background Noise

There has been no *unanimous* scientific evidence on the impact of music on studying. The best course of action is simply to *experiment* and discover what works best for you.

That being said, silence (an absence of music) has been consistently linked to *better* performance and memory retention in tasks compared to when different types of music were present.[14] However, it must be taken into account that the sample sizes for the studies were very small, so results may not be representative.

For those who insist on listening to music while studying, it's important to remember that listening to music while doing repetitive homework or coursework tasks is significantly *different* to listening to music when we're revising.

During homework or coursework, many of us listen to music as it helps to relieve the 'boredom' we associate with repetitive tasks. In many cases, music even *stops* us from getting distracted by whatever is going on in our immediate environment. Many of us find that we can 'zone-in' with our headphones on, as if they create a *barrier* that prevents our mind from being distracted by our surroundings, and even our own thoughts.

However, revising for exams or learning new content is *very* different.

The purpose of revision is to focus on getting our brain to *remember* or *understand* a process or fact which has not been committed to memory beforehand. Listening to music distracts the brain from the content we're trying to revise, and makes it harder for our brain to process the information and commit it to memory.

If you *still* insist on listening to music while you revise, it may be worth considering that listening to instrumental music in the background at a low volume may be a better alternative to music that contains *lyrics*, especially at higher volumes. Listening to music with lyrics can be compared to having someone talking in the background – except that you might be tempted to want to *join in* with the conversation!

If you find it difficult to work in silence, it may also be worth considering ambient background music with few instruments and little variation throughout, or natural sounds like falling rain or birds chirping. Another option is to *read your content out loud*, whether it's directly from a textbook or as you're writing notes.

On an interesting note, some people might find that they can quite easily create memory associations between the content they are revising and a song playing in the background.

Having done this myself, I admit that it does work…but also that it may ruin the song forever!

After this incident, I decided to opt for other memory devices that didn't involve ruining my favourite songs and stopped listening to music while revising.

However, listening to music during my 5-minute Pomodoro breaks was one of my favourite methods for resting my mind (soft, instrumental hip-hop jazz beats) or pumping myself up (upbeat hip-hop or soul music) for the studying ahead.

Will this work for you? Try it and find out. As mentioned at the start of this section, the effect that music has on your studies *depends on you as an individual.*

Activity 2.5: Reflect on how you use music when studying. Is the music you are listening to helping or hindering your studying? What can you change in order to improve your situation?

Minimising External Distractions

Distractions are everywhere. Here are 5 of the most common sources, as well as actions we can take to prevent them from becoming distractions:

1. **Phones/ Tablets (texts, social media, apps etc.)**

   - Store them away from your workspace, put them on 'flight mode', or turn them off completely.
   - Allocate set time periods to address text messages or social media (for example, during 5-minute breaks of Pomodoros) – but be disciplined!

2. **Laptops/ Computers (social media, YouTube, Reddit etc.)**

   - Shut down/ sleep mode if they are not needed for study purposes.
   - Close distracting tabs as soon as you are finished with them.
   - Allocate set time periods for recreational Internet use.
   - Set up search engine add-ons which prevent you from accessing specific websites at certain times.

3. **Television/ Netflix**

   - Allocate set time periods for watching TV/Netflix shows.
   - Avoid revising with the TV on in the background.

- Do NOT start a new TV series close to exams! Seriously. Just don't.

4. People (family, friends, partner, colleagues)

- Inform family and friends of your study timetable so that you don't get disturbed – they'll be happy to support you in your efforts.
- Set aside time for fun activities with friends, ensuring that your *priority tasks* (Principle 1) are being fulfilled first.

5. Physical Needs (hunger, thirst, motion, sleep)

- These will be discussed in-depth in Principles 5, 6 and 7.

However, just because we've done our best to anticipate these distractions, they may still crop up occasionally.

As such, we also need to understand *when* we become most susceptible to distractions. I'll discuss 4 very common examples below:

1. Tired or *fatigued*

When we become **mentally fatigued**, our studying becomes unproductive. Our frustration and dissatisfaction increases, and we become easily distracted. Once distracted, it also becomes harder to return our attention to our work.

- If your fatigue stems from low energy, consider taking a brisk walk outdoors or doing some exercise. This is covered in greater detail in Principle 5. Ensure that you are drinking healthy amounts of water and avoid foods that cause energy to 'spike' and 'drop'. This is covered in greater detail in Principle 6.

- If your fatigue stems from tiredness, your productivity will only continue to decrease. Consider taking a nap, or even going to bed early. This is covered in greater detail in Principle 7.

- If your fatigue stems from low motivation, grab a pen and paper and explore *why* your motivation is low, and focus on what you can do to increase it *now*. This is covered in greater detail in Principle 3.

- If your fatigue stems from stress or anxiety, consider doing exercise, taking a walk outdoors, listening to music, doing some mindfulness practices, and generally doing relaxing activities. This is covered in greater detail in Principle 3.

2. Not enjoying or *bored* by the content that we're studying

If we find ourselves distracted because we're **not enjoying the process of studying**, we need to remind ourselves of the *purpose* of our study process and the goals that we're trying to achieve.

The most simple and effective way of doing this is to grab a pen and sheet of paper, and *write down* the goal that we're trying to achieve through our studying.

The physical action of writing not only breaks the mental aspect of distraction, but by *writing* our goals down again, we realign with our reason for *why* we're studying. This is covered in greater detail in <u>Principle 3</u>.

3. Offered a *more desirable alternative* (MDA) to studying

A **more desirable alternative (MDA)** to studying can mean anything from seeing friends or going out for dinner, to participating in leisure activities or watching Netflix. We have to be aware of the consequences that giving in to these temptations may have on our studies.

In some cases, we may check our plans and find that we can easily adapt our schedule. We can then make a choice to take up the offer of the MDA. Studying doesn't *have* to be an arduous, boring process, and this is exactly what planning allows us to do – study effectively, but also participate in the activities that we enjoy completely guilt-free.

However, in other cases, we become distracted by MDAs in a bid to *escape* from our study commitments, despite the setbacks we know it may cause.

Jane was a client of mine who would always encounter this problem. She'd start studying, but would constantly stop and check her phone for MDAs. Replying to a WhatsApp message, a quick walk to the grocery store with a friend, a coffee break with her sister – any of them were *more desirable* than studying.

But Jane, like many of us, would also feel *guilty* about this. As we worked together, Jane realised that she was no longer able to *fully enjoy* any of the activities she was doing because she knew that she should be studying.

Jane realised that if she did her studies *first*, she could enjoy all her MDAs guilt-free!

This is something that most of us recognise when we're reminded of it. However, by bringing it to our awareness and having it at the forefront of our mind, we can use that reasoning to avoid the temptation of MDAs.

Jane and I created a plan which would allow her to focus on doing her studies first. She decided to change her sleeping habits. Instead of sleeping at 4am and waking up at midday, she made the shift to sleeping at 11pm and waking up at 7am. This allowed her to study uninterrupted until lunchtime. A great way to start the day!

We also created a document where she explicitly wrote down her *priorities* and *why* she wanted to achieve her study goals. Whenever she was tempted by an MDA during her study hours, she'd look at that document and remember *why* she wanted to study.

4. In the *gap* between finishing one task and beginning another

The **gap between finishing one task and starting another** can be our best friend or our worst enemy.

At best, in can be a short, relaxing break; an opportunity to refresh our minds, replenish our hunger for knowledge, and recover our focus to attack the task at hand.

At worst, it can set off a crazy cycle of procrastination…

One YouTube video becomes thirty; messaging a friend on Facebook becomes tagging our friends on meme-pages for the next hour; replying to a text becomes trawling through Snapchat stories while we wait for our friend to reply...

By becoming aware of how we use the *gap between tasks*, we can set ourselves boundaries to ensure that we stay within the *'optimal rest time'* category, instead of entering a crazy cycle of procrastination.

Set firm time intervals or reminders to return to work. Avoid texting or social media activities until later in the day when you feel comfortable with the study progress you have made. Realign with your goals by reminding yourself of *why* studying will help you achieve what you want.

Activity 2.6: Write down your main sources of distraction. How can you manage them more effectively? How can you set measures in place to stop yourself from becoming easily distracted?

Now that we have a better understanding of our optimal study environment and how we can minimise the distractions within it, we can consider *when* we study.

2.3 When You Study: Finding The Perfect Study Time

In the debate between 'daytime' and 'night-time' studying, scientific research is yet to provide any evidence for an objective 'best time' to study. It comes down to individual preference, and an awareness of the advantages and disadvantages of each.

The majority of us are familiar with **daytime studying**. Most academic institutions run courses and lessons during the morning and afternoon. We study in the evening, and sleep at night in anticipation of the next day's lessons. Keeping to this structure has various advantages:

1. Society is structured in such a way that we're active by day and asleep by night. Libraries, coffee shops and other public locations are often only open during the day. Courses and lectures are also mostly run during the day. In the event of needing help, teachers, friends and colleagues may also only be available during daytime hours.

2. As human beings, we respond to natural light differently to artificial light. Artificial light is worse for our eyesight. It can also disturb our biological body clock and natural circadian rhythms, causing detrimental shifts in our sleep patterns. This is discussed further in Principle 7.

3. Exams are often carried out during the morning or early afternoon. Daytime study prepares our mind to be working at its optimum *during* the time we'll have our exams.

Night-time studying has become increasingly popular, although many more factors need to be considered in implementing it successfully. It's important to establish a consistent routine to ensure that our body adapts to night-time study, instead of fluctuating back and forth between night-time and daytime study, which creates a feeling akin to bad jet-lag.

Maintaining a well-lit room is important to night-time studying, both in terms of keeping our mind alert and preventing excessive straining of our eyes. It's also easier to lose track of time at night, making it vital to manage and track our time effectively. Setting a timer to drink water regularly is also recommended. We should ensure that we have a supply of good-quality food, since supermarkets and coffee shops are likely to be shut.

In terms of sleeping patterns, some people prefer to nap more frequently during the day to account for less sleep each night. Others shift their sleeping habits entirely, sleeping anytime between 2pm and 6pm in order to wake up between 10pm and 2am!

Night-time study does have some advantages:

1. The 'feeling of peace and quiet' is one of the most prominent advantages of night-time study. The decreased intensity and activity around you can create a more relaxed atmosphere in which to study.

2. There are fewer distractions – people are sleeping, and there are no lessons to attend or activities to join. It becomes easier to lose yourself in a work 'flow' when interruptions around you are at a minimum, which can translate to more effective studying.

3. Many people find that their creativeness increases at night-time. Concepts and problems may be looked at from different perspectives, some of which might be more conducive to remembering or understanding content.

Personally, I considered myself to be a 'night-owl' that became more productive after midnight. However, I soon realised that the true reason why I *became* a night-owl was poor organisation throughout the day. I would start to panic about how little I had achieved during the day, and find the energy and focus to do a lot of work until the early hours of the morning. Unfortunately, I realised that this wasn't sustainable. As well as the mental stress it created, I also found that my energy was lower throughout the day when I would want to participate in sports and other activities.

I came up with various reasons why it would be to my benefit to shift my sleeping habits. Most of my sports commitments were during the daytime, and feeling more energetic would be a huge advantage. It was reassuring to know that my friends, family and teachers were awake and available if I needed them. The idea of having a few more hours of blue sky and sunshine was also very appealing – though good weather is rarely guaranteed in the UK!

I opted for a 1:00am – 9:00am sleeping pattern during my study leave, and shifted it to 11:00pm – 7:00am as exams approached.

As of the time that I'm writing this book, I have found that sleeping earlier and waking up earlier has actually *increased* my productivity and creativity levels compared to my old night-owl habits, as well as *improving* my physical health while *decreasing* my levels of stress.

I sleep between 10:30pm and midnight, and wake up between 6:30am and 8:30am. When I wake up, I follow a routine of journaling, exercising and meditating for up to 45 minutes, followed by 90 minutes of uninterrupted, productive work on my *most difficult task*.

To conclude, there is no *right* time to study. As individuals, we need to assess what works best for us, and always keep in mind the time which we're going to be sitting each exam.

Activity 2.7: Reflect on your most productive study times during the day. Are these optimal to ensure that you are awake and focused when sitting your exams? If not, what can you do to change this?

In summary:

- We have discussed the importance of *how* we study and looked at different techniques we can use to prepare more effectively for our exams.

- We have analysed the impact of *where* we study in the context of our personality, work environment and susceptibility to distractions.

- We have considered the advantages of *when* we study in the context of day-time and night-time studying.

With a better understanding of how we study, where we study and when we study, we can move away from the *practicalities* of studying and focus on the *mental* aspect of studying. In Principle 3, we focus on understanding the different problems that our mind can create for us. We'll discuss different tools we can apply to resolve and manage these problems in order to cultivate the optimum studying mindset.

3. Principle Three: Mind-Management

Managing our mind is the key to cultivating the optimal studying mindset. We first need to understand some of the most common problems that our mind creates for us, and *why* it creates them.

The problem areas we'll discuss are:

1. Anxiety
2. Outer & Inner Pressures
3. Low Confidence & Self Doubt
4. Low Motivation

Once we have an understanding of these common problems, we can equip our mindset with a range of tools to resolve them. These include:

1. 'RUDMA' Framework
2. Owning Our Stress Response
3. The Motivational Fire Formula
4. Progress & Quick-Win Tracking
5. Self-Dialogue Transformation
6. The Path of Least Regret
7. Mindfulness Practices
8. Visualisations & Affirmations

I recommend trying each of the tools at least once. Some tools will feel more natural to us than others. Other tools will make us feel slightly uncomfortable. We shouldn't avoid these because of the discomfort they cause; they may be pushing us beyond our 'comfort zone' and into our 'stretch zone', which is where we actually make the *most* progress towards overcoming our problem areas.

The most important point to remember is to get into a *habit* of using the tools that we find useful. The more we practise applying these tools, the *easier* they become to apply, and the *better* we become at managing our mind and addressing problem areas *quickly* and *effectively*.

As funny/complicated as the names sound, these tools are simple to use.

Let's begin with the 4 common problem areas.

3.1 Problem Area 1: Anxiety

The circumstances that trigger anxiety differ for each of us. However, all triggers have a common root – on some level, they all involve our mind moving *away* from the *present* moment and *towards* the *future*.

We open our notebooks and begin to feel overwhelmed by how much we still have left to do. We fast-forward to Exam Day and imagine the feeling of dread as we open the paper, only to find out that we aren't prepared for the questions in front of us. We may even fast-forward to 'Results Day' and imagine ourselves getting terrible results.

For some of us, anxiety manifests as *small waves* that periodically come and go. This roughly corresponds to a thought pattern along the lines of: "oh no, exams are coming up, I should probably be studying...oh well, perfect time for lifting weights/ Harry Potter movie marathon/ anything else to distract myself from it..."

However, some of us experience *anxiety tsunamis* that quickly spiral out of control. The self-dialogue we encounter might be more similar to: "oh my God, I'm going to fail, I'm a failure, my life's a failure, what's the point – I just want to curl up in bed with a tub of Nutella/ Ben & Jerry's/ dairy or nut-free alternative..."

These anxiety tsunamis can even lead us to experience panic attacks because of our natural 'fight-or-flight' response to stressful situations. Symptoms of these panic attacks include sweating, nausea, chest pains and palpitations.[1] If your anxiety is causing you to experience these physiological responses, I highly recommend seeing a doctor or psychotherapist, and enquiring about possible solutions like Cognitive Behavioural Therapy.

In the context of exams, our anxiety arises because the outcome of our exams *matters* to us. However, the root causes of *why* our results matter could stem from much deeper reasons, for example: fear of failure; fear of letting ourselves down or not living up to our potential; fear of disappointing our parents; feeling ashamed and embarrassed if our friends do well and we don't; losing confidence in our ability if we don't get the results we desire; feeling worthless if we don't get good grades; and so on.

There's often *more than one* root cause for anxiety, though we can normally identify one or two which are most dominant. They differ for each of us based on a combination of the influence of our external *environment* and the internal *values* we consider to be most important in our lives. Only we can truly determine where the roots of our anxiety lie.

Some of the mindset tools we can use to aid us in understanding and overcoming our anxiety include:

- 'RUDMA' Framework (includes anxiety as a case study)

- Owning Our Stress Response

- Mindfulness Practices

- Visualisations & Affirmations (after RUDMA or Mindfulness)

3.2 Problem Area 2: Outer & Inner Pressures

Many of us experience *pressure* to perform well in exams. The pressure we feel can be divided into two types. The pressure that comes from outside ourselves, which we will refer to as *outer* pressures, and the pressure that comes naturally as a result of our own personal expectations, which we will refer to as *inner* pressure.

Outer Pressures

The most common outer pressures include:

- Expectations from our teachers/ parents/ loved ones.
- Influence from social media
- Influence from our peers

Expectations from our teachers/ parents/ loved ones:

Expectations matter more to us when we *respect* the source that they are coming from, and so the pressure we feel from them is greater.

We may feel pressure from the expectations of our teachers if the teacher is someone whom we respect and admire. These are often the teachers whose lessons we look forward to, who are passionate about their subject, and who truly want to bring out the best in their students.

However, we may feel *extra* pressure to perform from some teachers. Some genuinely believe in our ability and want to motivate us to excel, and so persistently apply pressure on us to perform to our full potential. Others apply pressure because they are conscious that the grades we achieve will unfortunately represent how *they* are assessed as a teacher, and so it's in *their* best interest to see us do well.

However, parents and loved ones express their expectations in different ways. Some will directly tell us what grades they expect us to achieve, or what career they want us to pursue. Others will more subtly direct us towards certain options, expressing disappointment or disapproval in a more delicate manner and gently trying to influence our views.

Specifically, in the case of parents, some will *insist* that they are putting *no pressure* on us if we confront them about the issue. Unfortunately, the extent to which they are telling the truth is *irrelevant*.

If *we* perceive pressure coming from them, then *the pressure exists*, regardless of whether it was their intention or not.

Many of us love and respect our parents. We therefore attach a lot of weight to their expectations, or what we perceive their expectations to be. We feel that it would be ungrateful or disrespectful to go directly against their views.

However, when the pressure becomes unbearable, we may *overreact* by rebelling completely. This doesn't necessarily serve us well in the long-run. As well as damaging our relationship with our parents, rebellion may potentially compromise our own future if we behave in a way that could be harmful to our health and well-being.

The key to dealing with our parents is to remind ourselves that they are *not perfect,* and that they may be acting out of *fear*, not just love.

In other words, as much as they love us and want the best for us, they *fear* that we won't achieve what *they* believe will give us the best chance in the future. This is based on what their *own* experiences show to be the definition of success, health, happiness, and so on.

We must remember that their reasoning aligns with *their own values*, which are not necessarily the same as ours. This is why we often find ourselves feeling conflicted about the direction that our parents are trying to push us in.

Many of our parents were influenced by *their* parents – our grandparents – and the world was a *very* different place back then! Poverty, famine and scarcity were much more prevalent, so *security* was heavily valued. In the modern world, security translates to getting a well-paid, stable job – which is more easily achieved with a good degree from a good university.

Our parents may also have been heavily influenced by their own cultures, some of which placed tremendous importance on academic qualifications and the prestige attached to them. However, globalisation and technological developments have meant that our generation don't feel the same obligation to culture that our parents felt. Many of us grow up with friends from various backgrounds and will be influenced by their cultures. Internet access and social media also expose us to various cultures and lifestyles; this may lead us to question or challenge those we were brought up with.

All of these may create conflict between our parents' expectations of our lives and our own expectations of our lives. Our parents are not at fault here! They want what's best for us – they just aren't aware that what was best for *them* in the world that *they* grew up in may not be what's best for us in the world we're being raised in.

However, some parents *fear* what other people would think if we took a different path or achieved low grades, because they believe that our actions reflect on *them*. They use threats such as 'letting your family down', 'after all we've done for you…', and so on. This is a difficult burden to manage, as it's *their* shortcoming that we have to suffer.

Another issue we may face is that people have a habit of meddling in the lives of others when they're *unhappy* with their own lives. Due to a lack of control over their own happiness, they try to control the lives of others around them. We may experience this with parents, siblings or cousins.

The key to dealing with this, and all the other sources of outer pressure, is to *block out their voices* and treat them with *compassion* instead of resentment.

Compassion is a vital part of this process. By placing ourselves in their shoes and imagining the setbacks and adversities that they've faced during their upbringing, we begin to understand *why* they're behaving in this way. Instead of feeling resentment for how they're trying to control us, we can cultivate compassion towards them instead.

There's no value in wasting time and energy on emotions like resentment, when we could instead focus our time and energy on the immediate challenges in front of us.

In the case of both parents and teachers, the easiest way to do this is to recognise that to a large extent, what *they* want for us very often aligns with what *we* want for *ourselves*. They want us to achieve good grades – so do we! They want us to succeed in the future – so do we! Their *reasons* may be *different* to ours, but the end *outcome* we seek is the *same*.

And if it does frustrate you when they're constantly telling you the same thing – you're not alone! I once had a client who complained that, even if he was about to start studying, hearing his parents remind him of it made him want to *not* do it.

I remember feeling *exactly* the same way during my GCSEs and A-Levels!

When this happens, we need to remind ourselves that *we're all aiming for the same thing*. By satisfying our *own* goals and desires, we will *automatically* be satisfying *theirs*. So, block out their voices, and act as if only *you* were directing *yourself* to achieve *your* goals.

Being able to block out this external noise leaves us with only one type of pressure to resolve: inner pressure, that which stems from within us. We'll address this shortly after discussing two other sources of outer pressure: social media, and our peer group.

Influence from social media:

Social media may be causing us more stress than joy.

In fact, a good or bad mood can actually spread *through* social media. Researchers found that exposure to positive posts helped to improve moods, but exposure to negative posts worsened moods.[2] This phenomenon is called "emotional contagion" and is similar to what we experience when we're around other human beings – if they're in a bad mood, it worsens our mood; if they're in a good mood, our mood improves.

Sadly, it seems that most of our news feeds are filled with content that worsens our mood. A 2014 Austrian study found that participants reported lower moods after using Facebook for 20 minutes.[3] This was attributed to a 'forecasting error' – people expected their time on Facebook to be more valuable and mood-enhancing than it actually was. They felt that their time was *wasted* – and the longer they spent on it, the worse their mood was.

So, why do we check social media so often?

Sadly, the answer is that we may be *addicted* to it. This isn't our fault – in fact, these applications were *created* to get us hooked on them, according to one of the founding presidents of Facebook![4] Notification alerts, likes and refreshing the news feed all signal the 'reward' centre of the brain to release dopamine, one of our *pleasure* hormones. So, when we're feeling down because our studying isn't going so well, we can find instant gratification by checking our social media.

This is actually quite scary when you think about it. We don't own our social media apps; *they own us*.

What does this mean for us?

It's unreasonable to tell someone to stop using social media entirely. For all its negative qualities, it can also have a positive impact on our lives. The key is to use social media *responsibly*. Curate your news feed to show posts from pages or friends which uplift you. Pick and choose who you follow carefully. And *don't use social media* simply because you're bored or dissatisfied. We don't want to programme our mind to rely on it as a source of momentary joy – especially as it generally leads to a worse mood shortly after!

My rule is to be *vigilant* about my social media use. Whenever I find myself about to check social media because I'm unhappy or bored, I stop immediately and find something else to do. I also turn all notifications off. This means that I check my social media when *I choose* to check it; not when the app *tells me* to check it.

We also have to consciously remind ourselves that most of *what* we're seeing on social media every day is a collection of two things:

- The *highlight reels* of our lives: holidays, expensive restaurants, night-outs, concerts, etc.
- The image that we *want* others to have of us: study selfies, gym sessions, expensive clothes, motivational quotes, etc.

None of these are *real*.

We're only creating more dissatisfaction in our own lives by comparing the *highlight-reels* of others with our *full, uncut movie*. It's incredibly unfair on ourselves to keep comparing the highlights of other people's lives with the 'behind-the-scenes' work and 'blooper reels' that we experience in our own movie. The images others portray of themselves and their lives are only what they *want us to see*.

We're *not* missing out on anything. They're *not* having more fun than us. They're *not* living a better life than us. They just want us to *think* that they are. Believe me – no matter what you see on your news feed every day, everyone is still facing their own *relative* struggles. Their challenges might be different to yours, but they *do* exist.

Life isn't a popularity contest. And even if it was, social media is a *terrible* way of judging it. Instead of focusing on a thousand surface-level 'friends' or followers, focus on building a handful of close friendships with people who bring you joy every single day.

My test is always this: Do I know the date of their birthday (without a Facebook notification reminding me)? And if not, do I even *want* to know their birthday? If the answer to either of these is no, we don't seem to think too highly of our relationship with this person, and it's unlikely to be adding much value to our lives.

It's the *quality* of our true friends that matter, not the *quantity* of people who follow us – most of whom we barely know, and don't necessarily even *want* to know.

So, let's stop comparing our lives through Instagram filters, Snapchat stories and the number of followers we have. It only leaves us feeling disgruntled with our lives and pressured to think of ways to quickly create more highlight-reels in our lives in the present moment.

Let's stop squandering our time and energy on sources of instant gratification – which ironically, leave us feeling *guilty* and *frustrated* afterwards. Instead, let's focus on *long-term satisfaction* by taking small actions every single day that move us closer towards our long-term goals.

Ironically, these *still* leave us feeling *fulfilled* in the short-term because we've accomplished something meaningful. Think about it – you never feel *bad* about yourself after going for a run. You don't feel *bad* when you finish your homework or do a few hours of solid revision. You feel *great*!

We owe it to our present-self *and* future-self to block these negative images out and resist the temptation to compare our current lives to the highlights of others. We need to keep our focus on *ourselves* and what *we* are trying to accomplish. Instead of spending time choosing the perfect filter on Instagram, why not do our future-self a favour and choose to spend our time on our study plan?

After all, it's the behind-the-scenes work that we do now which can give us the opportunity to experience *many* more highlight reel moments in the future. We should strive to maintain a *balance* between creating highlights in the present moment, meanwhile honouring our future-self by committing to the behind-the-scenes work that will eventually benefit them.

Influence from our peers:

When we're surrounded by high-achieving peers, siblings and cousins, we may feel pressured to do the same. Some of our peers will *appear* to do very little, yet achieve very highly. Others will portray themselves as perpetually stressed, constantly talking about how much they are working, how they feel they haven't done enough, and how scared they are about exam day.

This can be *constructive* to an extent, motivating us to work harder to succeed in our exams. However, it can also be a cause of unnecessary stress. It can be easy to push ourselves into burnout by trying to study in a manner which damages our physical and mental health.

Just as with social media, we must remember that the images our peers portray of themselves and their work habits are what they *want us to see*. These are *not* an accurate representation of what they are actually doing or how they actually feel.

I'm not going to be so cynical as to describe it as psychological warfare, but there are certainly some who create these images of themselves to 'psych out their competition'.

Don't add to the pressure you're already putting on yourself – *block out* their images, and *block out* their noise.

We must recognise that the only competition we need to focus on is between us, studying at *this moment*, and the *best-version of ourselves*, whose top grades we *know* we can achieve with hard work and determination. By removing the external element of competition, we can once again turn this outer pressure into inner pressure. This is much more manageable and far less stressful to deal with.

In some situations, we encounter our peers using 'study drugs' to increase their concentration and stamina. There have been studies showing that, in the long term, taking these substances can lead to various cognitive *deficits* and withdrawal symptoms.[5] Psychologically, they also make many students feel that they can't perform well *without* the aid of these drugs.

This dependency can even extend further into their adult lives. I know students who took study drugs in university. They're *still* taking them in their jobs because they feel that they can't perform without them.

Please resist the temptation to take study drugs! Your long-term health is far more important than an exam grade. Best of all, the tools outlined later in this chapter will allow you to *naturally* increase our motivation, productivity, concentration and stamina, without the risk of harmful side-effects.

Believe me – I achieved a 1st class grade in Manufacturing Engineering from the University of Cambridge without *ever* taking study drugs. I don't even drink coffee! And it's not that I was naturally intelligent – my A* in Further Maths had been carried by my high Mechanics and Statistics grades (I got a B in my FP3 exam despite putting a lot of work into it)! I also scored the lowest mark of all the Natural Sciences students in my college during my 1st year at Cambridge.

So, don't allow yourself to create excuses about how others have an unfair advantage over you. Trust that the tools outlined in this book will *absolutely* be enough to help you achieve the best grades possible.

Our peers' influence doesn't stop there. Other times, we're surrounded by students who claim *not to care* about how they perform. They sit in the back of the room, disrupt classes, talk about how little work they have done and how unbothered they are about it.

This is a façade. Many of these students are simply too *afraid* to admit to themselves that they care. They doubt their ability to succeed – but instead of working hard and simply doing their best, they prefer to project their own insecurities upon others. They hope that their behaviours will nourish the small seeds of doubt that *we all have*, and that we too will succumb to their mindset.

They would rather fail with company than experience failing alone. Or even worse in some cases, they would rather convince *others* to sabotage their grade, while they *secretly* do enough work to pass. The sad truth is that, if they are charismatic enough or considered cool enough, they often succeed in achieving this.

Is it right to not care about your future? Is it fair to project your own insecurities about your own abilities onto others, in order to alleviate how bad *you* feel?

You owe it to yourself to *block these people out!* Your future is *yours* to decide. The pressures you feel should stem from yourself, not from others.

Speaking of which…

Inner Pressure

When we succeed in blocking out the excessive noise of outer pressures, we will realise that there's one voice left.

Our own.

This includes the pressure we feel because of, for example:

- Our expectations of what we should be achieving.
- Our pride in wanting to perform to the best of our ability.
- Our desire to keep our future options open.
- Our fear of not being good enough no matter how hard we try.
- Our fear of failing and then regretting not trying hard enough.
- Our fear of working hard, but then having a bad paper on the day and feeling that all of our hard work has gone to waste.
- Our fear of disappointing our parents, loved ones, etc.
- Our fear of missing out on having experiences with our friends etc.

Any form of pressure which stems *authentically* from within us is a form of inner pressure. And we *don't need to fight these!* Instead of blocking these pressures out and denying their existence, we need to *explore* them, *listen* to them and *learn* from them.

Some of the mindset tools we can use to aid us in understanding and managing the inner pressures we feel include:

- 'RUDMA' Framework (to recognise, understand and manage the pressures)

- Owning Our Stress Response (to overcome the stress we feel from our expectations)

- The Motivational Fire Formula (specifically the *intention* and *expectation* components)

- Mindfulness Practices (to ease the feeling of pressure or stress)

3.3 Problem Area 3: Low Confidence & Self-Doubt

Low confidence and self-doubt are problems we often encounter on the path to Exam Success.

The most common questions that create this doubt are:

"Even if we do our best, are we even capable of achieving a 'good' grade?"

The answer to this question is *yes*. Exams aren't about how much we know or understand about the subject; they're about knowing how to do *exams*. We're all *capable* of getting good grades in our exams. Following the Principles outlined in this book will enable us to give ourselves the best chance to achieve this.

So, where does this doubt come from in the context of exams?

Doubt often enters our mind when we struggle to grasp concepts, answer questions incorrectly, or have attained poor results in past examinations or Past-Paper questions.

Our mind is unfortunately very skilled at remembering what we have done *badly*. We remember the mistakes we've made, the number of times we've failed to grasp a concept, and the bad grades we've achieved.

However, we very rarely remember the things which we've *done well*.

Instead of letting our mind remind us of the evidence for why we should *doubt* our ability to perform well in our exams, we need to train it to remember the *positive* progress we've made – and are continuing to make. For more on this, please read the Progress & Quick-Win Tracking tool.

"Is exam preparation even worth all this time, effort and stress?"

One way to approach this question is by identifying the course of action that would leave us with the *least possible amount of regret*. This is properly addressed in The Path Of Least Regret. No matter how much we doubt our ability to get the grade, or doubt whether the work we need to do is worth the effort, the question we can ask ourselves instead is:

'Would we rather *not* get the grade and feel *disappointed*, knowing that we gave it our best shot; or would we rather *not* get the grade because we put in less effort, and *always wonder* what we could have truly achieved had we actually given it our all?'

Being honest with ourselves, most of us find our answer to be the first option.

Or as famous Irish playwright, Oscar Wilde, eloquently put it: 'It is *better* to *know* and *be disappointed*, than to *not know* and *always wonder*.'

On a personal level, I wouldn't have met my Cambridge offer had I not asked myself this question. I received my offer in early January, but it required an A* in Further Maths…and I had just scored 28% (a *fail*) in my December mock exams!

I had a choice.

I could either accept that I would *never* get the A* because it was so far out of reach, and simply try for my offers that required an A or less. This would be an easier option, as I would never have to experience *failure* if I didn't meet the almost-impossible target of achieving the A* grade.

Or I could give it all I had to achieve the A*, knowing that I would be *disappointed* if I didn't achieve it, but also knowing that I would never have any regrets about what *could have been* had I actually done my best.

I am very grateful to my 17-year old self for choosing the latter option. I planned diligently, did my best and trusted that in doing so, the outcome would be right for me, no matter how disappointing it might initially feel.

I wasn't nervous when it came to Results Day, as I *knew* I had given it everything I had without compromising my physical health and mental well-being. I am sincerely grateful that my efforts were rewarded.

"Even if we do study hard, is there any guarantee that we'll get the grade we desire?"

The answer, simply put, is *no*. There is no guarantee.

However, there is a considerable amount that we can do to *increase the probability* of getting the grade that we desire.

Within our studies, there is **one** element that we *can* control: our preparation. Our study strategy, the effort we put in on a daily basis and our mindset on the day all fall under this category.

However, there are **two** elements that we *can't* control: the examiner who writes the *questions* in the exam paper, and the person *marking* our exam paper.

Since we can't control these two elements, it's best to simply recognise and accept them, and then focus on addressing what we *can* control. This can be frustrating to admit, but letting go of these uncontrollable elements is the key to unburdening ourselves from them.

To summarise, when it comes to low confidence and self-doubt, the key is to remember our *past successes*, to act on the elements that we *can* control, and to minimise the time that we spend thinking about the *outcome itself*.

So, make your study plans. Execute them. Adapt them when needed. Frequently remind yourself of the wins you have had and the progress you have made. And work diligently to the point where you leave no room for regret *regardless of the outcome*.

Some of the mindset tools we can use to aid us in understanding and managing low confidence and self-doubt include:

- 'RUDMA' Framework (to recognise, understand and manage the issue)

- Progress & Quick-Win Tracking (to build confidence in our abilities)

- Self-Dialogue Transformation (to reinforce confidence in our abilities)

- The Path Of Least Regret (to drive us to do our best, irrespective of the final outcome)

3.4 Problem Area 4: Low Motivation

Low motivation can be a consequence of all the problems described above. By dealing with those problems, we will also resolve our motivation issues.

However, low motivation can also be caused or intensified other problems, for example:

- An 'Unsustainable' Source of Motivation
- Fatigue
- Poor Planning/ No Plan
- Boredom

An 'Unsustainable' Source of Motivation

Unsustainable motivation refers to a source of motivation which was *initially empowering*, but is *now depleting* our energy.

One of the most common examples of this is being motivated by the desire to *prove someone else wrong* – for example, teachers, parents or peers who tell us that there is no way we will achieve a top grade.

Our motivation to achieve the grade becomes the satisfaction that we will get by proving them wrong and creating an 'I told you so' or 'you shouldn't have doubted me' moment.

Unfortunately, while this can be the kick-start that we need to carry out our tasks and drive us towards our goals, it's emotionally and mentally draining to *maintain*. It's unsustainable to create an adversary in our mind, and use our defiance and desire to *prove them wrong* as the driving force for our actions. The stress and pressure that we create for ourselves can exhaust us, leaving us closer to burnout and ultimately further away from the outcome that we desire.

Recognising this, it's our responsibility to find something within us that motivates us to succeed *for ourselves*, not to defeat an opponent we've created in our own mind. The most sustainable source of motivation accessible to us is our own set of authentic, internal *values* that drive our actions. The 'Motivational Fire Formula' tool outlined later in this chapter can assist you in identifying what these are.

Fatigue

Fatigue intensifies low motivation levels. To resolve this, we need to identify and resolve the source of our fatigue.

As mentioned in Principle 2:

If your fatigue stems from *low energy*, consider taking a brisk walk outdoors or doing some exercise. This is covered in greater detail in Principle 5. Ensure that you are drinking healthy amounts of water and avoid foods that cause energy to 'spike' and 'drop'. This is covered in greater detail in Principle 6.

If your fatigue stems from *physical tiredness*, your productivity will only continue to decrease. Consider taking a nap, or even going to bed early. This is covered in greater detail in Principle 7.

If your fatigue stems from *stress* or *anxiety*, consider doing some exercise, taking a walk outdoors, listening to music, doing some Mindfulness Practices, and generally engaging in relaxing activities.

Poor Planning/ No Plan

Poor planning causes us to feel demotivated when we fall behind on our schedule. The further we fall behind, the less able we feel to 'make up for it', and the more likely we are to give up on our plan entirely.

Having *no plan* can be demotivating due to the lack of direction or guidance in bridging the gap between 'Today' and 'Exam Day'. It can feel as if there are so many modules to cover or Past-Papers to complete, and the feeling of not knowing where to start can decrease our motivation further. It can also make us feel unproductive, introducing elements of doubt as to whether we're doing *enough* of the *right* kind of work to prepare for exams.

Poor planning or a complete absence of planning can also lead to procrastination. Falling behind on our plan and feeling like we can never catch up is an invitation to throw the plan aside entirely. The gap of time between setting the old plan aside and creating a new one is a perfect opportunity for procrastination.

In addition, without a guideline or direction as to the tasks we need to do, we're more likely to *extend* the time spent *before* we start our task with non-value-added activities (e.g. Instagram, Snapchat, Facebook, YouTube).

This is why it's so important to create flexible, adaptable plans (Principle 1). The direction it gives us allows us to start tasks *immediately*. The long-term view allows us to fill it with content we consider to be *relevant*, ensuring that no major modules or Past-Papers are being missed out. The *slack* we leave allows us to adjust and adapt our plan as necessary in case we fall behind. We can also *track* our progress, which is a small yet effective source of motivation.

Boredom

Being bored by the content we're studying is a strong source of demotivation. The less enjoyable we find the content we're studying, the more likely we are to procrastinate and delay starting the task – remember the Pit Of Eternal Procrastination? When we do finally start the task, we're also more likely to be distracted (see Principle 2 for more on distractions).

Realistically speaking, it's unlikely that we'll be able to magically convince ourselves to find a topic interesting.

However, we can find *other reasons* why it's in our best interests to study the topic and use these to motivate us instead. The <u>Motivational Fire Formula</u> tool can be used to help us identify motivators that allow us to push beyond boredom and avoid the procrastination it may result in.

To conclude this section, some of the mindset tools we can use to aid us in understanding and managing low motivation include:

- <u>The Motivational Fire Formula</u> (to identify and align with our key motivators)

- <u>Progress & Quick-Win Tracking</u> (for immediate motivation)

- <u>'RUDMA' Framework</u> (to recognise, understand and define the source of our low motivation)

- <u>Owning Our Stress Response</u> (to move from a stressed, unmotivated state to a resourceful, motivated state)

- <u>Mindfulness Practices</u> (to rest and refresh our mind for the task ahead)

- <u>The Path Of Least Regret</u> (to help with decision-making)

Having understood each of the 4 common problem areas, we can move on to the mindset tools that we can use to tackle them.

There are 8 Mindset tools outlined in this book that we can use to address and manage each of the common problem areas described above.

3.5 Tool 1: 'RUDMA' Framework

RUDMA is an acronym that stands for Recognise, Understand, Define, Manage and Accept. It's a diagnosis tool that pushes us to identify our problem areas and their root causes, as well as beginning the process of managing and resolving the problem.

In the example below, I will describe how it can be used to deal with one of the most common, yet complex, problem areas – anxiety.

R - Recognise *what* is triggering the problem and *how* it manifests.

In the case of anxiety, for example, did that annoying friend of yours mention how they were getting nervous about exams? Or were you just spacing out for a minute, and your mind decided to remind you of how much studying you had left to do?

How would you describe the feeling of anxiety *physically* (heart rate increase, stomach discomfort, etc.) and *emotionally* (overwhelmed, afraid, panicking etc.)? How does your anxiety affect the task that you're doing?

Recognition is the self-awareness component required when dealing with any emotion. By asking ourselves *questions* to stimulate our awareness of the issue and distinguish the *symptoms* of the problem, we enable ourselves to quickly recognise the problem that we're dealing with and swiftly proceed towards an effective solution.

When we practise self-awareness, we begin to notice that there is a 'thought-gap' between the trigger occurring and our response to the trigger. With practise, we can use that 'thought-gap' to replace our initial response (which would likely involve negative emotions or actions) with a positive, constructive response of our choosing.

U - Understand *why* the problem is occurring or the feeling is arising.

The 'Understand' step of RUDMA allows us to identify the **root causes** of our problem area.

This is by far the most difficult part of the framework, as it requires us to chase down emotions to their source, often encountering a lot of uncomfortable baggage along the way. For example, in many cases, anxiety arises because the outcome of our exams *matters* to us.

But the root causes of *why* it matters could stem from much deeper reasons, for example: fear of failure; fear of letting ourselves down or not living up to our potential; fear of disappointing our parents; feeling ashamed and embarrassed if our friends do well and we don't; losing confidence in our ability if we don't get the results we desire; feeling worthless if we don't get good grades; and so on.

We need to overcome our pride and approach each of these *without judgement* towards ourselves. We all have insecurities – it's not *weakness* to feel this way! We're simply trying to understand *why* we're feeling anxious in the most rational and non-judgemental way.

Don't be afraid if there are tears – it's nothing to be ashamed of to confront our demons! I'm a firm believer that understanding our demons requires *more* strength than simply suppressing them. I'll openly admit that I've been reduced to tears on many occasions as I've tried to understand my insecurities – and I consider myself to be *stronger* and more *resilient* as a result of it!

Tears are just a *signal* showing us that we're on the *right track*. Think of them as an indicator that you're making positive *progress* towards identifying the source of your problem. Don't fear your demons – shine the light of awareness on them and observe what they show you *without judgement.*

D - **Define** the problem.

The 'Understand' stage may lead to our mind running around in circles as we confront some thoughts and feelings and flee from others. The sooner we can turn this *undefined mind-chatter* into *concise, defined statements*, the quicker we can progress.

As part of the 'Define' stage, we need to **WRITE DOWN** the thoughts and feelings that we've uncovered in the 'Recognise' and 'Understand' stages of RUDMA. We can write them in a diary, journal, iPhone notes sheet, Word document, etc.

Studies have shown that writing in a journal when we're emotionally distressed helps us to improve our mood and mental well-being. Brain scans on volunteers showed that expressing their feelings on paper reduced activity in the *amygdala*, a part of the brain responsible for the perception of negative emotions, such as anger, fear and sadness.[6]

By externalising our thoughts and bringing our feelings *physically outside* of our mind, we put ourselves in a position of greater control over them. For example, one of the key reasons why anxiety occupies our mind for long periods is the discomfort caused by our mind hunting its source. But if we have already *defined* the source of our anxieties by covering all of the root causes, we only need to read what we have written in our notepads in the past in order to *skip* that entire 'hunting' stage.

It's important for us to keep our written thoughts non-judgemental. Our words are just a reflection of how we *feel* at this moment in time; they do *not* define who we *are*. We may *feel* angry, sad or weak, but that doesn't mean that we *are* angry, sad or weak. No one else needs to see these words if you don't want them to – they're for you, and you alone.

This saves time and energy, accelerating the process of overcoming our anxiety and allowing us to recover quicker and return to the process of Exam Success.

M - **Manage** the problem.

This is where we make the transition from processing our emotions to creating practical solutions.

It might be that just truly understanding and defining *why* we're feeling a certain way or experiencing a problem is enough to handle it. This may be the case for smaller waves of anxiety or other small issues that bother us on a day-to-day basis. However, in the case of giant tsunamis of anxiety or other significant problem areas, we may need a *plan* to manage it further.

This is where **scenario analysis** comes in.

There will be various future scenarios which might occur depending on the *extent* to which our problem manifests. A well-defined scenario analysis gives our mind a chance to understand the *consequences* of the problem, depending on the extent to which the problem manifests (e.g. worst-case scenario, best-case scenario).

It also allows us to visualise the *Ideal Case* scenario that would occur if the problem didn't exist *at all*. In other words, "how would we be acting if we weren't experiencing this problem or negative emotion?". This gives us an optimum case to strive towards. We can then identify and experiment with making small changes that take us closer to that state.

In the case of anxiety, our mind tries to anticipate one scenario in particular - **the worst-case scenario**.

Our mind runs towards this because it sees it as a *threat*. Our mind is always trying to prepare us for the unknown, and in this case, it wants to prepare us mentally for what it feels is an especially threatening 'unknown' scenario.

However, instead of helping our mind to define this scenario, we feel the emotional discomfort and pain of approaching it, and so we *resist* by trying to pull our mind away from it. Our mind tugs us towards the worst-case scenario again, and we pull back from it again! The cycle continues, resulting in the build-up of anxiety.

If our mind does eventually succeed in reaching that worst-case scenario, we're often so *emotionally compromised* that we can't *rationally* take advantage of the situation by analysing and managing it.

(The Chimp Paradox by Dr. Steve Peters is very effective at describing how our 'rational' brain and 'emotional' brain interact through some very easy-to-understand analogies – I highly recommend the book to anyone interested in this area.)

So, the next time our mind starts to run off towards the worst-case scenario, we need to *let it* do so!

Once it reaches the worst-case, we can be aware of our emotional discomfort, but make a conscious choice to allow our *rational* thought process to seep in with *no* judgement.

We can then *define* our worst-case scenario, and *write it down* in terms of:

- **Short-Term Emotional Consequences:** The initial feelings of disappointment, shame, fear, anger, failure, jealousy of others, and so on. In the context of exams, this may include the disappointment of not getting our grade, the fear and shame in telling our parents about it, feeling like we're worthless for failing, feeling unmotivated to continue, being jealous of our friends who achieved the results that they wanted, and so on.

- **Long-Term Practical Consequences:** The chain of events that could occur as a result of our worst-case scenario. In the context of exams, this may include retaking an exam, taking a gap year and reapplying, taking offers from other universities.

Once we have these written down, we can try to *account* for them by writing about how we would deal with them *if* they arose. This helps our mind to realise that our worst-case scenario *isn't* the end of our world. It may be inconvenient and disappointing, but it's *manageable*.

One of my clients, Maria, was extremely anxious about Exam Results Day, to the extent where she couldn't even enjoy her summer break! She was petrified of getting bad grades, and especially afraid of two Short-Term Emotional Consequences: telling her parents about her grades, and feeling embarrassed in front of her friends if they achieved the grades they wanted but she didn't.

I shared my own solution to these problems with her.

When I was waiting for my A-Level results, I had no idea if I would achieve the A* in Further Maths to meet my Cambridge offer. My final FP3 exam had gone especially badly.

I let go of these thoughts at the start of summer but found myself becoming consumed by them as Results Day approached. To help me process my anxiety about potentially failing to meet my offer, I found it useful to prepare imaginary 'speeches' that I would give to my parents and friends!

An example speech to my parents: "I unfortunately didn't meet my offer this year, and it's incredibly disappointing. I really appreciate your love and support, and I know I might have disappointed you as well as myself. But I know that I did my best, and even though my best wasn't enough this time, I'm going to learn from this and let my actions speak louder than words when I go into my second-choice university." (University tuition fees were going up threefold in the next academic year, so retaking a year or taking a gap year was not an option for me!)

An example speech to my friends: "I'm so happy for you, and I'm so glad all your hard work has paid off. Unfortunately, I didn't meet my offer and I'm really disappointed, but I know that I did my best and I have no regrets. But forget about me for now, I'm going to be fine. I hope you have an awesome time celebrating this with your family and friends!"

Maria found this exercise very helpful for managing her anxiety about Results Day. It helped her feel more prepared that, even if things didn't go her way on Results Day, she knew how she would handle it.

Thankfully, in both her case and mine, neither of us had to use our backup speeches! I attained my A* in Further Maths (despite a B-grade in my FP3 exam!) and she achieved the grades she needed to meet her offer to study at University College London.

If you do want further guidance on dealing with Exam Results Day Anxiety, I've created a 2-part video on YouTube. You can watch the video by searching: "Own It – How To Relieve Exam Results Day Anxiety"

Once we have our worst-case scenario defined *and* managed, our mind will have nothing further to run to, and we can then focus on the final stage…

A - Accept that it's absolutely *fine* to be dealing with this problem.

Finally, we need to accept that neither the feelings we have nor the problems we're experiencing are worth *resisting*. They're not weakness, they're not something to fear, and they're not something to run away from.

Resisting our problems only perpetuates them further. In psychological terms, we turn 'Type-1 Thoughts' into 'Type-2 Thoughts'. A **Type-1 Thought** is simply a self-aware reflection of the sensation or emotion we're experiencing, for example, "I feel stressed" or "I'm angry". However, a **Type-2 Thought** occurs when we start to layer on thoughts about our thoughts, often leading to destructive spirals of negative emotion.

For example, have you ever been anxious, and then noticed that you're feeling anxious – and then started to get *more* anxious *because* you're feeling anxious? Or perhaps you're feeling stressed, but then you notice that you're feeling stressed – and you've started to stress yourself out more *about* being stressed! Or you notice yourself getting angry about something small, and then feel *guilty* for getting angry? These are all common examples of Type-2 Thoughts.

How can we deal with this effectively? By not judging ourselves about the emotion we're experiencing, and by not resisting the emotion.

Emotions are like quicksand – the more we struggle with them, the deeper we sink. Fighting our emotions only intensifies them. *Bottling* and internalising negative emotions only buries them temporarily. During that time, these suppressed emotions poison us from within, creating tension and dissatisfaction. Eventually, they emerge with a vengeance, exploding to the surface in an uncontrollable display of rage, sorrow and pain. Meanwhile *brooding* endlessly about our emotions causes them to spiral, building up strength like a hurricane. Type-1 Thoughts rapidly evolve into Type-2 Thoughts, and we get caught up in an emotional maelstrom of pain and distress.

The quicker we accept that we're experiencing a certain emotion without judgement, the quicker we can let go and move beyond it.

One of my closest friends (let's call him Charlie) was a successful lawyer, Cambridge graduate, and a tremendously talented tennis player. His focus and determination were inspirational. He always seemed so calm on the surface. He would mentor us and guide us with words of wisdom.

One day, Charlie came to a training session with a broken wrist. He claimed it was a tennis injury. We didn't give it a second thought and wished him a speedy recovery.

A few years later, Charlie went through some very difficult life experiences. As part of his healing process, he opened up to me about his past. He told me how, from a young age, he'd internalised his negative emotions because he didn't feel comfortable talking about them. He admitted that he always felt the need to appear strong in front of his family and friends.

But because of this, the negative emotions would stay locked up within him, eating at him from the inside – until a random trigger would set them off in a ferocious, uncontrollable manner.

Charlie admitted that his broken wrist hadn't come from a tennis injury. It had come from punching a wall as a result of his pent-up anger erupting to the surface. The trigger for his action had been very small. But as the old idiom goes, "it's the last straw that breaks the camel's back". A minor action or event can lead to an unpredictably large reaction because of the cumulative effect of small actions.

Unfortunately, the issues that he'd faced in recent years had led him to a breaking point beyond doing damage to walls. He realised that he risked doing serious harm to himself and his loved ones if he didn't seek help.

Thankfully, he's approached the challenge of solving his emotional problems with the same determination that earned him his Cambridge degree, tennis accolades and successful law career.

Charlie's story shows us that no matter how successful we look from the outside, no one truly knows what's going on within us. It also shows us that it's never too late to change; to stop resisting and to begin accepting; to confront our demons, to make peace with them and to release them.

Charlie also knows that his journey is just beginning. His tendency to internalise emotions won't magically disappear. His triggers won't mysteriously vanish. His inclination to respond with anger won't miraculously transform into love and compassion.

After all, acceptance is also about understanding that we don't *permanently* overcome negative emotions or experiences – nor do we need to!

By becoming aware of our emotions and diligently applying frameworks like RUDMA, we can manage our response to triggers so effectively to the extent where they have a minimal impact on our lives. We can ingrain positive *habits* which allow us to rewire our default response and replace it with an empowering, constructive response. The moment that our old response is triggered, our brain runs on autopilot to manage it. We learn how to control our issues, instead of letting them control us.

In the case of anxiety, as we become more familiar with the R-U-D stages of the framework, we'll reach a point where we're able to feel the symptoms of anxiety as soon as it arises, and understand and define why it was triggered. We can then train ourselves to create a *positive response* where we immediately apply the M-A stages of the framework to guide ourselves through our anxiety.

Each time we do this, our anxiety will pass quicker and less painfully than before. We're then free to introduce more positive thoughts and visualisations before getting back to taking action towards Exam Success.

Activity 3.1: Get a notepad or journal. Create a habit of writing in it as a method of managing your anxiety (or other mindset-related problem area), using the RUDMA framework to structure your journaling.

3.6 Tool 2: Owning Our Stress Response

Funny story. After hours of writing, I was finally reaching the end of this section about Owning Our Stress Response. All good – until my laptop decided to spontaneously restart and update.

Only one problem.

I hadn't saved my work.

And, *oh boy*, did I notice my stress response starting to go into overdrive…

I waited nervously and anxiously for my laptop to load up again. I felt my stomach starting to twist and turn in anticipation. A part of me felt hope – maybe I'd saved my work earlier? A part of me felt hopeless – who was I kidding? I felt anger beginning to well up within me…

I reopened the file.

I'd lost all my work.

All my emotions burst to the surface. Angry, frustrated, overwhelmed, out of control – I was swearing profusely! I wanted to *punch* my laptop into pieces, set each tiny piece on fire, and laugh manically as it melted while crying at the same time because all the burning in the world wouldn't bring my lost work back.

(Yes, in case you haven't guessed, I struggled with anger issues when I was younger!)

My mindset training started to kick-in. A tiny rational voice in my mind informed me that my laptop was expensive. Instead, I picked up my chair, raised it over my head, ready to throw it to the ground…

…and then my training *really* started to kick-in.

I didn't want to damage the floor. I didn't really want to break the chair either. I tried to pick a spot to gently throw the chair, more out of symbolism at my frustration than out of sheer anger.

But by that point, the anger had dissipated. All that was left was resignation that I had indeed lost my work, and that it was *my fault* to a large extent. I wasn't angry at the laptop. I was angry at *me* for not saving my work.

I put the chair down. I immediately dropped to the ground and did push-ups while holding my breath. And when I couldn't do anymore, I sat up on my knees and took some deep breaths.

I felt a lot better. But I still couldn't face having to write this entire section again…

So, I went for a 10-minute walk. I listened to some calming music. I started to think about the positive lessons and blessings from this incident. A reminder to save my work more often and not leave my fate in the hands of technology. The fact that I only lost a few hours of work, instead of a few days' worth of work. The chance to improve on this section the second-time I wrote it. And…adding *this* incident to the section!

Why? So that I can show you *exactly how* each technique I'm sharing for stress management actually helped me to transform my intense, stressed state into a relaxed, calm state where I felt productive and ready to work again. It's cool to learn these things in theory; it's even cooler to *know* that they really work in practice!

Owning Our Stress Response is based around the idea of understanding our stress response, managing our stress response effectively, and ultimately changing the way we perceive stress.

What Is Our Stress Response?

Stress is not inherently *good* or *bad*. It's a *survival mechanism* designed to help us respond and adapt to threatening situations. Our stress response is actually an *optimised* biological response to a change in our environment or situation.[7]

Whenever there's a change in our environment, our brain rapidly processes the sensory input that we're receiving. It links this with our own database of experiences and memories. These inputs allow our brain to assess whether we're in a stressful situation. If we are, our stress response is triggered.

Let's consider our hominid ancestors for a moment. If a sabre-toothed tiger appeared, we wouldn't have time to *rationally* think through our strategy to survive before the tiger mauled us to death!

The purpose of our stress response is to react quickly and effectively so that our chances of survival increase. Several things happen at once when our stress response is triggered. Our brain signals our body to release a cocktail of neurotransmitters and hormones, such as *adrenaline* and *cortisol*, to influence our physiological and emotional response.[7]

Adrenaline causes our heart rate, blood pressure and perspiration to increase. This means that more oxygen reaches our muscles at a faster rate so that we can *run for our lives*, and our body can also regulate its temperature more effectively as we *run for our lives*![7] Meanwhile *cortisol* tells our body to release stored glucose, curb our appetite and halt all non-essential body processes.[7] After all, it would suck to be thinking about how hungry we are or whether we've learned the right content for our exams (did cavemen have exams?) as we're *running for our lives!*

Our brain also sends us *vivid images* of us being chased down and eaten by the sabre-toothed tiger. We feel these emotions intensely to motivate us to *run faster* as we *run for our lives*!

However, there are no more sabre-toothed tigers for us to run away from. In war-torn, poverty-ridden countries, our survival mechanisms are still needed. But being at the top of the food chain in a first-world country means that our stress response survival mechanism is less necessary…

Instead, our stress response decides to go into *overdrive*. It activates in the *modern-day equivalent* of a threatening situation: important exams, sports fixtures, job interviews, public speaking, embarrassing ourselves at a party, confronting people, being punished by teachers or parents, and so on.

Stress is often a *learned* behaviour – we observe what other people are stressed about, and create our responses based on how *they're* dealing with stress.[8] Stress is also *contagious* – if other people around us are exhibiting symptoms of stress, we unconsciously pick up on these symptoms and begin to mirror them.[9] But not being aware of this, we don't know *why* we're feeling so stressed. And to make matters worse, we get *more* stressed out *because* we notice we're getting stressed and we've read somewhere that stress is bad for our health.

So, now we're stressing out because we're stressed. This is the reality of stress in a world where we're *fighting for exam grades* and not *fighting for survival*.

Our problems with stress lie in our *negative attitude* towards it and our inability to *respond effectively* to stressful situations. We allow our stress response to activate *too easily* and we spend *too long* in a state of stress.

So, let's completely transform the way we perceive and handle stress.

Dealing With High-Stress Situations: Association vs Dissociation

The first step to dealing with a high-stress situation is to *recognise* and become *aware* that our stress response has been triggered, just like in the RUDMA Framework.

In case of the tragedy that befell me as I wrote this chapter, my eyes sent a signal to my brain that my Microsoft Word document had closed, and my laptop had begun to restart and update. My brain linked this with past occasions when this had happened, and the experiences and emotions associated with those memories, such as anger, frustration, and being disheartened by the thought of having to do all the work again (I really should save my work more often).

Based on this, my brain decided that this scenario fit the definition of a *stressful situation*. Adrenaline and cortisol surged through my system. My breathing became shallower and faster. Vivid emotions of anger and helplessness surged through my mind. I noticed that my stress response was in full flow. I pulled my fist back, ready to punch my laptop to bits...

So, how did I get enough control over myself to avoid destroying my laptop? How can we stop ourselves from having a breakdown in the middle of an exam, having an emotional outburst around our family and friends, and generally managing our response to a high-stress situation?

Unlike the RUDMA Framework, we don't necessarily have time to *understand, define* and *manage* the problem when we're in a stressed state. Our stress response doesn't allow much room for rational thought – so we need to *create* that room.

We do this by *dissociating* from the stressful situation.

At any point in time, we're either in an *associated state* or a *dissociated state*.[10]

When we're *associated*, we're 'inside' our own bodies. We're immersed in our reality, seeing through our own eyes and fully experiencing our emotions. An analogy I use with some clients is that they're playing a video game in *first-person* mode. They're seeing *through the eyes* of their character.

In an associated state, we experience life *intensely* and don't notice the passage of time. This is very useful for paying attention, practising or learning a skill, enjoying an activity or memory, and entering the state of *flow* that I describe in <u>Principle 2</u>. However, because of their intensity, associated states are not ideal for experiencing stress, feeling negative emotions, or confronting fears and phobias.

When we're *dissociated*, we see ourselves as if from the 'outside', for example observing our body from above or watching ourselves on a screen. We're not as immersed in our experience and are able to *detach* ourselves from the emotional intensity of the event. Using the video game analogy, we're in *third-person* mode. We're not seeing through the eyes of our character, we're *seeing our character* move and act as we control them.

Dissociated states are useful for taking a step back from unpleasant situations, creating a sense of control or awareness, reviewing and learning from past situations, and keeping track of time. Dissociation has been used successfully as a treatment to help patients overcome phobias and handle post-traumatic stress disorder (PTSD).[11]

We can practise association and dissociation by recalling positive memories. We can first *associate* with the memory and experience it as if we're reliving it in that moment – seeing what we see, hearing what we hear, and feeling what we feel. We can then *dissociate* from the memory and observe ourselves reliving that moment. We can imagine the memory happening on a screen in front of us, or imagine ourselves looking at the memory unfold from a distance. In doing this, we'll notice that the memory feels less intense.

The more familiar we become with our associated and dissociated states through practise, the better we become at dissociating from stressful situations and injecting a sense of *control* over our stress response.

Activity 3.2: Recall a positive memory and practise associating with it. Notice how your emotional state is affected. When you're ready, dissociate from that same memory. Notice how your emotional state is affected. Practise entering an associated state when studying. Practise entering a dissociated state on any occasion when your stress response is triggered.

In my case, I first *dissociated* when I was about to punch my laptop screen into oblivion. I saw myself about to break the screen and added a thought that it would be very expensive to replace! This stopped me in my tracks…

But the intensity of my stress response was very high, and I *associated* with the situation again. I picked up the chair, ready to throw it – and then I *dissociated*. I saw myself from a different angle, holding the chair above my shoulders. I imagined myself throwing the chair against the floor, breaking both in the process. I added a thought that replacing the floor and chair would be both expensive and inconvenient, and that I'd probably regret this action. I forced myself to stay in my dissociated state until the emotional intensity subsided, and I was able to put the chair back down.

Although I'd successfully taken control of my stress response, my *emotional state* was still quite terrible. I wasn't in a constructive frame of mind to resume my work and rewrite this section – if anything, I was considering not including it *at all!* I wasn't thinking clearly, and I still felt anger towards myself for not saving my work. I also felt quite drained and tired after the sudden rush of negative emotion.

So, how did I move from this *unresourceful, stressed* and *angry* state to a more *resourceful, calm* and *focused* state?

State Management: Transforming Negative States to Positive States

Our negative emotional states may linger even after our stress response has passed. For example, we may feel tired, drained, demotivated, angry, overwhelmed, sensitive, overly alert, and so on. All of these states are considered to be *unresourceful* – they aren't positive, and they aren't constructive in helping us achieve our Exam Success goals (or any goals for that matter!).

The better we become at transforming these unresourceful states into resourceful states, the quicker we can return to our optimal level of performance.

To do this, we must understand that we can't go *directly* from a negative state to a positive state. First, we need to *break* our negative state in order to enter a *neutral state*. Once we're in a neutral state, we can *then* consciously choose to *create* a positive state.[12)]

Breaking state is very simple and easy – in fact, we do it all the time without being aware of it. We can break state by changing our environment, changing our physiology or changing our behaviour.

Just by walking into a different room, we've broken our state. By stretching or standing up, we've broken our state. By stopping our task to drink a glass of water or do push-ups, we've broken our state. By dissociating from an event (as discussed in the last section), we've broken our state.

However, as we're normally not *aware* that we've broken our state and entered a neutral state, we tend to *return* to our previous state immediately. This is because we revert to the same thought, action or behaviour that we were doing prior to breaking our state. So, although we may go from a negative state to a neutral state, we end up going straight back to a negative state.

Instead, we need to *consciously create* a positive state once we've entered our neutral state. There are several easy ways of doing this:

- **Listening to music** that puts us in the mood that we want to create. For example, if we're recovering from our stress response, we may choose to listen to calming music. If we're about to go and see some friends, we may choose to listen to upbeat music.

- **Recalling and associating with a memory** that puts us in the mood that we want to create. By associating with a memory which helps us feel calm and peaceful, and we'll create a calm and peaceful state. Associating with a memory of a time when we were energised and excited creates an energised and excited state.

- **Changing our physiology** to transform our emotional state. When we're sad, tired or depressed (emotions), our shoulders slump and our chin tilts downwards so that we face the floor (physiology). When we're confident and positive (emotions), our chest pushes out, our shoulders broaden and our chin tilts upwards (physiology). Our physiology and emotional state are so intertwined that by changing our *physiology*, our emotional state will also change. So, if we're sad or tired but decide to push out our chest, broaden our shoulders and tilt our chin upwards, we can *create* a positive and confident state. Try it for yourself and see!

- **Changing our breathing** to transform our emotional state. When we're stressed or anxious, our breathing moves 'higher' up in our chest and becomes shallower, and our shoulders may begin to move up and down. However, in a calm state, we breathe 'lower' and deeper into our abdomen using our diaphragm. By consciously focusing on taking deep breaths, we can change our state from stressed and worried to calm and relaxed.

Let's return to my (heart-breaking) story of losing my first draft of this chapter.

After putting the chair down, I immediately dropped to the ground and did some push-ups. This *change in physiology* helped me to return to a neutral state. It also helped me dissipate some of the nervous energy that had built-up inside me. I then took some deep breaths to elicit a state of calm.

But I still wasn't ready to work. So, I went for a 10-minute walk in a nearby park. This *changed my environment* and allowed me to recall many pleasant *memories* of the peaceful walks I've taken in the past. I also listened to calming *music* to release the tension left behind from my stress response and to reinforce feelings of tranquillity and peace.

I was ready to get back to work again – but I wasn't *excited* to get back to work yet. So, I decided to spend a few minutes thinking about the ways in which I could *reframe* this incident and look at it with a positive perspective. Some reframes were lessons that were practical but not exciting: remembering to save my work, only losing a few hours of work, and being able to improve on what I'd written.

But one of the reframes I came up with was *very* exciting. The idea of incorporating *this* incident into the section on Owning Our Stress Response so that you readers would have a real-time example! By the time I was back home, I was *eager* to start writing again.

I transformed my unresourceful, stressed state into a calm state in less than 3 minutes. And because I had the luxury of time, I then transformed that calm (but emotionally tired) state into an excited, eager state in an additional 15 minutes.

There will be situations where we don't have this amount of time, for example during an exam, dealing with immediate deadlines, or in-between points during a tennis match. Sometimes this is *helpful* – once we've changed our stressed state to a calm state, our sense of urgency will give us enough drive to get back to work. But when you have time, like I did in this case, it's worth investing extra time to create as resourceful a state as possible.

There will also be cases where the stressful situation is a *recurring event*. In this case, it may be worthwhile to use the RUDMA framework to help you understand the underlying cause behind your stress, and to create a strategy that you can use to manage that stress. Strategies for reducing stress may include Mindfulness Practices, increasing your Physical Activity & Movement (Principle 5), changing your Nutrition & Hydration habits (Principle 6), getting more Sleep (Principle 7), and surrounding yourself with a positive Support Group (Principle 8).

So, next time you're confronted with a stressful situation, remember the following three steps.

1) Recognising that your stress response is *natural* and that there is no need to *resist* it.
2) *Dissociating* from the stressful situation to reduce the intensity of your stress response.
3) Breaking your *negative* state to enter a *neutral* state, and then consciously creating a *positive*, resourceful state.

Activity 3.3: Make a list of 5-10 recent occasions which caused you to experience stress. Use the RUDMA Framework to run through each example. When you reach the 'Manage' stage, make a note of what actions you can take in the future to manage your stress response more effectively.

Our Attitude To Stress Matters

As mentioned before, our stress response is not inherently good or bad; it's an *optimised* biological response.

And yet we're constantly being told that stress is *bad* for us. We're led to believe that stress is harmful and should be avoided at all costs.

However, not *all* stress has negative effects. In fact, stress can actually have *positive* effects in the short-term; it can boost our immune system, overcome lethargy and enhance performance.[13] This has been termed *eustress* by Hans Selye, a pioneer of modern stress. This *eustress* is the stress that athletes leverage to gain a competitive edge, public speakers use to deliver enthusiastic speeches, and that *you* can use to perform optimally in an exam. In short bursts, this doesn't cause long-term consequences for our physical and mental health.

However, stress can be negative when it exceeds our ability to cope, fatigues our body systems and causes physical or behavioural problems. This is *distress* – it can cause overreaction, confusion, poor concentration and performance anxiety.[13] If this is experienced on a constant basis, it can become *chronic stress,* which can have adverse impacts on our physical health and mental well-being.

So, how do we differentiate between *eustress* and *distress?*

A lot of it comes down to *attitude.* If we *perceive* stress to be *positive,* it will have a positive impact on our physiological and emotional response to it. If we perceive stress to be negative, it will have a negative effect on our performance, health and well-being.

Don't believe me?

A study carried out at the University of Wisconsin looked at 30,000 people over an 8-year period. Each person was asked two questions. First, they were asked to rate how stressed they were. Second, they were asked about how they believed stress affected their health.[14]

The researchers then checked the National Death Index to find out *who died!*

Unsurprisingly, they found that those most likely to die were the people who rated themselves as being highly stressed, and who also perceived stress to be *harmful* for their health.

But who was *least* likely to die? Surprisingly, it wasn't the people who were least stressed!

The least likely to die were people who rated themselves as experiencing high levels of stress, but *believed* that stress *wasn't* harmful for their health!

Crazy, right?

Some Harvard University researchers thought so too, so they conducted a study to find out *why* our *beliefs* about stress could potentially prevent us from dying earlier.[15]

One of the reasons why stress kills us prematurely is that it causes our blood vessels to constrict, which in the long-term can lead to heart disease and high blood pressure. However, the Harvard researchers discovered that there was no blood vessel constriction in people who *believed* stress to be *positive.*[15] Their *belief* about stress changed the way their body responded to stress!

I don't know about you – but learning about this absolutely *blew my mind.* If you want to learn more, I recommend a Ted Talk by Kelly McGonigal called "How To Make Stress Your Friend".

What does this mean in the context of Exam Success?

Well, the definition of Exam Success is achieving our ideal grades with the *least amount of stress.* After all, while short-term stress can have some benefits, being stressed isn't a sustainable state to maintain for a long period of time.

So, *optimise your lifestyle* to reduce the likelihood of it. As mentioned earlier, strategies for reducing stress may include <u>Mindfulness Practices</u>, increasing your Physical Activity & Movement (<u>Principle 5</u>), changing your Nutrition & Hydration habits (<u>Principle 6</u>), getting more Sleep (<u>Principle 7</u>), and surrounding yourself with a positive Support Group (<u>Principle 8</u>).

However, if you feel yourself getting stressed, *embrace it.* Don't *resist* it. Understand that your stress response is perfectly natural. Recognise that having a positive attitude to stress will help in preventing negative physiological and mental consequences in the long-term. And then *manage* your stress response and *use* it to perform optimally in the short-term.

3.7 Tool 3: The Motivational Fire Formula

This is probably the most empowering tool in this book. Done correctly, this will become a *sustainable source* of *motivation* that can be applied throughout our lives to *anything* that we want to do.

Motivation is not something that we find. Motivation is something that we *create*. We can create sustainable motivation by applying the *Motivational Fire Formula*:

Motivation = Intention + Realisation + Action − Expectation

All fires require 3 components: *heat, fuel* and *oxygen*. Intention is the *heat*. Realisation is the *fuel*. Action is the *oxygen source*. If any of these are not present, the fire won't start. If any of these are present in small amounts, the fire won't last.

In the context of our Motivational Fire, Expectation is the fire blanket that specifically denies oxygen (Action) and therefore extinguishes our motivational fire.

For maximum motivation, we therefore want to have *high intention, high realisation, high action* and *little/no expectation.*

You can use the **MIRAGE** mnemonic to remember this. For (M)otivation, just add (I)ntention, (R)ealisation, (A)ction…and (G)et rid of (E)xpectation!

Let's take a deeper look at each of these.

Intention

Intention is the *heat* we provide to light the fire of motivation. Strong intention is like a magnifying glass. It will direct and focus heat towards lighting our Motivational Fire. Weak intention has no direction or focus. It's scattered, unreliable and ultimately a waste of our energy.

Intention is composed of the '**what**' and the '**why**'.

The **what** is our goal. The more clarity we have about *what* we want, the better we'll be able to align our *actions* with our *intention*. In the context of Exam Success, our *what* is to achieve our ideal exam grades in the least stressful way possible. However, your definition of 'ideal' exam grades for each subject will be unique to you. 'Least stressful' is also something that you will need to define – it may be related to the amount of time you spend working and relaxing, doing the activities that you enjoy, getting enough sleep, and so on.

But having clarity about *what* we want isn't enough. We need to have clarity about **why** we want it. For our intention to be truly powerful, we need our *why* to be aligned with our **values**.

Intention – Value Identification

We all have our own set of values which represent the things that are most important to us in our lives. Every action we take is a *means* to an *end*, and that end is the fulfilment of a value (or combination of values). In other words, our values show us the 'why' behind every action that we take.

There are two types of values that we need to distinguish between: **'towards'** values and **'away-from'** values:[16]

'Towards' values are those which leave us moving *towards* general **pleasure** emotions when fulfilled. Examples of these include, but are not limited to:

- Success	- Fun	- Authenticity
- Security	- Being Loved	- Peacefulness
- Freedom	- Approval	- Purpose
- Health	- Honesty	

Note that *money* and *family* didn't come up in that list – this is because they are *means* values, not *ends* values. By this, I mean that money is the *means* to an *end* value; which could be the fulfilment of *freedom*, *security, success* or any other value.

'Away-From' values are those which leave us moving *away from* general **pain** emotions when fulfilled. Examples of these include, but are not limited to:

- Anger	- Worry	- Loneliness
- Depression	- Boredom	- Guilt
- Disappointing Others	- Insecurity	- Regret
	- Rejection	

All of the words we use to describe our values are *abstract* – each word has a *unique meaning* to us based on what we *personally associate* with the word. Because of this, no one else can tell us what our values are. It's up to us to discover them for ourselves.

It's important to note that it's not *better* to have more *towards* values than *away-from* values. There is a common misperception that away-from values are *bad*, but this isn't true at all. As you read through the next section, you'll notice that no value is inherently bad; it's our *rules* for fulfilling them that may make them have a negative impact on our life. Once we're aware of these rules, we can *choose* to change them.

Intention - Challenges In Value Identification

Up until now, we've been driven by values that we may not have even known existed. As we look within, we need to be able to recognise that some of our values are *outdated* and *inauthentic* – they're there because they felt successful in the past, or because others told us they were the right thing to do.

However, they may need *upgrading* to match our present situation. Our values are not static; they can change throughout our lives. As long as we're *aware* of these changes, we can always adapt and manage them.

If you are struggling to identify your values, it may help to ask yourself the following questions. These are some questions which life coaches use to help their clients to elicit their own values:

- What accomplishments are you most proud of? *Why* are you proud of these particular accomplishments?

- Describe a time when you felt most fulfilled. What was it about that occasion which made you feel fulfilled?

- For any goal that you have set yourself, what motivated/ is motivating you to achieve that goal?

- Describe a recent time when you felt like you let yourself down. What was it that made you feel like you let yourself down?

- What do you fear your friends finding out about you? How would it make you feel if they found out?

Another challenge is that we have *many* values, and how we rank them is often ambiguous. We often rank values by what we *want* them to be, or think they *should* be. Being honest with ourselves is vital; it's very difficult to motivate ourselves by trying to align with values that we *don't really have*!

If you are struggling to rank your values, consider asking yourself the following question: "If I fulfil priority value number 1, but not number 2, would I be okay with it?". If the answer is no, switch them around. You can then do this with the other values that you identified.

Activity 3.4: Identify 5 of your key 'towards and 'away-from' values. Rank them in order of which has the most influence over your decision-making.

Finally, just as important as knowing our values is knowing our **value fulfilment conditions**, or '**rules**' as they are called by the renowned life strategist, Anthony Robbins.[17]

These are our beliefs about exactly what must happen to *tick the box* for fulfilling one of our values. In other words, *how do we know* when we've achieved success, attained freedom, avoided disappointing others, and so on? How do we know when we've attained pleasure, or avoided pain?

Not being aware of them in the past, it's likely that we have set ourselves *disempowering rules* throughout our lives.

These are rules which are either *impossible* to fulfil or require things to happen that are *out of our control*. Remember – value fulfilment leads to feeling *pleasure* emotions. Not fulfilling our values leads to feeling *pain* emotions. We want to give ourselves the *best chance* to feel pleasure, not pain!

By identifying the rules that we have created for ourselves for the fulfilment of each of our values, we can begin to think about how we can *transform* these disempowering rules into ones which empower us to fulfil our values with greater ease.

For example, our rules for the fulfilment of a *move-towards success* value could be:

1. Achieve the highest grades in my year group.

2. Get accepted into Cambridge University.

3. Get accepted onto a top banking/consulting Graduate Scheme.

These are great, ambitious goals – but if they are just the *conditions* for fulfilling our value, they are immensely disempowering. Although they're not impossible to fulfil, they are very unlikely! However, the biggest issue with these rules is that they all involve elements which are *out of our control.*

1. We don't decide exam questions; we don't mark the paper; we don't control how our peers prepare for their exams.

2. We don't control who interviews us or what questions they ask; we don't know how the quality or quantity of other applicants.

3. We don't control who interviews us or what questions they ask; we don't know the quality or quantity of other applicants.

It would be more empowering to set our value fulfilment conditions as:

1. Aim to achieve grades which represent my full potential.

2. Prepare as well as I can for university interviews. Leave the interview room knowing that whatever the outcome, I've given an accurate representation of who I am and what I'm capable of.

3. Do my best to achieve the grades needed to allow me to pursue any job option. Leave every interview knowing that I've represented myself and my capabilities to the best of my ability.

All of these elements are *within* our control, giving us a greater opportunity to fulfil a *move-towards success* value and feel the *pleasure* that comes with it.

Our goals can still remain the same as our original, disempowering rules. However, we should never let these goals become *expectations*. We need to ensure that the fulfilment of our values is *not conditional* on whether the goal or outcome is attained. This means that we have a greater chance of feeling pleasure and avoiding pain regardless of the outcome.

Activity 3.5: Write down your value fulfilment conditions for each of your towards and away-from values. For each, identify whether it's empowering or disempowering. For any disempowering rules, write down a suitable empowering rule to replace it with.

Intention - Value Alignment

Once we've identified our values, we can use them as a *driving force* for taking action towards our goals. We do this by *aligning* our values with the action we need to take. This involves creating a *strand* (a link) between the action we're going to take and how it's fulfilling one (or more) of our values. No matter how thin or weak this *strand of alignment* seems, it still gives us *something* to drive us forwards.

Let's discuss this in the context of Exam Success.

We have exams that we need to revise for. It isn't happening. We feel stuck and unable to motivate ourselves to study.

We can align the *studying we need to do* with the *values we have*. For example:

- If we value **moving-towards *success***, we can link studying with the success that we'll feel when we achieve our ideal examination results.

- If we value **moving-towards *security***, we can link studying with achieving high exam grades which will increase our chances of getting a good, stable job (and the financial security that comes with it).

- If we value **moving-towards *freedom***, we can link studying with high exam grades that will allow us to explore job options and make new opportunities more available to us.

- If we value **moving-towards *loving* and *being loved***, we can link studying with achieving high grades that will allow us to have a well-paying job to provide a good life for the family we wish to have in the future.

- If we value **moving-away-from *regret***, we can link studying with reducing the chance of getting poor grades that we may regret.

- If we value **moving-away-from *disappointing others***, we can link studying with increasing the chance of getting good grades, and therefore avoiding disappointing our parents or loved ones.

- If we value **moving-away-from-*boredom***, we can link studying with getting good grades which will enable us to pick from a broad selection of careers and avoid having to settle for a job that we consider boring.

Being honest, some of those links/strands of alignment are *very thin!* However, even a thin strand aligning each of our values with the task at hand is still a powerful motivating tool. It may even help to visualise a *physical strand* connecting our present action to the fulfilment of our value in the future.

This is what I personally did in my 3rd year in Cambridge. You can see a photo of my **'Intention Sheet'** in Appendix 2 – including the shoelace I used as my 'strand of alignment' connecting my to-do list (my *what*) with my values (my *why*)! I also include an explanation of how it links with the components of the Motivational Fire Formula.

Activity 3.6: Use Appendix 2 as an example to create your own 'strands' linking your values with the studying, revision or other tasks you need to complete.

There may be times when all our strands are lined up, but we still feel *stuck* and unable to progress. In these cases, we may be experiencing **value conflicts,** where our *values* are not aligning with *each other*. Value conflict leaves us feeling frustrated, indecisive and stagnant, sabotaging our goals in the process because of our inability to take action.

For example, if we have a move-towards *freedom* value, but also a move-towards *security* or move-away-from *risk*, it can become difficult to make decisions or take action. The decision or action may fulfil one value (freedom), but go against the other two (security, risk).

By *ranking* our values, we can reconcile these value conflicts by understanding which values we really *prioritise*. We can consider actions that would fulfil our *priority* values first, and then figure out how we can also honour our lower-priority values as well.

In the case of exams, for example, a move-towards *success* can easily conflict with a move-towards *fun*, or move-away-from *boredom* value. With these values, we will constantly find ourselves getting distracted or taking up offers to do 'more desirable' alternatives to studying. We will feel guilty and assure ourselves that we will work later...and then the cycle will begin again.

We will be more driven to study if we *consciously choose* to prioritise our move-towards *success* value by creating a *strong strand* linking studying to the fulfilment of this value.

At the same time, we can also ensure that we leave time for 'fun' activities in our plan to also meet our move-towards *fun* value. We can also consider ways to make our work more interesting or less monotonous to satisfy our move-away-from *boredom* value.

Now that we have a firm grasp of how to create **strong intention** to provide intense heat for our motivational fire, let's take a look at the other components in the Motivational Fire Formula.

Realisation

Realisation is the *fuel* for our motivational fire. Powerful realisation requires an abundant supply of good quality fuel. Weak realisation is like wet wood or low-quality coal. The fire won't start; and if it does, it won't last for very long.

Realisation considers two definitions of the verb 'to realise'. The first definition is causing something to happen – for example, "realising our goal". The second definition is becoming fully aware of something and understanding it – for example, "realising what we know and what we don't know".

Realisation is concerned with two questions.

Question 1): *"Can* we realise our goal?"

This question uncovers our *belief* in our ability to achieve our goal. In other words, do we believe that our goal realistic given the time, energy and resources that we have available to us? But more importantly, do we believe that we have the skills, capabilities and determination to achieve our goal?

The Planning tools outlined in Principle 1 helps us address how realistic our goal is in terms of time and resources.

However, if we don't *believe* that we have the potential to achieve our goal in the first place, our motivational fire won't ignite at all. We need to have an *abundance* of belief in our ability to be diligent, persistent and fearless in pursuing our goal. And if we feel that we're lacking certain skills or capabilities, we need to have an *abundance* of belief in our ability to learn and develop them given time and practice.

Several of the tools outlined in Principle 3 can help us to cultivate this self-belief, including Progress & Quick Win Tracking, The Path Of Least Regret and Self-Dialogue Transformation.

Question 2): "*How* can we realise our goal?"

This question focuses on *how* we achieve our goal. We need to realise that achieving our goal requires *knowledge* about the goal topic. The higher the *quality* of our knowledge, the more relevant it is in helping us create the action steps we need to take to attain our goal.

I've worked with multiple clients who have struggled with low motivation as a result of *poor realisation*. Not having a firm grasp of the knowledge relevant to our goal lowers our confidence and self-belief, which in turn lowers our motivation.

In the context of Exam Success, knowledge may refer to:

-   Knowing the content of each subject we're being examined on.
-   Knowing the right revision strategy for each subject we're being examined on.
-   Knowing the right exam technique for each subject we're being examined on.
-   Knowing the resources available to us that can help us to achieve our ideal exam grades.
-   Knowing the right people to speak to who can help us achieve our ideal exam grades, for example teachers, tutors, older siblings or peers.
-   Knowing how to manage stress caused by pressure, anxiety, low confidence, and so on.
-   Knowing how to motivate ourselves to study.
-   Knowing how to maintain our physical and mental well-being.

We may already possess some of this knowledge. This can be used to create a plan of action regarding *how* we're going to achieve our goal in the most effective manner. This is discussed in-depth in the Prioritisation and Planning sections of Principle 1.

However, we also need to realise what knowledge is *missing* – in other words, what *don't* we know that we *need to learn* about in order to attain our goal? And more importantly, *how* we can learn about it? For example, this may require spending more time studying a particular subject, speaking to a teacher or tutor who specialises in a subject we're struggling with, or speaking to someone who can help us with the mindset-related challenges we're facing with regards to stress or anxiety.

I always recommend that my clients learn *everything they can* about the topic their goal relates to.

If they're studying for exams, I urge them to consider all of the points I mentioned above pertaining to Exam Success. If they're trying to lose weight, I urge them to learn about nutrition and exercise so that they understand *how* they can lose weight in the most effective manner. This might involve reading books or speaking to a dietician, doctor, personal trainer, or an expert in another relevant profession – but the point is not just to follow instructions, but to learn *how* weight loss actually happens and *why* specific actions will help us to achieve it.

It's also important to realise that things *change*. Our goals and values change over time, so our *intention* changes. New scientific studies reveal more effective methods for achieving our goals, so our *realisation* changes, influencing the *actions* that we take.

Fuelling our Motivational Fire isn't a one-time job! But the more we know and understand about *how* we can achieve our goal, the more confident we will feel about pursuing our goal – and the more good-quality fuel we will have to feed our Motivational Fire!

Activity 3.7: For any goal you're striving to achieve, write down a list of the knowledge and resources you already possess to help you achieve your goal. Write down what knowledge and resources are *missing* – for each of these, make a note of how you can acquire them.

Action

Action is the *oxygen* that breathes life into our Motivational Fire.

All the *intention* and *realisation* in the world are meaningless until we take *deliberate action* and actually begin *moving* towards our goal. The more high-quality actions we take towards our goal, the more motivated we feel to *keep* taking action.

So, what stops us from taking action? We talk ourselves out of taking action for many reasons:

- *The action seems challenging or difficult; we're afraid of making a mistake or finding out that we can't do something.*

  We need to focus on the *realisation* element of the action. By increasing our knowledge about the actions that need to be taken, the task becomes easier. The things that we don't know can be learned with time, effort and the right resources. The mistakes that we make can be corrected, and we'll often learn valuable lessons from them.

- *The action will take up a lot of our time; we'd rather spend that time doing something else.*

  We need to address both our *intention* and *realisation*. Strong intention will help us to reinforce why our actions align with our values and resolve any value conflicts that we have. Powerful realisation will help us to plan out exactly *how* we can break our time-consuming actions down into smaller, more manageable action steps.

- *We create excuses about why today isn't the 'right time' to take this action (we're tired, we don't have enough time, etc.) , and that we should wait until the 'right time' to begin taking action.*

We must remind ourselves that *mood follows action*. We don't wait to feel good and *then* take action; we take action, and *then* we feel good as a result of it! For example, we rarely feel good about doing a homework assignment – but we feel great when we've finished it. We may not feel great before we go for a run, or even during our run – but we feel incredible when it's done!

It's important to focus on how *good* we'll feel *after* we've taken the action, instead of how *bad* we feel *before* we've done it. There's no better time to take action than in the present moment. As the old proverb goes: "The best time to plant a tree was 20 years ago; the second-best time is now."

- *Once we take action, we're committed to our goal – which means that 'failure' becomes a possible (unpleasant) outcome that we'd rather not face at all.*

It's absolutely possible that we won't achieve the outcome that we desire, especially if there are elements that aren't in our control. However, whether we choose to define that as *failure* is up to us. We can all benefit from redefining failure.

Failure isn't an outcome; it's our *response* to an outcome. If we get up after we fall, we haven't failed. If we learn from our mistakes, we haven't failed. If we bounce back after a setback, we haven't failed.

We don't fear failure; we fear the *emotions* we'll experience if we fail. We fear feeling the pain, disappointment, humiliation, shame, and other negative emotions that accompany failure. It's important to remember that failing to achieve an outcome is often disappointing and painful – but those feelings are not *permanent!* It might feel humiliating to tell your family and peers that you've failed – but they're more likely to be *supportive* and *helpful* as opposed to being judgemental and cruel.

It was painful and disappointing when I received a 2.2 for my 2nd year in a row in Cambridge. I had invested a lot of time and energy into getting a 2.1 grade, and I failed to achieve my goal. How did I respond? I *allowed* the disappointment to manifest instead of suppressing it. I didn't resist my emotions. I cried and wrote journal entries. I took some time to nurse my wounded pride and dented confidence. I even opened up to my parents and expressed my fears about how I'd disappointed them – they responded by telling me that I was an idiot, and that all that mattered was my health and happiness.

And then I got back up again, knowing that this pain will absolutely fade, and that the many valuable lessons it leaves behind may guide me to success. Had I given up, I wouldn't have achieved my 1st class grade in my 3rd year.

- *We don't trust the process; we want guarantees that our actions will lead to the outcome we desire.*

Outcomes are rarely guaranteed in life, primarily because there is so much out of our control. Instead of becoming attached to a specific outcome, we need to remind ourselves to embrace the journey. If we focus blindly on the peak of the mountain, we'll miss the beauty of the climb.

In addition, the lessons we learn about ourselves on the climb are arguably *more valuable* than reaching the peak. They don't just translate to Exam Success; they translate to success in *all* areas of our lives.

Activity 3.8: For any goal you're trying to achieve, write down the reasons which are stopping you from taking action, and what you can do to overcome them. Reinforce to yourself that taking action will motivate you to take *more* action. Make a commitment to start carrying out the action steps you've defined in your plan.

So – you've got clarity about your *intention*. You've accumulated the knowledge that you need to *realise* your goal. And you've started to take *action* towards achieving that goal.

What could stop you now?

There's one final factor that we need to consider…

Expectation

Expectation is the *fire blanket* which stops oxygen from reaching our Motivational Fire. When it seeps into our psyche, it stops us from taking further *action* towards our goal. Our *intention* and *realisation* may still be powerful, but the Motivational Fire requires *all* 3 components to feed it.

No *action*, no fire.

So, what do I mean by expectation?

Expectations are *attachments* to a future outcome that hasn't yet occurred.

The most common form of expectation in an exam context is our **'ideal' future outcome**. This is when our *goal* or *hope* evolves into a full-blown *expectation*, such that achieving a 'pleasure' emotion (e.g. happiness, worthiness, success, relief, relaxation) becomes *conditional* on the fulfilment of the goal or desired outcome.

In the context of exams, this is when we start to attach our happiness, self-worth, confidence (etc.) to getting good grades. As a result of this, we begin to place an immense amount of internal pressure upon ourselves to achieve that outcome – along with the external expectations our families and friends might be imposing upon us, as discussed in the Outer & Inner Pressures section of Principle 3.

Unfortunately, this means that we're putting our happiness, satisfaction and self-worth in *someone else's* hands. After all, the reality is that we're *not fully in control* of our grades – we don't choose the questions in the paper, nor do we choose who grades our paper. This conflicts with our *expectation* that if we work hard, we'll get the results that we've attached so much importance to.

This conflict between *expectation* and *reality* causes even *more* pressure to build up. We recognise that we've attached so much to a result that we're not even in control of. We begin to question whether our hard work is worth the time and effort. We start to doubt whether our best efforts will be enough. We remind ourselves of how important our exam grades are for our future, and how failure to achieve a good outcome will shake our confidence and disappoint our loved ones.

Eventually, the pressure arising from our lofty expectations creates so much tension and anxiety within us that we *stop* taking *action*. It becomes easier for us to distract ourselves with other tasks than to take action towards our Exam Success goals and have to confront the pressure of our expectations again.

We still have the heat of our *intention* (what we want and why we want it) and the fuel of our *realisation* (how we can achieve it), but we smother our oxygen source (our actions) with a fire blanket (our expectations) and put out our Motivational Fire in the process.

We can manage this by consciously *acknowledging* our expectations and making a decision to *downgrade* them from expectations to hopes and goals. We can recognise that we *want* to succeed and achieve our goals; but that our happiness and self-worth are not *conditional* on our success. We can also accept that, as we're not fully *in control* of our results, we should focus our energy solely on what we *can* control.

Simply becoming aware of our expectations in relation to the reality of our situation causes them to lose a lot of the power and influence that they have. This allows us to focus our energy on the small actions that we need to take on a day-to-day basis to move closer towards our goals, instead of wasting our energy feeling pressured and anxious because of the expectations we've created.

One of my life mantras for expectations is:

"Act, without expectation. Do, without condition. Strive, without attachment. Hope for the best, but don't *need* the best. Prepare for the worst, but don't *fear* the worst."

In other words, take action without *expecting* your actions to achieve a certain outcome. Do your tasks without creating *conditions* that need to be fulfilled for that task to have been worthwhile. Strive to achieve your goals without *attaching* your worth to whether the goal is achieved. *Hope* that your actions will help you achieve your goal; but don't let your *fear* that you won't achieve your goal stop you from trying.

Activity 3.9: Make a list of all the expectations you've placed on yourself (and others have placed upon you) to achieve a goal. Go through each one using RUDMA, and make a choice to *downgrade* it from an expectation to a *hope*. If necessary, use the 'Manage' stage of RUDMA to confront and resolve the worst-case scenario if your expectations aren't met.

So, let's return to our **Motivational Fire Formula:**

Motivation = Intention + Realisation + Action − Expectation

For maximum motivation, we want to have *high intention, high realisation, high action* and *low expectation.*

Keep this formula in mind whenever you notice your motivation diminishing. Ask yourself the following questions. Are you still clear about your *intentions*? Do you still know how you're going to *realise* your goals? Are you taking *action* every single day towards your goal? Are you managing your hopes and goals and preventing them from escalating into expectations?

If the answer to any of these is "no", use the RUDMA framework to help you understand what has changed, why it has changed, and what you may want to do about it to reignite your Motivational Fire.

If the answer to all of these is an honest "yes" – then take a rest! Fatigue can skew the way we perceive our progress towards our goals. Every hill looks steeper when we're tired. So, go for a short walk. Do some light exercise. Get some sleep.

And then return to your goals with a clear vision, a focused mind, and a scorching hot Motivational Fire.

3.8 Tool 4: Progress & Quick-Win Tracking

Progress Tracking

We become easily dissatisfied when we feel like we're not making progress with our studying. We also become disheartened if we think too much about how much studying we still have left to do.

Tracking our *progress* helps us to understand *what* we're doing and *how well* we're doing it.

Knowing what we're doing means that we're more likely to stick to our study plan. It also allows us to quickly recognise if our plans need to be *adapted* in response to any deviations – this is why *tracking* is the 6th Law of Study Planning.

Knowing what we're doing also allows us to identify what we're *missing*. Perhaps a few weeks down the line, we realise that we've missed out certain modules for our revision notes, or that we're missing some Past Papers. It's much more valuable to learn this three *weeks* before our exams than three *days* before our exams.

Knowing how well we're doing something allows us to manage our expectations effectively. It allows us to set realistic targets for ourselves, so that we don't risk losing confidence and motivation chasing *unrealistic expectations*.

In addition, knowing how well we're doing something allows us to ask ourselves what we can consider doing to *improve* our performance. The small tweaks that we make to our studying preparation after asking these questions are often the catalysts for the biggest improvements.

It's useful to track:

- **Completion of a task:** Progress towards our goals is motivating, and every tick in the box represents a small step towards achieving that goal. As you complete tasks, physically cross them off your to-do list or highlight them on your planner.

- **Energy levels:** Use an arbitrary 1-10 scale to gauge this throughout the day. When are you most focused and productive during the day? When do you feel most fatigued? How does eating, sleeping or exercise affect your energy levels? How can you ensure that you do the most important work during the times you are most focused and productive?

- **Number of hours you work:** Use a timer or time-lapse video to record this. Is this number less than what you would like it to be? How much of this time was actually *productive*?

- **Number of *productive* hours you work**: What can you do to increase your *productivity ratio* – that is, the number of productive hours worked in relation to the number of hours you work overall? *When* are you most productive during the day?

- **Performance on individual past-paper questions:** Helps you to understand which topics you struggle with, and therefore need to focus your revision on.

- **Time spent on individual Past-Paper questions:** Helps you to understand which topics you spend longer on, and therefore need to get quicker at doing in exam conditions.

- **Mistakes on Past-Papers:** How many questions are you getting wrong because of simple errors (e.g. didn't read the question, wrong entry into calculator, spelling mistake etc.)? How many questions are you getting wrong, or missing out, because you don't *understand* the concepts needed to answer them? What do you need to focus on to prevent these mistakes?

- **Grades for Past-Papers:** Is our revision helping us to increase our Past-Paper grades? Keep in mind that your grade will largely be dependent on whether your stronger or weaker topics came up in that individual paper. Don't be disheartened by lower grades; it's a great way to identify what our weaknesses are in order to address them.

Whatever forms of tracking we choose, we need to turn them into a *habit* by applying them frequently and regularly. The more effective our tracking is, the better we become at identifying what needs to be *changed* to make the biggest difference, so that we avoid wasting time making unproductive changes.

Activity 3.10: Decide on which of the above options you want to use to track your progress during your studies, and how exactly you'll track them. Think about any other progress tracking options you can add that would be useful to you.

Quick Wins

Quick-wins are small improvements that yield immediate benefits. They're the small steps we take and the milestones we meet on our way to achieving our bigger goals.

Whereas a long-term-win can be as big as completing revision notes on an entire module or finishing three years of Past-Papers, quick-wins can be as small as memorising a new fact, learning a new concept, or correctly answering a question that we couldn't do before.

The problem is that many of us don't *allow* ourselves to celebrate our quick-wins. We're our own harshest critics. We devalue the small steps that make up the big achievements, focusing only on the end outcome itself. Instead of focusing on the 10 things we're doing *well*, we beat ourselves up for the one thing we did *wrong*.

And then whenever we do actually achieve something, we *punish* ourselves by saying that we should have been doing that *anyway*. Every time we meet a new milestone, we forget about it and look ahead to the next one. We feel fatigued and overwhelmed because we're only focusing on how far we still have left to go.

Other times we look at other people and focus on how much further ahead of us they are. This is insane – we can never truly *know* how others are progressing. Our perception of how far ahead we *think* they are is not a real representation of where *they know* they are. We're not comparing ourselves to a real person – we're comparing ourselves to a ghost we've created in our own mind. And we'll *always* create a reason why that non-existent ghost is ahead of us, no matter how much progress we make...

These are harmful mental habits that we need to change, and it starts with recognising quick-wins.

Simply permitting ourselves to *acknowledge* these quick-wins helps us to build confidence, motivation and a more positive mood.[18] By recognising the small actions that we're *successfully* taking to achieve our goal, we appreciate the *improvement* in our own abilities. This motivates us to *continue* progressing towards them.

We don't need to deceive ourselves into thinking our quick wins are *bigger* than we believe them to be. This is not about pretending that the Past-Paper we completed is a miracle cure for our confidence. We're just acknowledging *incremental* progress in our abilities and using that to motivate us to take *more action* towards our goals. Recognising quick-wins is a **habit**. It's a mindset that we need to proactively train and develop. As with all habits, it takes approximately 66 days to fully replace an old habit with a new one.[19]

Up until now, we've been focusing more on the things we've done *badly*, as opposed to the small steps we're taking in the right direction. As such, we should spend a few minutes at the end of each day identifying our quick-wins and writing them down in a diary or journal. Please keep in mind that these are *not* for anyone else to see or judge. *You* are the only true judge of your own progress. Monitor your quick wins, permit yourself to feel the confidence boost they give you, and use that momentum to drive you towards your bigger goals.

Activity 3.11: List down 5-10 quick-wins you have made in the last few weeks – they can be as big or small as you like. From today onwards, make a commitment to write down *at least 3* Quick Wins *every single day* in your journal/diary/planner.

3.9 Tool 5: Self-Dialogue Transformation

How often do you find yourself thinking thoughts such as: "I can't do this", "I don't know how", "I'm not good enough", "it doesn't make sense", "I'll never figure this out", and so on?

I can't speak for you, but I'll admit that I certainly find myself experiencing these thoughts on a daily basis.

All of these thoughts are *limiting*. They create *tension* within us. There's a sense of constriction and confinement, as if the thought is squeezing us and tightening around us. We don't think, feel or act effectively under the influence of these thoughts.

We can recognise which thoughts have these effects on us by noticing the *tension* or *stress* that they physically induce. Then, we can consciously choose to *replace* these thoughts with those that create a feeling of *space* and *expansion*. These thoughts give us room to think, feel and act. They create a feeling of freedom, lightness and ease.

In the context of exams, this means replacing **constricting** thoughts ('I don't know how', 'I can't do it', 'I'll never understand this', and so on) with **expansive** thoughts ('I'll figure it out', 'it'll come to me', 'I'll take it moment by moment', 'I trust the process', and so on).

Unfortunately, many of us have created *thought patterns* out of our limiting thoughts. They've become ingrained in us because we've repeated them to ourselves throughout our lives. In these cases, these simple *thoughts* evolve to become genuine *beliefs*. These **limiting beliefs** stop us from striving towards our goals and performing at our best.

To resolve them, we first need to become *aware* of when we think about them, and then recognise what triggered them.

For example, in my case, they became much more frequent when I was *fatigued*. The situations that triggered them included when *other people* would speak about their exam preparation, or when I started to get *anxious* that I wasn't preparing enough, or when I felt that I was certain to fail my exams regardless of how much I prepared.

Activity 3.12: Over the next week (or longer), write down each occasion you catch yourself having a *limiting belief* or *thought*. Describe the thoughts and the situation that triggered it. Come up with an alternative thought or belief that creates a feeling of *freedom* and *expansiveness* instead of *tension* and *constriction*.

Once we recognise our limiting beliefs and their triggers, we can begin to transform them.

First, we need to create **doubt** about the old belief, questioning whether it's still *valid* in our current life situation.

For example, if we have a belief that we will 'never achieve the grades that we desire', we need to recall a time (for example, a Past-Paper or mock exam), where we *did* achieve a good grade. This disproves our old belief that we will 'never' achieve the grade we wanted. By introducing *doubt* about an old belief, we make it invalid and give ourselves the opportunity to replace it with an updated, positively-framed belief.

Next, we associate *pain* with the old belief.

We recognise the pain that our belief has been causing us, both in the past and in the present moment. For example, we may think about how the belief caused us to lose our self-confidence, or the stress and anxiety we're currently experiencing because of it. We can also consider the *pleasure* that the old belief has been *depriving* us of. For example, the pleasurable feeling of working in a focused manner or being confident in our ability to succeed if we do our best. By making these new associations, we can replace this old belief with a new, empowering belief that brings us *pleasure* instead of *pain.*

It's especially important to change our negative beliefs which contain the words 'never' and 'always'. For example, 'I'll never succeed', 'I've always failed', and so on. These are absolute terms that imply a *permanent* situation. It would be in our benefit to erase (or at least replace) 'never' and 'always' from our vocabulary in the context of exams and studies.

You can follow this *8-Question Belief Transformation Process* to replace your own limiting beliefs with new, empowering beliefs:

1. What triggers this limiting belief?

2. Where did this belief come from? What is the *root cause* of this belief?

3. How has this belief been holding you back from your goals?

4. What evidence do you have that proves this belief to be inaccurate or invalid **now**, even if it may have been true in the past?

5. What's the new, empowering belief that you'd like to replace it with?

6. How will this new belief take you closer to your goals?

7. What evidence do you have that supports this new belief?

8. What habitual steps can you take to turn this new belief into your 'default' belief?

Activity 3.13: Address each of the limiting thoughts and beliefs you wrote down in Activity 3.12 in turn using the 8-Question Belief Transformation Process outlined above.

Another simple tool we can use is to add '…yet' to the end of our negative statements, for example:

- "I can't do it" becomes "I can't do it…yet"

- "I don't know" becomes "I don't know…yet"

- "I'm not good enough" becomes "I'm not good enough…yet"

- "It doesn't make sense" becomes "It doesn't make sense…yet"

This simple change to our self-dialogue gives a *time-perspective* to our limiting beliefs. We recognise that our limiting belief exists in the present moment, *and* that we have a *choice* to *change* it in the *future*. It also encourages us to ask ourselves empowering questions, such as:

- What's the *first step* I can take to: learn how to do it/ know it/ become good enough/ make sense of it?

- What's stopping me in *this* moment from: learning how to do it/ know it/ become good enough/ make sense of it?

Through these techniques, we empower ourselves to take *action* to change our beliefs, instead of resigning ourselves to being limited by them.

Activity 3.14: Begin applying the '…yet' technique to your own limiting beliefs as described in the above examples.

Another powerful self-dialogue transformation tool is replacing the use of disempowering statements that begin with:

- I should…   - I have to…
- I must…   - I need to…

These statements are disempowering because they create a sense of *obligation* or *necessity* to carry out the tasks. They take away our *choice*, limiting our options and making us feel more constrained. We become less focused on doing the action itself, and more focused on the *negative consequences* that would come with *not* doing the action. This negative focus drains us of our energy and may lead us to feel overwhelmed and tired.

These statements also impose *pressure* to carry out the task, making us feel stressed and tense. We may also feel *guilt* or *anger* towards ourselves because we know what we 'should' be doing but we're not doing it. This saps our energy; energy that we *could* be using to actually do the task.

We can replace these with more empowering alternatives that begin with:

- I could…   - I get to…   - I allow myself to…
- I would like to…   - It would be nice to…

These statements are empowering because they create a sense of *possibility* and *permission* to carry out the tasks. We recognise that we have a *choice* in carrying out the action. We don't *have* to do it; but we may *choose* to do it. This gives us *space* to make a decision without focusing intensely on the consequences of the action.

Whereas "I *should* study" creates a sense of pressure and tension, "I *could* study" creates a sense of choice and freedom.

"I *have to* study" makes us feel constrained and limited, whereas "I *get to* study" makes us feel grateful and appreciative.

"I *need to* study" focuses on the negative consequences if we *don't* study, whereas "it would be nice to study" focuses on the positive feelings we would experience if we *do* study.

These small language shifts can create a huge impact in terms of whether we feel *tension* to complete a task, or whether we feel *freedom* to do the same task.

Activity 3.15: Make a note of at least 10 disempowering "should/ must/ have to/ need to" statements that you make. For each one, replace it with a more empowering version using "could/ would like to/ get to/ allow myself to/ it would be nice to". Write this new, empowering statement down and repeat it to yourself whenever you notice yourself thinking or using the old, disempowering statement.

A final self-dialogue transformation tool is converting negative **identity** statements into **behaviour** statements.

- A **behaviour** statement is one that relates to *what we do*. Our behaviours are what can be observed from the outside.

- An **identity** statement is one that relates to *who we are*. We express ourselves through our behaviours, beliefs and values, but our identity runs *deeper* than all of these. Identity statements begin with "I am...".

Why is this so important?

Because behaviours are *not as difficult to change* as our identities! They're just things that we may have a *tendency* to do, to the extent that they've become habits. As we learned in Principle 1, it may take 66 days to break an old habit and replace it with a new habit.[19]

But habits *can* be changed.

On the other hand, our identities are much deeper-rooted. Not only are they harder to change – we don't necessarily *want* to change them because they make us who we are. Our egos *like* having an identity to cling onto, even if that identity isn't serving us positively anymore!

Unfortunately, so many of us mistake our behaviours for our identities. We convert simple behaviours into deep-rooted identities with statements such as, "I'm a procrastinator", "I'm a failure", "I'm stupid".

We need to remind ourselves that *we are not our behaviour*. We are not *procrastinators* – though we may have a procrastination habit. We are not *failures* – though we may have failed to achieve the outcome we desire before. We are not *stupid* – though it may have taken us a little while longer to understand some topics.

Knowing this, there are two actions that we should take:

1. Transforming **negative identity statements** into **behaviour statements** whenever we catch ourselves thinking about them or saying them aloud. You are *not* a mess – though you may have gotten yourself in messy situations in the past.

2. Transforming **positive behaviour statements** into **identity statements** on every possible occasion. You didn't just work hard for your exams – you *are* a diligent, hard-working person!

Practising this on a daily basis will help us to loosen the hold of negative behaviours that used to hold us back, while affirming our strengths and positive behaviours that will take us closer to our goals.

Activity 3.16: Write down some of the negative identity statements in your self-dialogue. Beside each one, write down a rephrased statement in which that identity is phrased as a behaviour. Recite this to yourself daily until you no longer associate that behaviour with an identity.

3.10 Tool 6: The Path Of Least Regret

The Path Of Least Regret is a very simple mindset tool. It dictates that, when we're faced with a decision, we should take the action that will lead us to the *least amount of possible regret.*

So, what does The Path Of Least Regret look like in the context of exams?

Simply put, it means that we won't have any regrets at the outcome of our exams, *even if* we don't achieve the results we want. We may be *disappointed* at the outcome itself; but looking back on our preparation and the effort that we applied, we'll know that we couldn't have done anything more. We'll know that we gave it our *best.*

What does our **best** look like?

First, let me tell you what it *doesn't* look like.

Our best doesn't look like slaving away for 15 hours in a dark library. It doesn't look like a state of constant stress and an overwhelming feeling of despair that we're not doing enough. It doesn't look like sacrificing the activities that we enjoy and cutting off all contact with our friends.

This only leads to misery, stress, burnout, and an increased chance that we *won't* perform well in our exams.

Our best also doesn't look like perfection. In fact, perfectionism is a trait highly associated with increased anxiety, burnout, rigidity and less healthy coping tendencies.[20]

I consider myself to be a *reformed perfectionist.* I used to be obsessed with perfection, whether in academics or sport. It only led me to dissatisfaction, procrastination and failure. Whenever I approached a task, I would end up talking myself out of it because I knew that I could never complete it perfectly. I was so afraid of doing something *wrong* that I wouldn't do it *at all.*

I made a choice to give up perfectionism when I realised how it was holding me back from achieving my goals. I learned that *done is better than perfect* – that it's far better to have completed something that I can improve on later, than to delay completing something because I'm trying to make it 'perfect'.

I used the 80-20 Rule to help me identify exactly how I could get the most out of each minute of work, so that I didn't waste unnecessary time chasing the illusion of perfection at the cost of all of my other tasks.

I also learned the value in striving for **excellence** instead of **perfection**. I used Progress & Quick Wins Tracking to notice the tiny improvements I was making every single day. I may have started off clueless and inept, but with time and practice I noticed myself becoming more competent and proficient. Mastery doesn't happen overnight; we need to embrace the journey from incompetence to excellence.

If it wasn't for letting go of perfection, this book would never exist! I could have spent years refining the content of the book, adding more and more tools, constantly updating it with new developments in the field of education and psychology.

If I did, you would never be reading this sentence.

Letting go of perfection is crucial if we want to do our best.

So, now we know what our best doesn't look like. What *does* it look like?

Our *best* looks like **balance**.

Our best is when we can honestly look back and feel that we've worked in a focused and efficient manner towards our end goal of succeeding in our exams – and we know that we *couldn't have done any more* without compromising our physical health and mental well-being.

Our best is knowing that we worked diligently and focused on the tasks at hand. It's knowing that we planned effectively, and that we applied our time and effort in an efficient way to cover the modules that we needed to revise. But it's also knowing that we stayed well-rested, exercised, ate well, did fun activities, and spent time with friends and family.

Our best is understanding that our exam results *aren't fully in our control!* There are three elements to exams: First, those who write the paper. Second, those who prepare for the paper and turn up to do the paper on exam-day. Third, those who grade the paper. Of all three elements, we're only in control of *one* of them – our preparation for the exam, and our performance on Exam Day.

Our best is recognising that, *because* we're not fully in control of our results, we should strive to give our energy and effort to the elements that we *can* control – our preparation and on-the-day performance – instead of *wasting energy* stressing over what we *can't* control. At first, this may not be easy to accept. But the more we revisit, embrace and internalise this fact, the better we become at focusing our time and energy on what we *can* control.

Our best is accepting that – yes, we may be incredibly disappointed if we don't get the results that we desire, *especially* because we've given it our best. But disappointment is temporary and will fade with time, whereas regret is permanent and will linger indefinitely. It's better to have failed trying our best, than to have been too afraid to try because of the fear that we might fail.

Failure is *not* a signal that we should give up. It's just a form of feedback telling us that what we did this time didn't work, that we should change our strategy if we want to achieve different results, and that there are many lessons that we can take from our 'failure' to help us *form* that winning strategy.

To put it poetically: **striving towards our goals, we either win, or we learn; we only fail if we fall, and don't get back up again.**

Finally, our best is knowing that our best has the potential to get *better* every single day. So, yes – our best may not have been good enough for our exams this year. And now, we have a *whole year* to take our best to a higher level. Our next-year-self has the potential to be *so much better* than our current-self; and therefore, to achieve much better results.

Sounds pretty good, right? Not so fast...

There are two factors that we need to be aware of if we want to walk The Path Of Least Regret.

First, we need to make a choice to *suppress* our desire for ***instant gratification***. To mitigate future regret, we need to be able to look ahead enough to understand how our current decisions can impact our future-self. We need to understand that *long-term satisfaction* and *short-term joy* are *not* mutually exclusive.

We can have *both*, because we feel short-term joy whenever we take an action that fulfils our long-term goals. You *always* feel good after finishing a set of revision notes in line with achieving your academic goals. You *always* feel good after going to the gym to fulfil your health/fitness goals.

The second factor that we need to consider is ***honesty***.

The most challenging aspect of walking The Path Of Least Regret is that only *we* truly know when we're being honest with ourselves. To minimise regret, we can't trick or deceive ourselves into believing that we're doing enough, when we *know* we could be doing *more*.

We need to make a commitment to ourselves to *keep it real* from the very beginning. One of the first steps to doing this is to start *paying attention* to what our mind and body are telling us.

For example, we're *all* familiar with the feeling of *guilt* that we get in the pit of our stomach when we've been procrastinating by watching hours of Netflix, browsing through too many YouTube videos, or playing FIFA for hours on end.

We have to *redefine* this feeling as a signal to take *control* and *act*.

As soon as we become aware of this feeling of *guilt*, we can use it to snap back to the present moment and ask ourselves whether the actions we're currently taking are the correct ones to minimise regret.

It may be the case that, honestly, we're really tired and just need some time to switch off from exam preparation. This is absolutely fine! Simply clarifying this in our mind will allow us to continue with what we're doing *completely guilt-free*. The guilt will only remain if we *know* that we're fully capable of carrying out exam preparation tasks, and so are leaving room for regret by continuing with what we're doing.

In my personal case, I redefined the feeling of guilt to mean a signal from my body and mind saying, "Listen to me! I'm refreshed, refocused, and ready to learn!". I would then *immediately* close my Internet tabs, open my textbook and start making notes – without even *thinking* about what I was doing.

Only when I had pen on paper would I permit my mind to think *just enough* to realise that I was *actually* studying – and that it might be a good idea if my mind popped by to help me *actually* understand the content I was writing about! By this point, I was already *committed* to the act of writing revision notes, and so my mind wouldn't have the time nor incentive to convince me to procrastinate.

And if it were to do so, I would simply remind it that, whether I liked it or not, making notes was honouring the path that I chose to walk: The Path Of Least Regret.

Activity 3.17: How can you apply The Path Of Least Regret to help you in your studying? What feelings can you 'redefine' to trigger you to take positive action towards your exam preparation?

3.11 Tool 7: Mindfulness Practices

Some of the mindset tools that I found most helpful were those that can be described as *mindfulness practices*.

Teaching mindfulness in schools has become increasingly common to aid students to perform better in their studies. In fact, several academic studies have reinforced the *benefits* of mindfulness – it's been positively correlated with increased resilience, self-awareness and focus in students, as well as reductions in stress and psychological distress.[21]

Mindfulness & How To Practise It

Jon Kabat-Zinn, a world-renowned expert on the subject, defines **mindfulness** as: "paying attention in a particular way; on purpose, in the present moment, and non-judgementally".[22]

In other words, whatever we're doing, we can do in a *mindful* state. Mindfulness doesn't have to come in the form of *seated meditation*, although the two are commonly associated with one another. But whether we're studying, washing dishes, listening to music or playing a sport, mindfulness is simply the act of 'filling our mind' with what we're doing in such a way that we *immerse* in it in the present moment.

When other thoughts or feelings arise, we can simply observe them (without judgement), and then gently bring our awareness back to the moment or task at hand, letting the thought go in the process.

I've always found it helpful to imagine myself sitting on a bench at a train station. When a train of thought comes, I let it come. And when the train of thought leaves, I let it leave. And if the train stops and the doors open, I remember that I don't need to board it. I can stay on my comfortable bench, watching the world around me and gently observing as the train departs.

Nevertheless, we can also *choose* to mindfully contemplate on our thoughts and feelings. It's our ability to recognise and be consciously aware of what we're doing in the present moment that makes an act mindful.

There are several ways in which we can practise mindfulness. Here are 4 methods to consider:

- Bringing awareness to our **senses**: How does the action *feel*, and what does it *look, taste, sound* and *smell* like? Instead of focusing on *describing* these experiences with words and labels that we instinctively think about, focus more on *enjoying* seeing, tasting, touching, hearing and smelling them.

- Bringing awareness to our **breathing**: For example, by keeping 'count' of the seconds we're inhaling and exhaling for, or by using a repeated sound, word or statement (mantra).

- Bringing awareness to our **body**: Feeling the sensations of an action on our body itself (for example, the feel against our skin, increased heart rate, whether it's pleasurable or painful).

- Bringing awareness to an **object**: Associating the 'present moment' (in terms of becoming aware of our senses/breathing/body) to an object we carry on our person, for example a necklace or bracelet. Once this has been done, the object can act as our *anchor* to pull our focus back to the moment at hand if our mind tries to run away. In making this a habit, we can train ourselves to return to the present moment by simply *touching* or *holding* the object.

Many clients that I work with express concerns about practising mindfulness meditation. These include:

- I don't have the time to sit down and meditate for 10 – 20 minutes a day.
- I'm not flexible enough to sit cross-legged.
- I get stressed about whether I'm practising mindfulness correctly or not.
- I keep getting distracted and losing myself in my thoughts.
- I tried it for a week and didn't notice anything, so I stopped.

I completely understand these issues. Here are some points which my clients have found useful in addressing them.

Timothy Ferriss, the author of the 4-Hour Workweek, proposed that when starting a new project, task or routine, we should always ask ourselves one question: ***"What would this look like if it were easy?"***

In other words, how can we make what we're doing as simple, easy and enjoyable as possible for ourselves. We can always add complexity and difficulty to the routine in the future. But to start with, how can we make it *easy* for us to stay motivated to continue with our routine?

Remember - we're not trying to become Buddhist monks; we're trying to enjoy some simple benefits of mindfulness!

So, to start with, don't worry about *needing* to practise mindfulness for 10 – 20 minutes a day. Start with 5 minutes (or even 3 minutes!) of sitting comfortably, closing your eyes, and becoming aware of your senses, your breathing, or your surroundings. With time and practise, you'll start to *enjoy* mindfulness so much that you won't *want* to stop!

Don't worry about your sitting position. Light Watkins, a renowned Vedic meditation instructor and the author of 'Bliss More: How To Succeed In Meditation Without Really Trying", talks about how we can begin our meditation practice by sitting in the same comfortable position that we watch TV in.

Don't fret about whether you're practising mindfulness meditation correctly or not. If thoughts come, let them. If emotions arise, let them. Even if you spent your entire 10 minutes of meditation completely lost in thought, the fact that you *realised* how you spent those 10 minutes is something to celebrate! It means that you're practising and cultivating the skill of self-awareness.

Mindfulness should be practised daily to yield sustained benefits. After all, you don't go to the gym for a week and expect your body to be fit for the rest of your life. The key to creating a routine is to make it as *easy* and *enjoyable* as possible to the extent that you look forward to doing it.

So, just start with 5 minutes. Sit on your couch or go for a walk. Notice your surroundings, your senses, your breath, your thoughts and your feelings. Enjoy the experience!

During my university studies, I came up with my own mindfulness practice that was specifically tailored towards addressing my anxieties and fears about exams.

Kam's Mindfulness Practice

Twice a day - normally after-lunch and after-dinner - I would take mindfulness breaks (15-30 minutes depending on time available and my personal need). I would go for a walk around nearby fields or sit on a park bench, as being in nature helped me to relax. In your case, it doesn't matter where you go, as long as you move *away from your usual study area.*

My routine was as follows:

1. **3-5 minutes of gentle walking while listening to music.**

   This helped me to relax, take my mind away from thinking about the content that I was revising, while also allowing room for my fears and anxieties about exams/studies/anything else to come up.

2. **5-10 minutes of quiet, mindful contemplation.**

   This involved turning my music off, opening up my 'Notes' page on my iPhone and carrying out the 'R-U-D' steps of the RUDMA framework outlined in Tool 1. I would start by writing down whatever anxiety I was feeling (e.g. feeling like I was afraid of failing, that I wasn't working hard enough, that I was overwhelmed etc.) in a non-judgemental manner. You can use a pen/paper or laptop - the key is simply to *write* your thoughts and feelings down.

3. **5 minutes of mindful resolution.**

   With everything written down, I would begin the 'M-A' steps of the RUDMA framework, resolving the fears and anxieties that had come up during my contemplation period.

   I would seek out the root source of the anxiety, and then assess the extent to which I had *control* over it (e.g. how much I revise = control; who chooses the questions in the paper = no control). If it was controllable, I would write down a plan of action to address it or reinforce how I was already addressing it. If it was out of my control, I would grapple with the thought and the implications it could have on my result, take a deep breath, and simply say *'forget it!'* as I exhaled. After all, by doing whatever was in my control, I would be leaving no room for regrets regardless of the outcome.

(Okay, I'll admit that I used a *different* word beginning with 'f'. 4-letters, somewhat profane… I think you've figured it out by now! Use any expression that you feel empowers you the most – as long as it doesn't get you in trouble!)

In addition, if I was feeling demotivated, I would also take a moment to realign with my values (which we talked about in 'The Motivational Fire Formula').

4. **5 minutes of mindful breathing** (minimum - enjoy for longer if you have time).

   With my anxieties addressed, I allowed myself to relax and immerse myself in my walking/sitting. Focusing on breath is my preferred method, and I highly recommend the practices put forth by Vietnamese Zen-Buddhist monk, Thich Nhat Hanh. I found three of his books – Peace Is Every Step, The Miracle of Mindfulness and The Heart of the Buddha's Teaching – to be very helpful to developing my mindfulness practices.

Aside from this practice, I also have a necklace that I use as an *anchor* to reconnect me with the present moment and stimulate feelings of peace, focus, gratitude and joy.

How did I create this *anchor*?

Whenever I watched a sunset, I would immerse myself in the experience. Nothing else mattered, regardless of what I'd experienced during the day or the tasks I still had left to do. All my problems, challenges, stresses and worries would dissipate and dissolve. In doing so, I would experience feelings of joy in the present moment, gratitude for being alive, and a pure sense of concentration and focus.

During my time teaching in China, I bought a necklace with a jade Buddha pendant which I would wear under my shirt. Whenever there was a sunset, I would do my usual routine of immersing myself in the experience; but I also got into the habit of pushing the Buddha pendant of the necklace into my chest, taking a deep inhalation as I did so.

I did this so much that, even in the absence of a sunset, I could push my Buddha pendant into my chest, take a deep inhalation, and experience the *exact same feelings* of peace, focus, gratitude and joy flowing through my body.

I joke that the necklace has the **'Power of a Thousand Sunsets'**.

So, whenever I become aware that my mind is running away with anxieties about the future or regrets of the past, I only need to push the Buddha pendant of my necklace into my chest, and it creates those identical feelings of peace, focus, gratitude and joy. I become aware of my body and the sensations that I'm feeling, and I let my other senses immerse themselves in the moment.

This has been very useful for me when I've noticed my mind beginning to wander during studying, and even more beneficial when I sit the exam itself. I've also found it extremely useful during tennis matches and before giving presentations – peace, gratitude, focus and joy are a recipe for success in nearly all situations!

Activity 3.18: How can you incorporate mindfulness practices into your studying routine? Consider *when*, *where* and *how often* you will practise them in order to turn them into a habit.

To conclude, practising mindfulness gave me the following benefits:

- I would feel refreshed, re-energised and motivated to work.

- I noticed improvements in memory retention and increased focus during revision. Giving my mind a short break before returning to my studies helped me to absorb the content with greater ease.

- I was no longer stressed by anxieties or fears about exams (or other things). By mindfully contemplating on their sources and writing them down (as shown in the 'RUDMA' Framework), I was able to develop my self-awareness so that I could recognise and gently overcome my anxieties and fears with greater ease when they inevitably re-emerged in the future.

3.12 Tool 8: Visualisations & Affirmations

Visualisations and affirmations are positive reinforcement tools that target our conscious and sub-conscious mind. They have been used by elite athletes, successful businesspeople and other peak performers in various fields. [23]

Visualisation involves creating a *vivid* mental picture of the positive outcome that we want to manifest. Affirmations are positively-framed sentences that are written down and/or spoken aloud. In practice, we often combine the two.

Some of the main recognised benefits of visualisations and affirmations include: [24]

1. Keeping our mind *focused* on our goal.

2. Programming our mind to more readily *perceive* and *recognise* resources (those within us and those around us) that can help us to achieve our goal.

3. Stimulating our 'subconscious mind' to begin generating *creative* ideas to attain our goal.

4. Making us feel positive, energised and refreshed, therefore *motivating* us to take action to achieve our goals.

Before we look deeper into these, please note that these tools are *not* for the self-conscious. Simply put, too many of us are sceptical about using tools which are too *'out-there'*, *'esoteric'* or *'woo-woo'* (yes, vocabulary at its very best…), because they can make us vulnerable to the judgment of others.

We have *all* encountered judgmental individuals who look down on people who use these tools, describing them as *naïve, gullible, stupid,* and so on. As a result, we become insecure about using these tools because we fear facing similar judgement. Even if we succeed in blocking out the negative voices and attempt to use these tools, we *doubt* their effectiveness, rendering them far less powerful.

If you're going to practise affirmations and visualisations, *commit* to them. Block out what others would think of you. *Believe* that they're an effective strategy to employ. Set aside your doubt and really allow yourself to impartially observe the impact that these tools are having on *your* life.

Besides, if they've worked for world-class athletes, CEOs and leaders, does it really matter what your friends think?

Practising Visualisations & Affirmations

The most common form of visualisation involves creating a *vivid mental picture* of what we want to manifest. The picture might be an 'internal' picture focusing on *us* (e.g. completing our revision notes, feeling confident during the exam), or an 'external' picture involving *others* (e.g. our parents' excitement when we tell them our good results).

The key is in the *details*. We need to imagine what we *look* like, how we *feel*, and what we're *doing* and *thinking* in our mental picture. Visualisation is an *active* process – we *direct* the images that our mind is creating. This is different to daydreaming or fantasising, both of which are passive, unfocused processes where our mind creates images that we just *observe*.

For visualisation to be effective, we need to turn it into a *habit*. It's important for us to set a few minutes aside, perhaps twice a day, and practise at a time when we feel relaxed and peaceful (for example, when we wake up, after a meal, or before we sleep).

The last thing any of us want when practising visualisations is for our anxious mind to sabotage our positive image with *negative thoughts*. If we find our visualisations being sabotaged, we need to *stop*. We can then use the RUDMA framework to identify *why* our negative thoughts are influencing our visualisation practice, and then resolve them before attempting the visualisation again.

Because of this, I would normally practise visualisations *after* my mindfulness practices, or *after* using the RUDMA tool to address any anxieties or fears I had. Here are a few examples of visualisations I found useful while studying:

- **Revision Notes/ Past Papers:** An image of me walking into my room. I open my textbook and notepad. I feel the sensation of putting pen to paper. I have a peaceful half-smile on my face. I feel at ease with the content I'm studying. I feel focused, efficient and ready to learn.

- **Exam Room:** An image of the examiner starting the clock for the exam. I open my paper and begin looking through the questions. I feel myself smile and feel at ease as I look through the paper, recognising that I *know* how to do *every single question*. I feel focused, efficient and ready to do my best.

- **Sleeping** (especially if I was sleeping late): An image of me waking up in the morning to my favourite alarm song. I feel replenished, focused and ready to start the day. I feel pleasantly surprised that I have so much energy. I jump out of bed with a smile and begin my day.

- **Results Day:** An image of me checking the results on my laptop. I feel peaceful, knowing that I gave it my all. The page loads up. I see the result I desire. I feel grateful and excited to share the news with my family.

Our visualisations are highly personal, and therefore need to be authentic to us. Use my ideas if you wish, but add your own unique twist that makes them meaningful to *you*.

And don't forget – if you don't *believe* that visualisations are an effective strategy, you simply won't gain as much benefit from them.

Activity 3.19: Create 5 (or more) visualisations that you can use to aid you in your studies and during your examinations. Write down their exact description to aid you in this. Set aside 5 minutes, twice a day, to practise these.

We can use *affirmations* to supplement our already-existing visualisations. We can also create affirmations by themselves, and *then* attach strong mental images and feelings to them afterwards as we speak them aloud to ourselves.

When creating affirmations, we should consider the following 5 points:

1. Our affirmations need to be ***positively stated*** – we must avoid negative language, and state them in terms of what we 'gain', not what we 'lose' or 'give up'. (e.g. gain fitness and health, not lose weight – our subconscious mind doesn't want to *lose* or *give up* anything.)

2. Our affirmations need to be stated in the ***present tense*** – our subconscious mind uses this as a signal to get to work on them instantly.

3. Our affirmations need to be stated with ***emotion*** – we need to *feel* the words, not just speak them.

4. Our affirmations need to be ***realistic*** - we have to believe that they're plausible for us to achieve in real-life.

5. Our affirmations need to be ***personal*** – they must be authentic to us, and stated only with regards to what we can control (i.e. ourselves, not others).

It's important to *write down* our affirmations, whether on a sheet of paper or on a phone app. We can read them to ourselves whenever we have a moment to spare – it doesn't take more than a few minutes each time.

It can be helpful to create a *routine* or set aside specific times for practising our affirmations, for example after-meals, during walks, and after visualisations.

Kam's Study Affirmations

Examples of affirmations I used during my studies:

1. I am focused, efficient and ready to learn.
2. I am courageous and steadfast in striving towards my goals.
3. I am replenished, re-energised and ready to achieve my goals.
4. I am working to the best of my ability.
5. I am healthy and fit, mentally and physically.
6. I trust that I know when I need to work, and when I need to rest.
7. I am successful in achieving an outcome that represents my full potential.

I also used some specific affirmations *during* my exams (read Principle 4 for more on this):

1. I honour every minute in this exam room, knowing that *nothing else matters* during this time.
2. I am fully focused, efficient and performing to the absolute *best* of my ability.
3. I am *creative* and *resourceful*, and will always find an answer to the problem.
4. I am *calm* and *patient*, and I know my mind will lead me to the answer even if I don't remember it straight away.
5. I release onto this paper *all* the knowledge that I have accumulated during my preparation, honouring every moment of hard work I have put in.

As I mentioned earlier, your affirmations need to feel authentic to *you*. Feel free to adapt those I have suggested above (they *really* did help me a huge amount), but add your own personal twist to them!

Activity 3.20: Write down the affirmations that you want to include with your 5 (or more) visualisations. Write down 5 (or more) other affirmations that can aid you in your studies.

In summary:

- We have identified 4 key problem areas that can negatively impact our mindset towards studying. These are: Anxiety, Outer & Inner Pressures, Low Confidence & Self-Doubt, and Low Motivation.

- We have discussed 8 tools to create an optimised study mindset and deal with these problem areas. These are: 'RUDMA' Framework, Owning Our Stress Response, The Motivational Fire Formula, Progress & Quick Win Tracking, The Path Of Least Regret, Self-Dialogue Transformation, Mindfulness Practices and Visualisations & Affirmations.

We have (finally) come to the end of Principle 3. I hope that this section has clarified the causes of some of the mindset issues that you may be experiencing, and equipped you with a range of tools to optimise your Mind-Management as you continue your quest towards Exam Success.

4. Principle Four: On-The-Day Performance

The big day has arrived. All the months of planning, revision notes and ink refills have been building up to this. It's time to do our preparation justice and achieve Exam Success!

4.1 The Night Before

Ideally you've prepared enough so that you feel no need for last-minute cramming. A good night's sleep has been shown to improve memory recall and concentration, so resist the voice of doubt and anxiety that tells you to trade sleep in exchange for work. I am not going to go into any more detail on the importance of sleep in this chapter – Principle 7 is dedicated to that.

If you're feeling anxious or stressed, try some of the tools outlined in Principle 3. The mindfulness practices may be particularly helpful. Other than that, calming music, a warm shower or a bit of light exercise can also have a relaxing effect.

If you're struggling with a cold or illness, *rest earlier* than you would have done otherwise. Be sensible and realistic about your capacity to do productive work. You want to ensure that you feel as *alert* as possible for the entire duration of the exam the next day. A good night's rest will also *accelerate* your recovery for future exams. An all-nighter now would do more harm than good.

The physical symptoms of a cold can be managed through different forms of medicine. However, the *mental* aspect of the illness is more dangerous. It's easy to become frustrated and disheartened because we're not feeling at our best at the time when it's *most important*. It's tempting to feel like the victim of an unfair situation, as if our body is conspiring against our success despite all the preparation that we've done. We must *not* let our mind go down this path of thought.

Use the tools outlined in Principle 3 to *manage your mind*. No matter how bad you feel now, you *must* believe that you will be able to muster up the strength and clarity of mind to perform well for the duration of tomorrow's exam.

Finally, make sure that your bag is packed with all the documents and stationery necessary for the exam.

If you can't sleep once you get into bed, *don't worry*. Even the act of lying down and closing your eyes helps to rest and refresh the mind. And if you stay there long enough, sleep will eventually come. If you're especially worried about being unable to fall asleep, I've outlined some breathing exercises and techniques that may help in Principle 7.

4.2 The Morning Of The Exam

No matter how much you slept, or how well you think you slept, tell yourself that you feel *refreshed, re-energised* and *ready* to handle whatever lies ahead.

Pick some 'Motivational Morning Music' for yourself, and literally *jump*, or even *dance,* out of bed! Yes, it sounds stupid. Yes, it probably looks stupid too. And yes, it absolutely puts you in an *awesome* mood. No one is watching you. No one needs to know. Give it a go and see how you feel. (I *still* do this every morning…)

If your exam is in the morning, try to wake up *at least* 1.5 - 2 hours before you leave your house. This will give you ample time to eat a good, balanced breakfast (see Principle 6 for in-depth ideas on foods to eat), use the bathroom, and most importantly, give yourself time to *allow your brain to really wake up*.

Doing some light exercise before a test has been shown to improve mental performance[1], so it may be worth including a quick workout before breakfast or walking to your exam venue. This is discussed further in Principle 5, which is dedicated to the importance of movement and physical activity in the context of exams.

If you feel obliged to do some pre-exam revision, stick to *reviewing* your revision notes or looking through past-papers that you have *already completed*. Don't go through them with the goal of memorising content; simply use them as a tool to kick your mind into gear and prepare it for what's to come.

I strongly recommend *avoiding* revising new content or doing new past-papers on both the day before the exam, and on the day of the exam itself. There simply isn't enough time to understand new concepts, and it will only put you in a state of panic if something comes up that you realise you don't really understand.

You want to go into your exams feeling *focused* and *confident*. Leave any surprises to the exam paper itself, not to the anxious illusions your mind conjures *before* you've even set foot in the exam hall. If you're ill, *convince yourself* that no matter how you feel *now*, you'll be able to perform *at your best* for the entire duration of the exam.

Check your bags to make sure you have all the documents and stationery you need for the exam. Arrive at your exam venue *at least* 30 minutes before the start-time of the exam. While waiting for the exam to start, it may be useful to find a location where you feel comfortable, and where the chances of being interrupted by your peers is minimised. You need to focus on *your* mental preparation, not be influenced by *theirs*.

During my GCSE and A-Level exams, I would seek refuge in my favourite place in the school – the sports hall. It was a relatively private location where I could review my notes without being interrupted. Just before going to the exam room, I would sneak into the toilets to listen to my 'motivational' music – the school rules prohibited listening to music on our phones, and I highly doubt teachers would have approved of me playing 2Pac's 'Me Against The World' aloud anyway…

Finally, I would start chewing on gum just before entering the exam room. Chewing promotes blood flow to the brain by a mechanism that scientists refer to as 'mastication-induced arousal' (seriously, you can't make this stuff up…). Studies show that a burst of gum-chewing before testing improves a student's performance, but only after a 20-minute period from when chewing had commenced. Gum chewing was shown to help especially during memory-related tasks.[2]

Throughout university, I would walk to each of my exams. During the 15-minute walk, I would avoid thinking about the content I had studied or the exam itself. Instead, I would immerse myself in my 'motivational' music (Own Appeal by Oddisee, if you're curious), and repeat the affirmations that I created for myself (see Principle 3). I would isolate myself from my peers upon arriving at the venue, until the time came to enter the exam hall...

4.3 The Exam

Exam instruction time is mental preparation time. We can utilise positive affirmations (<u>Principle 3</u>) to focus our mind if it tries to run away into the realms of anxiety. We can also use a mindfulness *'anchor'* object (<u>Principle 3</u>), for example a necklace or bracelet, to keep us focused on the present moment.

When **reading time** begins, *use it*. Look through every question in your exam paper, and begin to mentally *plan* which questions you'll choose to do (if you have a choice between questions), and which order you'll attempt them in.

How you decide your question order is up to you. I would always choose to do the 'easiest' or 'quickest' questions first in order to build my confidence. In doing so, this would allow me to have more time later to attempt the more challenging questions.

In **numerical exams**, spot the questions where they *give* you the answer or formula that you need to derive ("show that…" questions). These are an effective way of building confidence by getting a guaranteed 'correct answer' under your belt early on in the exam. Even if you can't *derive* the formula (normally the first part of the question), you can still use the given formula to answer subsequent parts of the question.

One of my clients, Arya, refused to look ahead at the other questions in the paper because she felt that she would, "get anxious and panicky about not being able to do them". After coaching, she decided to attempt my strategy.

Arya told me after the exam (an A-Level Mathematics Mechanics module) that it was, "the best decision she made". The first question on the paper seemed very challenging, so by looking through the others and finding questions that were easier, it helped to put her anxiety at ease. She not only achieved her offer to study Law at Birmingham University, but she scored 93/100 on that Mechanics paper!

When reading time finishes and the exam begins, *don't feel pressured to dive straight in* and answer the questions. There are several productive options you can consider.

One of my favourite tactics was to grab a scrap piece of paper and write down any fact, date or formula that I was worried I might forget later in the exam. It only took three minutes, but it put my mind at ease knowing that I had it for later reference if needed.

For **essay questions**, consider creating an essay *plan*. The amount of time you spend on this should be based on the time or marks available for the question. In my case, I would give myself roughly 5 minutes to plan for a 45-minute question.

I would spend the 5 minutes interpreting the question, selecting the arguments I wanted to put forward in the main body, and structuring them appropriately. I would then use these arguments to roughly plan my introduction and conclusion. This saved me *significant* amounts of time as I wrote the essay, and reduced the likelihood of having to go back and make changes to my arguments or add new ones later.

Once you feel ready, *attack* the questions with focus and determination.

To prevent silly mistakes, *check* your answers, working-out, spelling, grammar (etc.) as you go through the paper. Don't forget to *show your working-out.* Even if silly mistakes occur, clear working can save you some marks.

You can also utilise **sense-checks**. For questions which describe a realistic situation, ask yourself if your answer *makes sense.* For example, if you calculated the length of an airport runway to be 350 km, you may have done something wrong in your calculations (unless it was the runway in Fast & Furious 6…). Similarly, a man would *not* be running at 180 m/s (even Usain Bolt after drinking copious amounts of Red Bull) under any realistic circumstances.

Throughout your exam, always keep an eye on the clock. I suggest bringing your own watch or timer. You should have a rough idea about how long you want to spend on each question. Set yourself a deadline for when you'll move on to the next question regardless of the progress you are making on the current one, unless you're *confident* that you can make up the lost time.

If you start to feel anxious, use your *affirmations* and mindfulness '*anchor*' object to bring you back to the present. **Deep breathing** is also a powerful tool to calm yourself down. I would do 5 sets of breathing with a 4-4 count. This involves inhaling for a mental count of 4, and then exhaling for a count of 4. I can't emphasise how many times the above breathing exercise (40 seconds in total) has calmed me down during a bad exam.

Many clients have asked me why deep breathing helps to calm us down. It's a very fair question, and I've personally found that understanding *why* something works makes me far more likely to do it! So, let's begin the brief science lesson…

In short, deep breathing helps to calm us down as it stimulates the *parasympathetic nervous system,* releasing hormones and neurotransmitters like acetylcholine that lower our heart rate and form our 'rest-and-relax' response (the opposite of our 'fight-or-flight' response).[3] It also activates slow adapting pulmonary stretch receptors (SARs) in our lungs, which cause an inhibitory signal to travel to our brainstem to suppress our sympathetic nervous system (which is responsible for our 'fight-or-flight' response).[4]

A 'tactical' 2-minute toilet break can also be useful to break out of mental slumps. As we mentioned in Principle 3 (Owning Your Stress Response), sudden shifts in body posture, such as standing-up and walking, can be used to 'break' a negative state. They allow us to get out of an unresourceful state of mind to re-enter a 'neutral' state. We can then build a positive, resourceful state through breathing exercises and affirmations. Return to the exam room feeling positive, creative and ready to focus on the task at hand.

If you're in a negative state but can't leave the exam room to use the toilet, just lean back and stretch on your seat, or take a drink from your water bottle. As we discussed in Principle 3, all of these actions also break our negative state, following which we can consciously create a positive state.

When we find ourselves stuck on multiple questions but there are no others that we can attempt, it's easy to put our pen down and wait for the exam to finish. However, I suggest that we *keep* our pen in our hand, grab a scrap piece of paper, and begin to write down ***everything we know*** about the subject we're being examined on.

Why?

In <u>Principle 3</u>, I shared some of my affirmations with you. One of them was: "I release onto this paper *all* the knowledge that I have accumulated during my preparation, honouring every moment of hard work I have put in."

And I meant every word.

Our *exam* may be over, in that there are no more marks we feel we can gain. But as long as there's still time and you're still sitting in that room, you *might as well make the most of it!*

In my view, I had put a *tremendous amount* of effort into preparing for these exams, and had *learned so much* in the process. Just because the examiner hadn't chosen a question that allowed me to honour this hard work and show how much I had learned, it wasn't going to stop me from letting out *all* the knowledge that I had accumulated.

So, I would proceed to write *every* quote, formula, mnemonic – anything related to the subject I was being examined on – on a scrap piece of paper. I let my mind *release* it all onto the sheet of paper in front of me during the time that I had left.

Two amazing things happened when I did this:

1. I felt good. Really good. I'd learned *a lot* during these months, and it felt great to be releasing that knowledge in the exam room – even if I wouldn't get marks for it.

2. After a few minutes of this, something amazing would happen. I would suddenly find myself writing down or remembering something *relevant* to one of the questions that I was *stuck* on! And in doing so, it triggered a 'light-bulb' moment in which I realised *how to answer that question.*

This was *exactly* the tactic that I utilised in four of my 3rd year exams. I don't know exactly how many marks that I gained through this, but I do know that my overall 1st class grade was *very close* to the grade boundary – so *every single extra mark* had made a significant difference.

Activity 4.1: Which of the exam day tactics discussed above are you going to try? Make a note of what you'll do and exactly how you'll do it.

4.4 The Aftermath

Congratulations – one more exam done!

As you leave the exam room, I highly recommend that you don't speak to any of your peers. The exam is *done*. Having a group discussion about it will only increase your chances of finding a mistake that you *can no longer change*. You do *not* need to be exposed to that kind of potential disappointment and loss in confidence, especially if you have another exam coming up.

But even when you escape from others, you may struggle to escape your own thoughts.

If you feel that the exam went well, be grateful. Assess what you did well, take a relaxing break, and then refocus your attention on the next one.

If you're feeling disappointed because the exam went poorly, you need to address it *immediately*. Set yourself a *specific* amount of time to deal with it. Apply the RUDMA framework to address the feelings that you might have about the exam. Use mindfulness practices to bring your mind back to the present moment. And then, when your time is up, *move on*. The past is gone and can't be changed – but you still have control over the outcome of your *future* exams.

One of the exercises that I do with my clients after each exam is called an *exam audit*. We split an A4 sheet of paper into three sections:

1. **Positive points:** What went well?

2. **Negative points:** What didn't go well?

3. **Action points:** How can I improve next time?

In the **first** section, we write down *at least 5 positive points* from the exam. We look at the *night before* (e.g. slept early and felt refreshed in the morning), the *morning of the exam* (e.g. breathing exercises helped to calm me down), the *exam itself* (e.g. great timing throughout, didn't get flustered on question 3, etc.), and *after the exam* (e.g. avoided talking to my friends when I left the exam room).

In the **second** section, we write down *every negative point* from the exam. This is a very effective way of venting any frustration that we might have about a silly mistake, a question that we weren't prepared for, or anything else still lingering in our mind. We can also note down other setbacks, for example feeling tired during the exam, panicking during the exam, or hearing from one of our peers that we got an incorrect answer.

In the **third** section, we write down *at least one action point for each negative point* that we wrote down. This might be a *constructive action point* that we can take (e.g. sleep earlier, check for silly mistakes, try breathing exercises to calm down, change revision techniques for the next exam, etc.) or *accepting* something that can't be changed (e.g. let go of a silly mistake, let go of our annoyance at an unclear question that was hard to understand).

I recommend spending 5 to 10 minutes after each examination carrying out an *exam audit*.

Due to the intensity of exams, it can be beneficial to take a break before resuming revision. Whether you grab a bite to eat, go for a walk, take a nap, do some exercise, see some friends (etc.), make sure that you set a *specific time* to return to your revision.

If you're ill, *rest*. Don't push yourself to work if you feel fatigued and unproductive. Focus on recovering for your future exams. Do some light physical activity. Stay well hydrated and eat good-quality foods. And most importantly, get a good night's *sleep*.

One more exam done. One step closer to the finish. One step closer to Exam Success.

In summary:

- **Night-before exam:** Sleep

- **Morning of exam:** Pump yourself up, physically and mentally.

- **During exam:** Stay focused and keep your mind on the task at hand. When you think you've done all you can, take a scrap piece of paper and write *everything* that you can think of relating to your subject, irrespective of whether it's relevant to the exam or not.

- **After exam:** Exam audit. Learn from it. Let go of it. Rest. Repeat.

Congratulations – this concludes the 'Optimising Your Studying Process' half of the book. Take a moment to reflect on the key learning points from the book so far, and complete the activities if you haven't done so already.

The second half of the book focuses on 'Optimising Your Studying Lifestyle', since the overall *effectiveness* of our exam preparation is determined largely by the lifestyle choices that we make during this time.

Thankfully, the 4 Lifestyle Principles will not be covered in as much depth as the 4 Studying Process Principles. The main purpose of the following chapters is simply to convey the *importance* of the lifestyle choices that we make with respect to exams, and to introduce you to *methods* by which you can begin to make changes to your own lifestyle.

There's also a *tiny* bit of science and the *occasional* reference to academic studies. Please ignore them if you wish; they're simply there for the sceptics and the curious ones among you who actually want to understand *why* physical activity, good food, staying hydrated, plenty of sleep (etc.) are so important on the journey towards Exam Success.

Here we go!

5. Principle Five: Movement & Physical Activity

Let me make this crystal clear. This Principle is *not* about telling you to become a gym monkey. It's not telling you to go running on cold, rainy mornings. It's not telling you how to lose weight, carve toned abdominal muscles and achieve the beach body you always (or never) dreamed of.

This is also *not* a biology lesson. We will not be talking about the differing health benefits of aerobic or anaerobic activities. We will not discuss the impact of exercise on your metabolic rate or VO₂ Max. We will not explore the qualities of fast-twitch and slow-twitch muscle fibres.

This Principle is solely about the benefits of physical activity and movement in the context of *exam performance*.

And the key message I want to convey is that **any movement is better than no movement!**

I will avoid using the word *exercise* in this chapter as much as possible. The word has a different meaning to each of us, and there are many who associate *negative* thoughts with it. Please do not let your prior relationship with exercise stop you from engaging in movement and physical activity.

By 'movement and physical activity', I am referring to anything that involves:

1) The motion of limbs.

2) The use of different muscular groups.

3) An increase in heart rate.

Examples include:

1. Brisk walking
2. Jogging, cycling, swimming etc.
3. Recreational or competitive sport
4. Yoga, Pilates, Zumba, other forms of dancing
5. Gym (to work-out, not to take selfies...)

5.1 The Importance of Movement & Physical Activity

So, why should we bother with movement?

In the short-term, movement results in improved blood flow to the brain, leading to improved *cognitive function* and the ability to sustain a higher level of *focus* for a longer time period. [1] Physical activity performed four hours after learning has been shown to improve *memory consolidation* of the content studied.[2]

In the long-term, regular movement has also been correlated with an increase in the volume of the hippocampus, a part of the brain responsible for *memory retention*.[3]

Physical activity stimulates the release of several hormones and neurotransmitters, for example:

- *Dopamine*: Positively correlated with learning and attention span.[4]

- *Norepinephrine*: Positively influences motivation and mental stimulation. [5]

- *Serotonin*: Contributes to regulation of sleep cycles and improved mood. [6]

- *Endorphins*: Linked with euphoria, decreased stress and enhanced immune system. [7]

In addition, the body becomes better at regulating the release of cortisol, commonly known as the 'stress' hormone (we talked about it in <u>Owning Our Stress Response</u>). Excess cortisol has been linked with higher levels of stress and lowered immunity[8], both of which are detrimental to exam preparation and performance.

Finally, a study conducted in the University of Illinois showed that as little as 20 minutes of physical activity led to an *immediate* increase in brain activity in the *basal ganglia* region, which is responsible for coordinating thoughts and actions. The students showed improvements in cognition and memory, and scored *higher* on tests and examinations carried out shortly after their activity.[9]

Having experimented with jogging, bodyweight circuit workouts and walking (to the exam venue) on the morning of my exams, I *absolutely support* the results of this research study. Doing these forms of activity made me feel much calmer, focused and energised during my exams.

5.2 Integrating Movement Into Your Lifestyle

Depending on the type of physical activities we choose to pursue, the time of day may be important to consider:

- **Before breakfast:** The longer our activity, the *lower* the intensity we should carry it out with. Even though 'fasted' cardio & HIIT (high-intensity interval training) are becoming increasingly popular for weight-loss, our primary focus is Exam Success. High intensity movement is taxing on the central nervous system (CNS).[10] After our activity 'high' (from hormones and neurotransmitters), the fatigue which stems from CNS exhaustion can be detrimental to studying. Not recommended unless you have a lot of experience with physical training.

- **After breakfast/lunch/dinner:** Blood flow to our stomach is increased after eating, and we may feel mentally and physically sluggish. Walking is a great option to aid digestion and prepare ourselves for the studying to come. I would personally go for a 10 - 15-minute walk after lunch during my exam preparation.

- **Between lunch and dinner:** If we've been studying efficiently in the morning and immediately after lunch, we may find our productivity start to wane. A run or workout anytime between 16:00 and 19:00 is a great option to give ourselves a break and boost our energy levels.

- **After dinner:** This depends on the individual. Some people find that physical activity helps to tire them out, enabling them to fall asleep easier. Others, such as myself, find physical activity to be energising. I would limit my after-dinner activity to a walk at around 21:30 as part of the Mindfulness Practice outlined in <u>Principle 3</u>. However, late night runs and gym sessions did come to my rescue on multiple occasions when I felt particularly stressed.

To integrate physical activity (aside from walking) into our schedule, we can use our planner to identify 3 or 4 days a week (minimum) when we can set aside time for at least 20 – 45 minutes of movement.

If we know *when*, *where* and *what* activity we're doing, it becomes easier to stick to our commitment and create a habit out of it. Remember – *motivation* may get us *started*, but *habit* is what *keeps us going* on the days when we feel tired, demotivated and lazy.

For those of us who worry about the challenge of maintaining our physical activity habits, an effective way to stay motivated is to frequently remind ourselves of the *benefits* of movement and how it aligns with our *values* (Principle 3).

If we value *success* (e.g. good exam grades), we should remind ourselves of how movement will actually *benefit* our mood, focus and memory retention, therefore allowing us to study more productively. If we value *health*, we can use the *long-term* benefits of movement to motivate us to stick to our schedule. If we value *fun*, we can think of ways to make movement enjoyable. For example, we can choose activities that we enjoy or are already familiar with, or gather a group of friends to run or work-out together.

If we're worried about wasting time during exercise, we can create a workout plan before our session to save time deciding on which exercise to do next (see Appendix 3 for my personal-trainer approved workout plans). Another option is to attend sessions or classes where an instructor tells us what exactly to do for the duration of the class.

If we're feeling ill, we should stick to *light activity* (e.g. walking, Yoga). Sweating is an effective way of removing toxins from our body and accelerating our recovery process. However, medium-to-high intensity activity can fatigue us further and be detrimental to our recovery.

We should try to avoid activities that may result in injuries – we're getting ready for exams, not hospital test results! I lightly sprained my ankle playing a competitive game of basketball the *day before* my first exam in my 2nd year at Cambridge. Thankfully, the injury wasn't too serious. However, hobbling to the exam hall was *not* enjoyable, and neither was the throbbing during the exam.

If you've had prior injuries or other health conditions, it's recommended to consult a physician or doctor before carrying out any form of physical activity.

Activity 5.1: Identify the days and times each week during which you are going to engage in physical activity. Which activity will you do? How long will you do each activity for? Think of 5 obstacles that might stop you keeping to your physical activity schedule, and consider methods by which you can overcome them.

5.3 Kam's 'Efficient Study Training' Routines

If you're new to movement and physical activity or don't have access to gym equipment, *don't worry*.

I've included 2 of my own 4-minute bodyweight circuit routines (approved by several personal trainers) in Appendix 3. Please check it for details on the exercises involved in the circuit and the length of time that each exercise should be carried out for.

There are varying levels of difficulty to select for each exercise depending on your fitness levels. To see how each exercise is done, search YouTube for a video titled 'Bodyweight Exercise Circuit Workouts – Kam Taj'.

These circuits have been tried and tested on many students, from complete beginners through to University-level rugby and tennis players. Circuit training is suitable for anyone because it allows *you* to decide the *pace* at which you do each exercise in the given time. This gives you *complete control* of the intensity at which you train.

It also allows you to gauge your progress relative to your prior performance on the same circuit, which some students find motivating. Exam Success *and* improving fitness levels? Sounds like a win-win scenario to me!

The 4-minute circuits can be repeated as desired to increase the overall time spent doing physical activity. For example, a 4-minute circuit on its own works very well as part of a quick morning routine. A 20-minute circuit (4 x 4-minute circuits with 1-minute break at the end of each circuit) works well as a quick, yet effective workout.

Activity 5.2: Check Appendix 3 (and watch the YouTube video) – if the bodyweight circuit routine appeals to you, how will you implement it into your schedule?

Some of the bodyweight exercises in my 4-minute circuits are considered to be 'high-impact exercises' which exert greater force on your body, so it may be worth consulting a physician or doctor if you've had prior injuries, joint problems or other health conditions.

For those of you who are worried about the *time* that physical activity will take up in your schedule (and take *away* from studying and other recreational activities), I hope that my experiences below will reassure you that it's not only manageable to fit it in your schedule, but that it's actually a *valuable investment* of time

On a personal level, I'm a bit of a fitness nut. I've *never* stopped training to prepare for exams. During GCSEs and A-Levels, I would be training for 1-4 hours per day, 6 days of the week (ah, to be 16 again...) for my three main sports: basketball, tennis and badminton. It was actually my desire to continue my high level of physical activity that *forced* me to learn how to plan effectively to ensure that I also did well in my studies (to keep my parents happy!).

During my time at Cambridge, I focused on tennis as my primary sport. I supplemented my training with basketball practice, gymnastic rings, sprinting and training with free-weights in the gym. Training and competition together took up roughly 1-3 hours per day, 5 days a week. I would also walk or cycle to my lectures every single day. The key to managing this was *good planning* (Principle 1). I would always ensure that there was sufficient time in my planner to meet my physical activity needs while maintaining my studying commitments.

In my case, frequent movement was not only vital to my physical health and mental well-being, but also ensured that I was productive, focused and efficient when I studied. By increasing the *quality* of the hours I studied, I was able to account for the reduced *quantity* in the number of hours I studied.

During the exam period itself, not only would I *maintain* my planned physical activity, but I would occasionally *add* spontaneous physical activity sessions.

In my first year at Cambridge, I had a horrific Physics exam. I walked home completely distraught. I'd also done terribly on my Materials Science paper the day before. I knew that I had to prepare a *huge amount* for my upcoming Chemistry and Mathematics papers in order to simply *pass* the year.

Having returned to my room and eaten lunch, I felt mentally and emotionally drained. I was still beating myself up about my Physics exam. I was in no mood to work, and was aware that my productivity would be significantly impaired.

Recognising this, I picked up my basketball and went outside to a nearby court to practise in solitude for an hour. Physically, this had very little effect on my heart rate. But mentally, it was *exactly* the respite that I needed. I vented all my disappointment on the court, and strengthened my resolve for what was still to come. I went back, studied effectively…and thankfully did better in my next few papers!

In summary:

- Frequent physical activity and movement has been shown to have many positive effects in the context of studying.
- Good planning is the key to making time for physical activity given our exam preparation priorities.
- After a bad exam, 'sweating it out' is a legitimate option.
- Kam likes sports. A lot.

I hope that reading through Principle 5 has shown you that physical activity and movement can be beneficial on the quest for Exam Success. Don't worry too much about what kind of activity you do – simply remember that, in the context of exams, *any* movement is *better* than no movement.

(And don't forget to take a look at Appendix 3)

6. Principle Six: Nutrition & Hydration

6.1 Nutrition

As with the last section, I want to emphasise that this book is *not* going to give you the key to your optimal diet for sustainable energy and health.

Having been a nutrition fanatic myself for the last nine years of my life (restaurant waiters and chefs wince in pain when they see me arrive…), I can inform you that most nutritional studies have *contradicted* each other *consistently* for the last thirty years. The only *real* conclusion that can be drawn is that we must experiment to identify the optimal diet for us as individuals.

In this book, we won't be assessing the benefits and drawbacks of intermittent fasting, paleo, gluten-free or low-carb diets. We won't be analysing the impact on health of organic produce in comparison to genetically-modified foods. We *certainly* won't be discussing how food companies have been feeding us lies about what to consume and when to consume it for their commercial benefit…

We will only be looking at the nutrition in the context of *exam performance*.

The 7 Factors of Optimal 'Exam Success' Nutrition

There are 7 factors to consider when looking at the food we eat in the context of Exam Success:

1. Consistent source of energy.

Our food should provide us with sustainable energy, as opposed to causing our energy to fluctuate, which makes us feel tired, lethargic and irritated. This means *minimising sugars* and avoiding foods with a *high glycaemic load (GL)*.

Without turning this into a biology lesson, blood glucose rapidly increases after eating these foods. This leads to insulin being secreted to allow cells to quickly absorb glucose from the bloodstream. The consequent fall in blood glucose results in a 'sugar crash', making us feel tired, easily annoyed and (still) craving more sugar.

The most common high GL culprits include snacks, such as soft drinks, fruit juice, sweets, potato chips, raisins and bananas. High GL foods also include white bread, pasta, white rice, potatoes, corn and most cereals.

For those interested, <u>Appendix 4</u> contains a description of *glycaemic load (GL)* along with a list of common foods and their GL score.

Realistically, many of us will continue to consume these foods. If so, it's worth considering minimising the *portion size* of high GL foods relative to the amount of lower GL foods on our plates. We should also choose the *time of day* during which we consume these foods carefully to avoid sugar crashes during peak study time.

Nevertheless, the best way to address this issue is to *replace* high GL foods and sugars with low GL alternatives. Cereals such as muesli and all-bran, sourdough bread, whole wheat breads, brown rice, and most fruits fall within the medium/low GL category.

2. Keep us feeling fuller for longer.

The less hungry we feel, the less likely we are to be distracted while studying. Replacing high GL foods and sugary snacks with low GL substitutes will aid with this by preventing sugar crashes and food cravings.

We can also ensure that our diet is full of *proteins*, good *fats, high fibre* foods, *vitamin-rich* foods and plenty of *water*.

Higher *protein* intake has been shown to increase 'fullness ratings' in various studies.[1] Increasing *fat* intake has also been shown to have a similar effect on satiety, though this is largely due to fats being more calorie-dense than proteins or carbohydrates. [2] Foods high in *soluble fibre* expand in the stomach, slowing the rate of gastric emptying (how quickly food leaves the stomach) and making us feel fuller for longer. [3]

Studies have also shown that eating vitamin-rich foods or multivitamin tablets to ensure *adequate vitamin intake* also suppresses appetite[4]. This may be attributed to the fact that our body craves food when it senses that there's a deficiency in a specific micronutrient (though it doesn't tell us exactly *which* nutrient we're missing, or which food contains it, so we just end up eating chips and chocolates!).

3. Strengthens the immune system to prevent us from falling ill.

Catching a bad cold during the exam studying period can set us back for a couple of days. Catching one *during* exams is even more frustrating. Selecting our nutrition wisely can not only aid us in recovering from illness, but may also help to prevent it in the first place.

We need to consume foods which are high in *antioxidants*, such as Vitamin A, Vitamin C and Vitamin E. Antioxidants have been shown to support the immune-system and restore cellular health.[5] Some, such as *flavonoids*, also have anti-inflammatory properties.[6]

Common foods which are high in antioxidants include:

- **Fruits**: Citrus fruits, blueberries, pomegranates, goji berries.
- **Vegetables**: Broccoli, kale, ginger, onions, red bell peppers, sweet potatoes.
- **Nuts**: Walnuts, pecans, almonds, cashews, brazil nuts.
- **Herbs**: Cinnamon, turmeric, oregano, cloves, sage, thyme.
- **Beverages**: Green tea, matcha tea, black tea, pomegranate juice, 'green' smoothies.
- **Other**: Dark Chocolate (over 70% cocoa solids).

4. Minimises likelihood of dependency on consumable 'drugs'.

Caffeine is a stimulant found in various foods, such as coffee, tea, energy drinks, soft drinks and dark chocolate. It's been known to increase wakefulness, focus and attention span.[7] In moderation, caffeine can have a positive impact on studying.

However, we must be careful not to consume too much caffeine. In terms of exam performance, side effects of over-consumption include insomnia, headaches and indigestion. Because caffeine is a stimulant, it also masks how fatigued we *really* are. This can make us more susceptible to illness, adrenal fatigue and burnout.

In my case, I didn't (and still don't) drink coffee. During exam preparation, I didn't consume more than one cup of green tea in the morning and a few pieces of dark chocolate throughout the day (never after 6pm). I used walking and exercise to boost my energy levels at different times of the day. Provided we're not sleep-deprived, we naturally get a *'second wind'* after even 10-15 minutes of light walking and exercise. Much healthier and cheaper than coffee! If my concentration was still waning due to tiredness, I would favour a power nap (Principle 7) instead of consuming caffeine.

For those of you above the legal age to consume alcohol, it's been shown to have negative impacts on studying – research studies show that it inhibits cognitive functioning.[8] I personally recommend avoiding alcohol as much as possible during the exam preparation period. If consumed as a means of relaxing, I recommend trying some Mindfulness Practices (Principle 3) or physical activity (Principle 5) instead. (I'm so fun at social events…)

5. Doesn't have a negative impact on our digestive system.

For optimal exam performance, we should try to avoid foods that cause us digestive discomfort. There are no *specific foods* to avoid. We each have different degrees of tolerance to different food groups, and it's up to us to find out what these are.

On any occasion that we suffer from stomach discomfort or intestinal distress, we should make a list of the foods that we've consumed in the previous 6-8 hours. Looking at these over time, we'll notice trends in the foods that come up more frequently on our lists. We should keep in mind that it may not be a certain food that triggers these symptoms, but a *combination* of different food groups.

If you've struggled with gastrointestinal issues in the past, it may be worth consulting a doctor or conducting allergy/ intolerance tests. Gluten intolerance, lactose intolerance and sensitivity to chemical additives (such as Monosodium Glutamate, Aspartame etc.) can be easily diagnosed. It's then your choice as to whether you want to adapt your diet to account for these.

6. Ensure that we stick to consistent eating habits.

Changing our eating habits, such as cutting carbohydrates or beginning an intermittent fasting diet, can cause various side-effects which are not conducive to studying or taking exams. If you insist on making changes, implement them *gradually* to prevent side-effects, and do it *as far away* from exam day as possible.

One of the most common side-effects of cutting carbohydrates is known as 'induction flu'. We feel tired, lethargic, irritable and occasionally nauseous as the body begins to adapt to using fat as a primary energy source instead of carbohydrates. We can experience headaches and 'brain fog', and feel unable to carry out simple, routine tasks. Our attention span and ability to focus on a task decreases significantly.[9]

Intermittent fasting (and other fasting variants) also leads to similar 'induction flu' symptoms as our body adapts to functioning in a 'fasted' state.

These symptoms normally disappear towards the end of the first week. They can also be relieved through a combination of increasing our water and salt intake.

Nevertheless, I recommend that for the purposes of exam performance, it's best to avoid making any *drastic changes* to our diets when studying for exams.

7. Consume responsible portion sizes to avoid overeating.

Many of us have experienced 'food comas' where we feel tired, lethargic and unable to function after overeating. This is mainly due to the *type* of food that we're consuming, as opposed to overeating itself.

When we overeat fats and carbohydrates, our parasympathetic nervous system is triggered, making us enter a "rest and digest" mode.[10] Even feeling slightly full from eating carbohydrates can make us feel tired as a result of increased 'sleep hormone' (serotonin and melatonin) levels triggered by the release of insulin.[11] Finally, overeating carbohydrates can lead to a "sugar crash", with the rapid drop in blood glucose causing tiredness and lack of focus. Great for lounging in front of the television on Christmas day. Not great for revision.

If we don't overeat in the first place, we won't have to deal with these problems. We should select our portion sizes responsibly, and drink water half an hour before eating to ensure that our hunger is not being intensified by dehydration. On the day of our exam, we should give ourselves *at least* 1.5 hours between eating a primary meal (breakfast or lunch) and sitting the exam.

If we do find ourselves feeling sluggish after a meal, we should consider engaging in some light movement. Studies have shown that a brisk 15-30-minute walk can aid in digestion and help in regulating blood sugar levels.[12]

With the 7 Factors in mind, I've compiled a list of 12 foods to consider including in an 'Exam Success Diet'. I will refrain from going into detail on the specific vitamins and minerals (known collectively as *micronutrients*) in each food.

1. **Cruciferous Vegetables:** Includes vegetables such as kale, cabbage, broccoli, collard greens and watercress. High in dietary fibre and crucial vitamins and minerals.

2. **Non-Cruciferous Vegetables:** Includes vegetables like squash, tomato, peppers, carrots and celery. High in crucial vitamins and minerals.

3. **Low-GL Fruits**: Include fruits such as citrus fruits, apples, blueberries, pears, avocadoes. For a longer list, consult Appendix 4. Good fibre, vitamin and mineral content. Avoid consuming in large quantities.

4. **Legumes**: Include beans, lentils, chickpeas and peas. Good source of protein, fibre and crucial micronutrients. Help to cultivate healthy gut bacteria. If you're not used to them, they may cause slight digestive issues!

5. **Oats**: Good source of fibre and micronutrients. Can be soaked overnight for easier digestion. ('Overnight Oats' also make a great breakfast.)

6. **Sweet Potato**: Good source of carbohydrates; high fibre and micronutrient content. Easy to digest.

7. **Quinoa:** Good source of protein; high fibre and micronutrient content. Can be tough to digest, so wash before you cook.

8. **Nuts:** Good source of healthy fat, protein and a range of micronutrients (differs in each nut type). Can be tough to digest, so it may be worth soaking them first.

9. **Seeds**: Includes seeds such as pumpkin seeds, sunflower seeds, chia seeds, flax seeds and sesame seeds. Good fat, protein and micronutrient profile. Great to sprinkle on cereal or salads. Avoid consuming in large quantities.

10. **Eggs:** Egg whites are a good source of protein. Egg yolks contains healthy fats and micronutrients, although they also contain high levels of cholesterol.

11. **Salmon**: Great source of protein and healthy Omega-3 fatty acids.

12. **Chicken & Lean Red Meats**: Lean sources of protein which contain crucial minerals.

Please remember - these are only *examples* of foods that you may consider including in your diet. There are many other foods that contain beneficial nutrients. In terms of recipes and food preparation, I will leave the experimenting to you. This is a book on Exam Success, not cooking!

That being said, if you make just *one* change to your diet, it should be to eat *more* vegetables. Don't worry about cutting things out of your diet; just *eat more vegetables*. Your body and mind will thank you for it.

I hope it goes without saying, but if you're vegetarian or vegan, you do *not* need to add the eggs, meat or fish suggested in this list of foods. Similarly, if you have nut allergies, do *not* eat nuts just because they are on this list.

I've been following a *plant-based diet* (in other words, vegan) since January 2018, and I've never felt more energised, productive or physically stronger! It's absolutely possible to succeed at exams (and life!) without eating meat or dairy. (Just make sure to take your B12 supplements!)

Activity 6.1: Having looked through the 7 factors and the food list, what changes can you make to your diet to aid with studying? Which foods are you going to add? Which foods will you consume less of or remove from your diet?

6.2 Hydration

In the context of exam preparation and performance, it's extremely important to stay well-hydrated. Scientific studies show that dehydration may be our worst enemy when it comes to exams (and life in general…). Dehydration has been linked with:

- Depressed mood, tiredness, increased perception of task difficulty, lower concentration and headache symptoms.[13]
- Impaired attention span, memory and motor skills.[14]
- Shrinkage of brain tissue, leading to an increase in the level of effort required to achieve the same performance level.[15]
- Increased susceptibility to illness.[16]
- Constant feeling of hunger.[17]

That's a lot of problems! And we're not even considering issues *unrelated* to exams such as weight gain, acne and skin issues.[18]

Keeping well-hydrated allows us to:

- Improve our **mood** and **state of mind**.
- Increase our **concentration levels**, **alertness** and **focus**.
- Feel **less hungry**.
- **Relieve headaches** - participants in a study[19] experienced 'total relief' from their headaches within 30 minutes of drinking (on average) 2 cups of water.
- **Flush out toxins** in our body, helping to prevent and recover from illness.

With this in mind, there are several steps that we can take to remind ourselves to stay hydrated. We should keep a full glass or bottle of water on our desk when we study, replacing it when empty. We can also set a timer or alarm to remind us to drink water as we study. If you're using Pomodoros (Principle 2), the 5-minute break in between carrying out tasks is a perfect time to sip some water.

Activity 6.2: How will you ensure that you stay well-hydrated? Think about how you can implement regular water consumption into your study schedule.

A study carried out in the University of East Anglia showed that students who brought a bottle of water to their tests performed better on their exams, even after accounting for the academic ability of the students.[20] Scientists proposed that this was a result of two things: first, the *physiological* effect of water consumption on thinking functions, and second, *alleviating anxiety* through water consumption.

Whatever the reason, it certainly won't do you any harm to take a water bottle with you into the exam. Don't worry about needing to use the toilet if you drink too much - as mentioned in Principle 4, a 'tactical' toilet break can be a very useful tool to break out of negative mental states.

In summary:

- Reduce sugary snacks and high GL foods.

- Increase the amount of vegetables, fruits, and sources of fibre, proteins, good fats and vitamins in your diet.

- Drink plenty of water when studying (and when not studying).

- Take a water bottle with you into the exam room.

I hope that reading through Principle 6 has conveyed the importance of good nutrition and keeping well-hydrated as you strive towards Exam Success. If you're feeling a bit tired – good news! Principle 7 is all about *sleep*.

7. Principle Seven: Sleep

You may be familiar with the idea of the 'Student Life Triangle', with the joke being that you can only pick *two* of the three components of the triangle:

1. Good Grades
2. Active Social Life/ Recreational Activities
3. Enough Sleep

For many of us, sleep is the first of these to be sacrificed.

We need to change this for two reasons. First, it's *entirely* possible to balance the 3 aspects of the 'triangle' – just because *someone else* wasn't willing to apply the effort to balance them, it doesn't mean that *we* should believe that we're doomed to the same fate.

Second, getting enough sleep is linked to *both* achieving higher grades *and* maintaining good health and high energy levels that allow us to fully enjoy social and recreational activities.

In other words, getting enough sleep is the *key* to balancing the triangle.

Don't believe me? Cue the research studies…

7.1 Benefits of Sleep

Studies have shown that sleep deprivation and sleepiness have adverse effects on cognitive performance, mood, response times, attention and concentration.[1] Even being *partially* sleep deprived has been found to reduce working memory (the processes used to temporarily store and manipulate information) and attention span.[2]

We also consume more calorie-dense junk foods (high-sugar, high-fat) when we're sleep-deprived because of a desire for quick sources of fuel. However, as discussed in <u>Principle 6</u>, this may lead to sugar crash symptoms which make us less productive, less focused and more irritable.

In the context of studying and exam performance, these are all side-effects that we want to avoid.

A Belgian study conducted on 621 first-year university students assessed the quality of their sleep during the exam period against their exam performance. It showed that students who slept seven hours per night during the exam period scored an average of 1.7 points *higher* (on a scale of 20) on their exams than their peers who got only six hours of sleep.[3]

Given this information, it's definitely in our best interests to optimise our sleeping habits.

7.2 Factors Affecting Sleep Quality

Brace yourself. Science is coming…

Sleep is regulated by two body systems: ***sleep/wake homeostasis*** and the ***circadian biological clock***.

Sleep/wake homeostasis tells us that we need to sleep because we've been awake for a long period of time. It also helps us *stay* asleep throughout the night to compensate for the hours spent awake.

Our internal circadian biological clock regulates the *timing* of periods of sleepiness and wakefulness throughout the day. It dips and rises at different times of the day. For adults, the strongest 'sleep drive' occurs between 2:00-4:00am and 1:00-3:00pm, but can have slight variations depending on whether we're a 'morning person' or a 'night owl'.

The drive to sleep because of these *circadian dips* becomes more intense when we're sleep deprived. The circadian rhythm can also cause us to feel more alert at certain times of the day, which is why we often feel an energy boost in the evening.

Studies have shown that our circadian rhythm shifts in adolescence, making it difficult to fall asleep before 11pm.[4] The circadian dips occur between 3:00-7:00am and 2:00-5:00pm, though these may *extend* depending on how sleep-deprived we are. No wonder so many of us feel like zombies during our morning lessons!

That said, next time your teachers complain that you're not paying attention in morning classes, I don't recommend blaming it on the "natural shifting of your internal circadian biological clock". I'm sure they'll be very impressed... as they give you detention!

Our circadian rhythms are why *regularity* is important for good quality sleep and performance. Constantly changing our sleep schedule causes circadian disruptions, which can inhibit cognitive function. We'll return to the idea of circadian rhythms when we discuss the optimum time for taking naps.

So, what magic actually happens when we sleep that makes it so beneficial for exam performance?

Without going into *another* biology lesson, sleep can be broken down into 4 stages which together compose a single sleep 'cycle': [5]

- **Stage 1 Non-Rapid Eye Movement (NREM) Sleep:** Light sleep, easily woken.

- **Stage 2 NREM Sleep:** Slightly deeper sleep.

- **Stage 3 NREM Sleep:** Deep sleep. Undergo body repair and physical restoration. Linked with consolidation of *declarative* (fact-based) memory.[6]

- **Rapid Eye Movement (REM) Sleep:** 'Dream' sleep. Undergo brain repair and mental restoration. Linked with consolidation of both declarative and *procedural* memory (process-based e.g. how to drive a car, hit a tennis ball, apply the quadratic formula etc.).[6]

In general, a complete sleep cycle takes between 90 and 110 minutes. The first sleep cycles each night are composed of short REM sleep and long periods of deep sleep. Later cycles have increased REM sleep and shorter periods of deep sleep. As brain repair, restoration and consolidation of memory occurs during REM-sleep, it's important to that we sleep *enough* to ensure that we get enough REM-sleep.

So, how much sleep is 'enough'?

In truth, it depends on the individual. The National Sleep Foundation recommends between 8-10 hours of sleep for teenagers, while 7-9 hours is recommended for young adults and adults.[7] However, studies have shown that both too little sleep (less than 6 hours) *and* too much sleep (greater than 9 hours) have been shown to be detrimental to cognitive function.[8]

To find out what our optimal sleep length is, we can *track* our sleep using phone applications (Sleep Cycle), or wearable devices (Fitbit, Jawbone UP etc.).

By looking at the *time* we sleep, the number of *hours* we sleep and the *quality* of our sleep, we can compare them with our relative *energy* levels throughout the day. This will allow us to experimentally determine our optimum time and amount of sleep, as well as identifying what factors may influence the quality of our sleep.

If using a phone app, I recommend setting up 'flight mode' before we get into bed to prevent texting, Internet distractions and exposure to screen light. Apps and wearable devices also have *alarm* options to increase the likelihood of waking us up during intervals of 'light' sleep as opposed to 'deep' sleep. This helps us to avoid the feeling of grogginess when we wake up.

Nevertheless, due to the countless number of variables that change from day-to-day, it's nearly *impossible* to keep them constant enough in order to draw concrete conclusions about the exact factors that influence our sleep. However, given enough time, we can still identify general *trends* that apply to us.

Some of my findings from over 5 years of using the 'Sleep Cycle' iPhone Application & 3 years of using a Jawbone UP bracelet are:

- Sleeping between 7.75 hours and 8.5 hours a night resulted in the *highest* energy levels during the day. Anything less than this and I would feel like taking an early afternoon power-nap. Anything more and I would feel sluggish until I did some exercise later in the day.

- For the same duration of sleep (tested with 7.5 hours), my sleep quality was *higher* when I slept *before* 12am.

- My sleep quality was *higher* on days where I engaged in more than one hour of *physical activity*.

- My sleep quality was *lower* when I had a heavy meal 2-3 hours before sleeping and still felt full.

Studies have also shown that alcohol *reduces* sleep quality. Alcohol has been shown to disrupt sleep quality in the *latter* half of the night, reducing the overall time spent in the beneficial REM sleep phase.[9]

Activity 7.1: Consider downloading the Sleep Cycle app (it's free!) and trying it out for a week. Make a note of any possible factors that influence the quality of your sleep. What can you change to improve the quality of your sleep?

7.2 Techniques for Falling Asleep

For those of us who have trouble falling asleep, there are several options we can consider:

1. **Don't *try* to sleep!**

    When it comes to sleep, the harder we try, the more likely we will be to fail. A study even showed that sleep-onset insomniacs who were instructed to lay in bed and try to stay awake with their eyes open fell asleep *quicker* than participants who were instructed to fall asleep. [10]

    Even if we have an exam in the morning, it's important not to work ourselves up about still being awake. Whatever you do, resist the temptation to look at your clock and fuss about the hours of sleep you can still get (believe me, I've been there – I used to get anxious about the fact I wasn't falling asleep, and then I'd get even more anxious *because* I was anxious about my anxiety stopping me from sleeping!). The more fuss we make about it, the harder it becomes to fall asleep.

    Now, I don't think about *sleep*, I just think about *being in bed*. I remind myself of how much I dislike leaving my comfortable, warm bed in the morning. This way, when I see it at night, I feel grateful and ready to embrace it. I also remind myself that just being in bed with my eyes closed is more *restorative* than if I was awake.

2. **Eat the right foods at the right time.**

    Science time. *Melatonin* is the hormone that signals to the body that it's time to sleep. *Serotonin* is another hormone which plays a role in the modulation of sleep. Both of these are produced by an amino-acid called *tryptophan*, which can be found in a range of foods such as sunflower seeds, pumpkin seeds, walnuts, chickpeas, yoghurt, soft cheeses, seafood, white and red meat. [11]
    Calcium is a mineral which helps the brain use *tryptophan* to produce *melatonin*[12], and can be found in green leafy vegetables (kale, spinach) and dairy, such as cheese and milk.

    Magnesium is also a mineral that aids in sleep[13], and can be found in foods such as dark leafy greens, pumpkin seeds, yoghurt, almonds, avocado and figs.

    We should give ourselves 2-3 hours between eating and sleeping, as both an empty or overfull stomach can make it more difficult to fall asleep. In addition, studies show that caffeine should be consumed *at least* 6 hours before we sleep to prevent sleep disruption. [14]

3. **Take a warm shower.**

    Taking a warm shower is not only relaxing, but it also increases our body temperature. As a result, stepping out of the shower into cooler air causes our body temperature to drop more steeply. This has been shown to slow our body metabolism at a faster rate, preparing our body for sleep. [15]

4. **Minimise exposure to light.**

    Darkness acts as a signal for the body to produce melatonin. Light of any kind can suppress the body's production of melatonin, especially unnatural 'blue' light from smartphones, tablets, computers and fluorescent lights. By reducing our use of these devices after specific hours, we can fall asleep quicker. We can activate 'flight mode' on our devices after a certain time in the evening to resist the temptation to use the Internet before we sleep.

I have a rule whereby I turn off all lights an hour before I sleep, with the exception of a small, weak torch. This torch provides the only light when I brush my teeth, shower and read through my affirmations before getting into bed.

I've also found that sleeping with an eye-mask can be very helpful if some light sources can't be avoided (e.g. from outside, other rooms), or if we're very sensitive to natural light in the morning.

5. Breathing exercises.

One of my favourite methods of falling asleep is by using the '4-7-8 Relaxing Breathing' practice, a technique pioneered by Dr. Andrew Weil based on ancient Indian *pranayama* practices.[16] We start by positioning the tip of our tongue in such a way that it makes contact with the roof of our mouth, just behind the upper front teeth. Then we begin the following breathing pattern:

- Inhale for a count of 4 (through the nose)
- Hold our breath for a count of 7
- Exhale forcefully for a count of 8 (it will make a 'whoosh' sound if our tongue is positioned correctly).

As long as we maintain a 4-7-8 ratio, the exact *time* that we're inhaling, holding and exhaling for doesn't matter. The more we practise, the longer we will be able to extend the count for.

(Don't let the tongue position bother you too much - even if the tongue isn't in the *right* place, the 4-7-8 exercise still helps.)

6. Counting down.

Another method I've used for falling asleep is counting down from 100 in multiples of 3 (100, 97, 94, 91…).

This simple task is 'mind-numbing' enough to require minimal attention, but engaging *enough* (due to the irregularity of 3's) to prevent the mind from distracting us with the thoughts that stop us from falling asleep. If we reach 0, we just should just repeat the exercise.

(I am yet to reach 0 more than three times…)

7. The 'Voice Memo'

I started experimenting with this technique after my mind decided that 'head making contact with pillow' meant 'get ready for hundreds of inspirational ideas!'

I would grab my phone (breaking my rules, but drastic times call for drastic measures – and I'd still stay on flight mode) and open a 'Voice Memo' application. I would then record myself speaking *every* idea in my head into the microphone. It doesn't take long – over the years, none of my voice memos have ever exceeded 4 minutes. When finished, I would put the phone aside, and promptly fall asleep with my mind unburdened of its thoughts and ideas.

This (slightly strange) technique works because ideas that stay in our head as thoughts tend to *repeat* themselves as they constantly circulate in our mind. By bringing them *outside* of our mind (i.e. by speaking them out loud or writing them down), they *stop* circulating and repeating themselves, leaving our mind free to shut-down and sleep.

Fun note: If you do this, it's quite amusing to listen to the voice memo in the morning and hear your half-asleep voice rambling on like an idiot.

8. RUDMA (Principle 3) for anxiety-related insomnia.

I've been kept up by anxiety on more (Sunday) nights than I can count. The only true, sustainable solution I've found is to resolve it at its source. I use my RUDMA Framework (Principle 3) to do this. Investing 10 - 30 minutes to confront, understand and resolve the issue may seem like a *nightmare* (sleep pun!), but it will save you from many sleepless nights in the long-term.

After applying RUDMA, we may feel emotionally fatigued (fighting demons is no easy task!), which can actually *help* in falling asleep. If adrenaline is still running high from the anxiety, follow up with the Mindfulness Practices outlined in Principle 3, or the '4-7-8 Relaxing Breath' technique described above.

Activity 7.2: If you have trouble sleeping, which of the sleeping techniques described above do you want to experiment with? Make a note of which nights you are going to try each of the techniques you selected.

Despite all this, we may *still* end up having a bad night of sleep, especially as we reach Exam-Day. It happens.

In this case, never forget the power of the *mind*.

If we *believe* that we haven't slept well, we *will* feel tired, and this will impact our mindset as we go and approach our tasks. It's up to us to ensure that, no matter *when* we sleep, how *much* we sleep, or how *well* we think we've slept, we wake up *believing* that we're replenished, energised and ready to handle our tasks.

One of the easiest ways to do this is to create a quick, energising morning routine. This may consist of:

- **Motivational, upbeat alarm clock music** - 'jump' or 'dance' out of bed.
- **Light stretching and exercise** – e.g. Yoga, walking, jogging.
- **Short, intense exercise** – e.g. 4-minute circuit of bodyweight exercises.
- **Journaling** – writing down dreams from the night before, random thoughts and ideas you have when you wake up, or even your to-do list for the day.
- **Taking a shower** – cold showers have been shown to increase alertness.
- **Mindfulness practices** – ideally *after* the above so you don't accidentally fall asleep – it happens!

I personally like to do a (roughly) 20-minute routine consisting of gentle stretching and a 4-minute bodyweight circuit (included in Appendix 3), 5-minutes of journaling (also to catch my breath!), and 10 minutes of mindful breathing. It doesn't matter what time I wake up – I'll always do my best to leave enough time to do the same routine.

If you decide to attempt a variation of this, make sure that you include some kind of *break* between exercising and mindful breathing – breathing mindfully when you're out of breath is not easy!

Activity 7.3: Create your own quick, energising morning routine to try tomorrow morning. Use the ideas outlined above or come up with your own. Make a commitment to stick to this routine for one week, and note down how you feel after doing it every morning.

7.3 The Power of Napping

We need to consider the *time of day* during which we nap, and the *length* of time which we nap for.

We generally feel the urge to nap between noon and 4pm, which matches the natural *circadian dips* of our internal biological body clock. It's been recommended by studies to avoid taking naps after 4pm, as it may compromise our ability to sleep at night.[17]

Napping when sleep-deprived is also unhelpful; there's always a chance of taking a 'power nap' at 3pm, sleeping through the alarm clock and waking up at 8pm feeling completely disoriented and baffled – yes, I write this from experience…

Depending on the location where we nap, it may be worthwhile to get an eye mask or ear plugs to aid with falling asleep in well-lit or noisy rooms. Different nap durations yield different benefits: [18] [19]

- **10-20-minute nap:** This has been shown to boost *alertness* and *energy*. As we remain in lighter NREM sleep (Stage 1), it's also easier to wake up feeling refreshed and focused. The cognitive benefits of this length of nap are short-lived (1-3 hours).

- **45-60-minute nap:** This has been shown to improve *declarative* (fact-based) memory consolidation. However, because we enter NREM deep sleep (Stage 3), we may feel sleep-inertia (grogginess and decreased motor dexterity) when we wake up. After the initial grogginess, cognitive performance is improved for several hours.

- **90-minute nap:** This has been shown to improve *both declarative* and *procedural* memory consolidation. This length of nap includes REM sleep and constitutes a full sleep cycle, and so typically avoids sleep inertia and grogginess upon waking.

We should avoid the 30-minute nap if possible, as we may wake up with symptoms of sleep inertia *without* the declarative memory consolidation benefits of a slightly longer nap. [18]

To ensure that we wake up on time, we should set *multiple* alarm clocks (again, I write from experience…). As well as the grogginess from a poorly-timed nap, we don't want to oversleep on any commitments or study plans we may have.

Some wearable technology devices have a 'power nap' mode which can detect our sleep phase. This reduces the likelihood of being woken up during deep sleep, so that we can avoid feeling groggy and disoriented.

In summary:

- Getting enough sleep is vital for optimal performance during revision.

- Aim to get plenty of sleep on the night before an exam, but don't obsess about it to the extent that it makes you anxious.

- We can create morning routines to energise us *regardless* of the quality or length of our sleep.

- Track when you sleep, how long you sleep for and the quality of your sleep to learn more about your *optimal sleeping habits*.

- Power naps can be beneficial, but require discipline to implement effectively.

I hope that reading through Principle 7 has clarified the importance of getting enough sleep and cultivating good sleeping habits to help you on the path towards Exam Success. Take a moment to congratulate yourself for reaching this point – and when you're ready, turn the page and begin reading about the Final Principle!

8. Principle Eight: Support Group

The final Principle of Exam Success involves surrounding ourselves with people who make us feel *supported*.

In the context of exams, support groups can be categorised as:

- **Academic Support Groups**
- **Mental & Emotional (ME) Support Groups**

Let me clarify this from the start; we do not *need* support groups. It's possible to achieve Exam Success without them – but it's also *a lot* more difficult. Creating support groups is *highly beneficial*. The mental comfort that comes with knowing that we're 'supported' is invaluable. And if anything does go wrong, whether academically or personally, we give ourselves the best chance to resolve it rapidly and effectively.

There are **5 Golden Rules** to remember whenever we need support from either our Academic Support Group or our ME Support Group:

1) **Make the first move** - If we don't ask, we *certainly* won't receive.

2) **Communicate concisely and effectively** – No one will *know* how to help unless we *tell* them what we need help with.

3) **Respect their schedule** – The people in our support groups have their own lives to lead; we shouldn't *assume* that they will be there for us whenever we call upon them.

4) **Take responsibility** – Our support groups are only as helpful as we *allow* them to be; to make the most of them, we must be *committed* to our own progress.

5) **Show gratitude** – Our support groups are doing us a *favour* by giving up their time for us; we need to ensure that they know their time is appreciated, and that we would be willing to do the same for them.

8.1 Academic Support Group

Our Academic Support Group refers to the people who help us with studying, understanding and learning the *content* relevant to our upcoming exams.

The most common examples include:

- Teachers & Teaching Assistants
- Private Tutors
- Lecturers & University Tutors/ Supervisors
- Study Groups or Study Partners

Most of us already have an Academic Support Group, though the *effectiveness* of our group may vary depending on the standard of our school or university, our financial background and our subject choices.

Activity 8.1: Consider your current academic support group as you read through the list below. Write down what you can do to ensure that you use them in the most effective way. Who else can you add to your academic support group?

Teachers & Teaching Assistants

Teachers may have a large number of students to educate, but we shouldn't *assume* that they won't have time to help us. In general, a *good* teacher will do their best to help a *committed* student – but it's up to *us* to convey to them our genuine desire to learn and improve.

The most daunting challenge is often making the first move; *we* need to take the initiative and approach *them*, instead of expecting them to come and help us.

Even if you've been a disruptive, low-performing student in the past, don't assume that your teachers will sneer at your request, tell you that you deserve whatever grade you get, and walk away. Just as you're likely to have surprised them by asking for help (and, if necessary, apologising for your past behaviour), they might surprise you by offering to help.

As an example, I'll always be grateful to my two Further Maths teachers. I was a disruptive and disrespectful student with a 'smart mouth' and a disdain for authority – in other words, an absolute *nightmare* to teach in my final year of A-Levels. I needed an A* in Further Maths to be accepted into Cambridge, but I wasn't anywhere *close* to achieving it. (I scored 28% in a mock-exam earlier on in the year...).

When one of our teachers gave our class 15 optional worksheets to attempt over study-leave (with answers but no written solutions), she certainly didn't expect *me* to be one of the students completing them. Over the next few weeks, I planned my time to ensure that I could attempt *every* question on those sheets. But in truth, I struggled tremendously and found myself losing confidence in my abilities. I got in touch with my teachers, and politely requested if they could spend some time discussing the questions with me. They were surprised, but said that they would be happy to help.

They ended up giving me 4 hours of *individual time* over the next two days. Their kindness in staying behind to help me significantly contributed to the eventual A* grade (and fulfilment of my Cambridge offer) that I achieved.

On a final note, many of us feel self-conscious about what our peers may think of us for asking a teacher for help. We worry that they might label us 'stupid' for needing help, a 'nerd' for requesting help, and a 'loser' for caring about our exams.

We need to block this out. We need to stop caring about what others think, and focus on how *we* are going to achieve *our* goals. This is *our* future that we're trying to build, and we should not permit *their* insecurities to interfere with it.

Private Tutors

If you can afford one, having a good private tutor is an opportunity to accelerate your learning tremendously – so take advantage of it! Consider the content that you need help with *in advance* and communicate it to your tutor before your session. Use your tutor to cover the topics which were poorly explained in school, or the concepts you feel you didn't grasp as comfortably as you would have liked.

If you can't afford a private tutor, don't worry – you're definitely not alone! It's absolutely possible to achieve great grades and get into a top University without one. I didn't have any private tutors during GCSEs, A-Levels or my university studies. It just meant that it was more important for me to utilise my teachers as academic support.

Lecturers & University Tutors/ Supervisors

Depending on the university or college you attend, lecturers will have different roles. Some deliver lectures and leave it to the tutors/supervisors to discuss with students. Others will take a more active role in ensuring that the students in their course have understood the content being taught.

In general, lecturers enjoy two things: talking about their subject, and talking to students who talk to them about their subject! (I'm only half-kidding…)

Take advantage of this and approach them at the end of lectures with any questions you might have. The worst they'll do is tell you that you should have been paying more attention, they're busy and you should email them later. In this case, you can also copy in your supervisor or tutor who may also be able to help.

With university tutorials and supervisions, we really do *get out what we put in*. If we turn up unprepared, we won't leave much better-off than before. However, if we prepare ourselves beforehand with the questions or topics that we want to discuss, we'll receive far more value for our time and effort.

Study Partners & Groups

In terms of academic support, these are not necessary. Those with a more dominant *social* preference (Principle 2) may benefit from a study group or partner far more than those who prefer *solitary* study.

There are generally 4 Incentives (A, B, C and D) for finding a study group or study partner.

Incentive A: To discuss, practise and test each other on content from our course.

If we're looking for a study partner to discuss, practise and test course content with, it's worth considering the following 5 criteria:

1. **Similar academic ability** – We don't want to be getting less from them than they are from us, and vice versa; it only breeds frustration, resentment and an ineffective partnership.

2. **Different strengths and weaknesses** – We can share our understanding of the course with each other to fill in individual 'knowledge gaps'.

3. **Non-competitive** – We need to consider ourselves a team and minimise as much competition as possible.

4. **Similar work habits** – If we get distracted every 10 minutes but our partner can work for an hour without losing focus, we're either going to end up feeling intimidated by their productivity (bad for confidence) or end up annoying them when we get distracted (bad for study partnership). Conversely, if we're *both* easily distracted, we need to be able to motivate each other to *stay* focused. We shouldn't become distracted *together* and end up doing *less* than we would have done individually.

5. **Not part of your ME Support Group** – We should try to avoid mixing the people in our personal ME Support Group with our Academic Support Group.

As an example, my ex-girlfriend and I studied the same course (Chemical Engineering) in our 2nd year of Cambridge. We lived together and became study partners out of convenience.

Let's see how that worked out…

1. She was *considerably stronger* than me academically. In fact, *considerably* is probably an understatement. (-1)

2. Owing to her academic ability, she was able (and kind enough) to help me fill out my 'knowledge gaps' – unfortunately, I was unable to return the favour. (-1)

3. Thankfully, we weren't competitive because she *knew* she'd achieve higher grades than me! (+1)

4. She could work non-stop for 2 hours without batting an eyelid. I would lose focus every 25 minutes. I would *try* not to distract her *every* time… (-1)

5. She was an integral part of my ME Support Group, but the above factors understandably led to her becoming slightly frustrated with me – not great for support. (-1)

That's a score of - 4. Not great for studying. Not great for exams. Probably not ideal for our relationship either!

<u>Incentive B: We feel more motivated to work when someone else around us is also working.</u>

If we're looking for a study partner to keep us focused and disciplined by working at the same time (and vice versa), it's best to choose people who *don't* study the same course as us. We also want to ensure that we share similar work habits with our partner, for example in terms of how long we can focus for. In addition, we should try to avoid selecting someone whom we consider to be part of our ME Support Group.

This prevents:

- One of us gaining *more* than the other from the arrangement.

- One of us holding knowledge back from the other for *competitive* purposes.

- Losing focus together and doing *less* than we would have done individually.

- Generally *getting on each other's nerves.*

Incentive C: We're afraid that we're not doing enough and want to know how much others around us are doing.

Feeling afraid that we're not doing enough and wanting to know how *much* others in our course are doing is *not* a good reason for wanting to find a study partner or group.

It *doesn't matter* how much others are doing. We can try to learn from the studying *approach* that they're using (for example, past papers vs. revision notes) – but even then, what works for them may not work optimally for us. We should not be deceived into thinking that their work habits are *appropriate* for us, or assume that they know how to study *better* than we do.

In the words of author, Timothy Ferriss: "**Focus on being productive instead of busy.**"

Most people around us are simply being *busy*. They feel that being busy means that they're not *falling behind* in an imaginary race they're running. They fill their time with things to do because they're too *afraid* of stopping. They don't spend time thinking about *what* they're doing and whether it's actually taking them towards their goals – they only exist in a state of *doing* or *not-doing*. And if they're *not-doing*, they feel guilt and fear that they need to be *doing more*…

But a lot of the time, *more* is actually *less*.

In other words, they do *more* – but they're *less* productive, *less* healthy, *less* focused on their goal, *less* relaxed, and generally *less* happy!

Remember our definition of *productivity* in Principle 2. Instead of being busy, we should devote our energy to doing the *most important* tasks effectively and efficiently.

We should *trust in our process* and be *honest* with ourselves.

We *know* when we're being lazy, procrastinating too much or simply not being productive enough. We also *know* when we're doing the best we can, and when adding more work would reduce productivity and adversely impact our physical and mental well-being. We need to focus on what *we* can do to address these issues, not risk becoming stressed because of how much more work others in our study group *seem* to be doing.

Incentive D: We're looking for someone that we can procrastinate and avoid doing work with.

Looking to avoid revision or finding an excuse to procrastinate with someone else is *not* a good incentive for finding a study partner.

We're well within our rights to make decisions that may have a negative impact on our *own* future, if that's what we choose to do. But we need to have the strength and self-respect to withstand the insecure need to sabotage someone else's future.

If this incentive describes you, *congratulate yourself* for your self-awareness and strength of character in admitting it to yourself. Finish reading Principle 8. Then please go back and read Principle 3 on Mindset-Management, where you can find some tools to aid you with the mental aspect of studying and exam preparation.

Activity 8.2: If you are looking for a study partner or group, identify which of the above incentives fits most with yours. Use this to find your ideal study partner or group.

8.2 Mental & Emotional (ME) Support Group

Our Mental & Emotional (ME) Support Group can help us to stay focused, motivated and free of anxiety and stress – all of which are vital to Exam Success!

Before we delve deeper into the subject, there are some students who feel that they don't *need* a ME Support Group, and would prefer to completely isolate themselves and focus on exams. If you fit into this category, I implore you to *read on.*

Why?

Because in my 3rd year, I considered *myself* to be one of those people.

Due to the personal issues I was dealing with, I had chosen to isolate myself from everyone apart from my closest friends (whom I saw or spoke to *at most* once a week), the university tennis team (for training), and my parents (through WhatsApp messages or FaceTime).

I would study alone, walk alone, shop alone, eat alone, sleep alone, and train in the gym alone. It was a personal choice that I had made for the following reasons:

- **Pride**: I felt that I had a huge amount to prove to myself, and to accept help or support from anyone else would show *dependence* and *weakness.*

- **Strength**: To achieve Exam Success in solitude would reflect my independence and *strength* of character. I would judge myself *weak* if I needed support.

- **Stress**: I refused to expose myself to the contagious influence of the stressed, anxious people around me working 10-15 hours a day. I promised myself that any pressure I felt would be *completely intrinsic.* (Principle 3)

- **Doubt:** I was studying using my own method – fewer hours, higher productivity. I didn't want to come across people who would feed the seeds of doubt that were ever-present in my mind as to whether I should be doing *more* like everyone else.

- **Fear:** In general, I was afraid of being negatively influenced, let down or hurt by people around me, so I minimised their presence in my life.

Activity 8.3: If you feel like you don't need a ME Support Group, which of the reasons above (if any) do you resonate most with for not needing one? If none, think about (and write down) what your personal reasons are.

If any of those reasons resonate with you, I implore you to *keep reading.*

Yes – by isolating myself from others, I was able to remove all of the *wrong* people who could potentially damage or interfere with my mental and emotional well-being.

However, even in my self-imposed solitude, I had still *unintentionally* created a ME Support Group of the *right* people. And not only had I formed a support group – I was inadvertently using them *every day* in some manner!

My pride was thankfully too blind to notice that I *was* being supported and helped by the *right* people, until I looked back on the year in retrospect. This was very fortunate for me – without my support group, I highly doubt I'd have achieved my 1st Class grade.

Given this, if you're someone who feels that they don't need a ME Support Group, read through to the end of this chapter *anyway.*

We don't *have* to face our challenges alone - nor should we *try* to!

With this in mind, let's discuss who the *wrong* and *right* people are in the context of our ME Support Group.

'Wrong' People: 6 Negative Roles

Simply put, these are the people around us who play certain 'roles' that can *hinder* us as we strive for Exam Success. There are 6 Negative Roles that we need to be aware of: The Stress Monster, The Drama King/Queen, The Trigger, The Executioner, The Tempter and The Vampire. (Awesome names, I know.)

The same person or group may play multiple roles. However, keep in mind that these roles do not describe what the person is *always* like – it just refers to the behaviours that they tend to adopt when faced with the stress of studying for exams.

Depending on the *extent* to which the person embodies a role, there are four actions we can take:

1. ***Talk*** to them about how their behaviour is impacting our well-being – sometimes they're not aware of how their actions are impacting us, and they'll be willing to change their behaviour around us after a short conversation.

2. ***Set boundaries*** or ***rules*** for how we interact with each other during the study period. We can also set boundaries and rules for *ourselves* about the impact we *allow* other people to have on us.

3. ***Block*** them out of our lives until the conclusion of our final exam.

4. ***Cut*** them out of our lives completely.

Yes – some of these may sound brutal. But if these people are having a negative influence in our lives, we're absolutely *within our rights* to do something about it.

That being said, I mostly recommend *communicating* with the person first, especially for some of the less-serious roles outlined below. It isn't always easy to confront someone to talk about their behaviour, but it's far better than ending a friendship or damaging a relationship.

Activity 8.4: As you read the descriptions of each *negative* role below, write down which roles some of the people around you embody, and think of what actions you can take to reduce their negative influence. More importantly, write down which roles *you* might have a tendency to play. Simply becoming aware of this can help you to address it and mitigate the negative effect you might have on others around you.

-----

1. The Stress Monster

The Stress Monster becomes extremely anxious in the build up to exams. During conversations, they always bring the topic back to studying and how stressed they are.

They'll often talk about how much work they're doing (often a very high number of hours), how much *more* work they need to be doing, how they're definitely going to fail, how others have an unfair advantage – and so on.

In other words, they're *venting*.

Constantly.

This is absolutely *fine*, provided that we're playing the role of The Listener (see 'Right' People). But if we aren't, we should communicate their behaviour to them and let them know how it's impacting us. If needed, we can then create some rules or boundaries about how we interact with each other. Spending too much time around a Stress Monster will feed the seeds of *doubt* that are buried in *our* minds regarding the quality of our own exam preparation. Their anxieties feed ours, and their stressful outbursts leave us mentally drained.

Set firm boundaries about how and when you interact, offer to play the Listener role for their venting, or simply block them out from your life during the exam period. Cutting them out completely is rarely necessary. Outside of exam time, they can be great people – exams simply bring out the 'monster' in them!

2. The Drama King/Queen

The Drama King/Queen is fuelled by (surprise, surprise…) *drama*. Small events in their lives are often exaggerated to become a source of controversy and grief for the parties involved. They seek attention, enjoying conversations and events that are focused around themselves. They will not hesitate to interrupt or message people around them at inconvenient times.

In the context of exams, we do *not* want to become the audience for their performance. They may choose to distract themselves by creating unnecessary drama outside of exams, and attempt to involve us in their affairs. They may also let exams *become* their drama, taking on a role similar to a Stress Monster.

Their antics are time-consuming, frustrating and mentally exhausting, none of which are desirable for our exam preparation. Boundaries may not be enough to manage them, so it may be worth blocking them out during the exam period.

Drama Kings/Queens are often drawn to their role even in the absence of exams. For those of us who consider drama to be a source of fun and excitement, the presence of a Drama King/Queen can be enjoyable.

However, if we have a very strong aversion to drama, we should consider whether it would be to our benefit to *cut* them out of our lives completely.

3. The Trigger

The Trigger causes us to feel a negative emotion (e.g. angry, sad, distracted, guilty etc.) whenever they're in our presence. Even running into them in the hallway or engaging in small talk leaves us feeling *worse* than we were before our interaction. These negative feelings may linger for anything from half-an-hour to days on end. Effective exam preparation requires focus, clarity and a positive, energised mindset. It's important not to let the Trigger take these away from us.

There are two kinds of Triggers to be aware of – *Blunt* and *Subtle*.

Blunt Triggers are people whom we *do not like*. Whether they've mistreated us in the past, act in a manner we disapprove of, or persistently interfere with the fulfilment of our own values (Principle 3) - we should consider *cutting them out* of our lives. However, this isn't always realistic. As such, we need to be ready to adapt our mindset to manage our response to their presence more effectively, while also setting firm boundaries.

In my case, one of my values is best described as *move-away-from 'being controlled'*. A negative response is triggered as soon as someone tries to exert their control over me by telling me what to do (e.g. teachers, parents). Nevertheless, I don't want to cut these people out of my life completely. Over the years, I've trained myself to become more skilled at managing this response. I take a moment to calm down, and then *reframe* their instruction in terms of why it would *benefit me* to act in accordance with it. I then *remind* myself that whatever action I take is ultimately *my choice*.

Subtle Triggers are harder to recognise and manage – we often *like* the Trigger or have shared meaningful *past* experiences with them.

Examples include the ex-girlfriend that leaves you with pangs of wistfulness every time you cross paths, the best friend that is always achieving higher grades than you (despite seeming to do less work), or the older sibling that you look up to but constantly teases you.

If we have time, it's definitely worth *talking* to our Subtle Triggers and communicating the impact that their behaviour has on us. It may actually help our relationship with them! However, if time is short, we can also *set firm boundaries* with them and try to realistically minimise the likelihood of interacting with them during the exam preparation period. We shouldn't do this with hostility – after all, it's not *their* fault that they elicit this response in us; it's a reflection of our *own* insecurities.

I highly recommend using the RUDMA Framework (Principle 3) to aid you in recognising the Subtle Trigger, understanding *why* they impact you in such a way, and then figuring out how to let go of underlying insecurities that cause this response. In some cases, doing this can resolve the issue completely, and you may no longer need to consider the person as a Trigger.

4. The Executioner

The Executioner is someone whom we love or respect to the extent that we feel *pressure* to perform to their expectations. We want them to be proud of our accomplishments and want to avoid disappointing them. Their judgement *matters* to us.

Often, our parents, older siblings or partners become our Executioners. We can try and talk to them about this, as they most likely love us as and want to be supportive. However, some parents find it difficult to have these conversations. Their *guilt* about the negative impact they're having on us conflicts with their *fears* about being a bad parent – they may end up becoming defensive or angry as a result.

In general, managing our Executioners involves *setting boundaries* for *ourselves* regarding the pressure we *allow* them to exert upon us.

In Principle 3, we discussed the idea of outer and inner pressure. We need to realise that our own goals and expectations (in terms of the grades we want to achieve) are often *aligned* with those of our Executioners. We want the best for ourselves, and *so do they*. Knowing this, we can *block* out their voices. The only Executioner that truly exists is *ourselves*. The only *real* pressure that we feel is intrinsic – it stems from within *us*.

5. The Tempter

The Tempter appeals to the metaphorical 'devil on our shoulder'. The Tempter knows that we're studying, and yet continues to tempt us with activities, events and alternative ways to spend our time. They invite us to go out to coffee, go for a walk, hang out for *one more* hour, have *one more* drink, and stay for *one more* song. They try to persuade us with statements like, "come on, you only live once!", and "you used to be so fun!".

We need to identify the extent to which someone is playing the role of the Tempter. Sometimes, they just genuinely enjoy our company and want to spend time with us. However, if they truly cared for us, they would respect our choice to study for our exams.

If they do simply want to spend more time with us (and the feeling is mutual), setting *boundaries* is the best option to ensure that we enjoy spending time with them without compromising our study plan.

Unfortunately, in some cases, the Tempter is simply using us to alleviate *their* guilt. By 'sharing' the guilt of succumbing to temptations with someone else, they feel that their lack of studying is more justified. In some extreme cases (see '**The Vampire**' below), the Tempter would rather *fail with company* by sabotaging someone else's exam preparation than risk *failing alone*.

If we feel that their incentives are based on 'guilt-sharing', we may need to *block* them out for the duration of the exam period. But if we feel that they're looking for a 'partner-in-failure', it may be worth *cutting* them out of our lives completely. Their harmful mindset may extend far beyond exams, and we have every right to end a friendship or relationship with someone who doesn't consider the negative impact that their actions may have on our future.

6. The Vampire

Vampires are people who can 'suck' our future opportunities away from us if we're not vigilant.

The Vampire claims *not to care* about how they perform in exams. They may sit in the back of the room and disrupt classes. They talk about how little work they've done and how unbothered they are about it. In many of these cases, the Vampire is simply too *afraid* to admit to themselves that they care, as they doubt their ability to succeed.

However, instead of working hard and simply doing their best, they prefer to project their own insecurities upon *others*. Their behaviour feeds the small seeds of doubt that *we all have*. We're all afraid of failing – the Vampire simply feeds this fear. Vampires would rather *fail with company* than risk *failing alone*.

It's the *easy* way out for them in the present moment – but with *hard* future consequences for themselves and anyone else who succumbs to their mindset.

We need to identify if the Vampire is *ignorant* of the consequences of their behaviour or not.

If they are '**Ignorant Vampires**', we can either *block* them out for the exam period or set firm *boundaries* to ensure their voice is muted in our mind. We may even try to help them by *talking* to them about the impact their behaviour has on others, and support them in overcoming the insecurities they have. (Maybe wait until *after* exams if time is short…)

However, some Vampires are fully aware of their behaviour. We can call these the **Toxic Vampires**.

Not only would they be content to fail with company, they may even try to convince others to sabotage their grade, while they *secretly* work hard enough to excel in their exams. The sad truth is that, if they're charismatic enough or considered 'cool' enough, they may succeed in achieving this. This behaviour rarely stays limited to exams, and may continue on into their future relationships and careers.

We owe it to ourselves to *cut* Toxic Vampires out of our lives. Our future is *ours* to determine, and we have the right to refuse anyone who tries to sabotage it to remain in our lives.

'Right' People: 6 Positive Roles

Having established who the *wrong* people are, we need to identify the *right* people to fill our support group with.

In every ME Support Group, we need the *right* people to play 6 Positive Roles: The Listener, The Balancer, The Motivator, The Mentor, The Coach and The Comforter.

The same person or group can play multiple roles. We should remember that these roles are *not* descriptions of a specific type of person – they're simply *roles* that we can *all* take. Nevertheless, some of us embody certain roles more naturally and effectively than others.

Activity 8.5: When reading the descriptions of each *positive* role below, write down which ones fit you most naturally, and which you would like to become better at. Think about who you can choose to play each role in your ME Support Group.

-----

1. The Listener

This is one of the most important roles, and yet one of the hardest to fill. The Listener is someone that we can completely unload our mental and emotional baggage upon – also known as *venting*. They do not need to offer solutions to our problems; they just need to listen sympathetically. They may even ask questions that can help us to clarify certain thoughts for ourselves.

In order to do this, the Listener should have a *high threshold* for *emotionally-charged situations*. We don't want our venting to leave them feeling mentally exhausted and frustrated.

The ideal person for this role would be a *councillor* – the client-councillor relationship is practical as opposed to emotional, so we can vent freely without becoming self-conscious. However, many of us can't afford this privilege. If so, we can consider a parent, sibling or friend who meets the criteria for a good 'Listener'.

To enforce this successfully, we need to set *boundaries*. Good friends, siblings and (especially) parents are emotionally invested in our well-being – they *want* to see us happy! If we begin venting without warning, they may feel unnecessarily worried or concerned about our state – or even worse, their lack of understanding may cause them to speak harsh words that leave both parties feeling worse-off.

To avoid this, we need to *explicitly state* that we're about to start venting even before we begin.

We should inform the Listener that things are *not as bad* as they may initially sound, that we're not complaining or moaning for no purpose, and that they should not feel worried or concerned. We can tell them that we're simply *unloading* emotional and mental baggage, and that we're not looking for solutions yet.

Finally, we should explicitly set a *timeframe* during which we will vent. After this time period is complete, we can resume normal conversation or even return the favour by being a Listener for *their* venting.

In my case, my mother was my Listener without me even realising it. My pride insisted that I was battling through my studies alone, and yet I would have an opportunity to speak to her and vent on an almost daily basis. I am immensely grateful that she had the patience and emotional capacity to handle my unsolicited venting, even though I had neglected to set boundaries.

I was very fortunate. Don't risk this.

In short: Find the *right* Listener. Set firm boundaries. Vent as needed. Feel mentally refreshed and ready to overcome the challenges at hand.

2. The Balancer

The Balancer is our reality check. They have the ability to put things in *perspective* and help us escape from the all-consuming bubble of exams. They may do this through conversation about different topics, lifestyle (sports and other hobbies) or through comedy and humour (a good use for YouTube videos!).

The Balancer offers a sense of *stability* and *reliability*. They shouldn't be someone who is easily flustered. If you're feeling like an anxious wreck, their support should help to bring you back to a state of calm – it shouldn't end up with *both* of you becoming anxious wrecks!

The Balancer is also *sensible*. Once we're feeling calm and relaxed, they won't become a Tempter and try to *stop* us from returning to our studies by offering further distractions. They're also disciplined, refusing to compromise or delay when it's time to return to *their* studies.

As mentioned earlier, no single individual is a Balancer *all the time* – it's simply a role. Nevertheless, I feel that we should *all* endeavour to develop the positive traits of the Balancer.

In my case, two of my closest friends played the role of the Balancer. I lived with them during my 4th year at Cambridge University, and I will always be grateful to them for their ability to keep me grounded and bring a sense of stability and perspective to my life.

But prior to them, the entire university tennis team played the Balancer role. Simply being in a group of like-minded people engaging in a physical activity that we all enjoyed was a helpful perspective check, gently reminding me that there was *more* to life than just exams. After a training session, we would briefly sit down, chat and joke around before everyone returned to their world of studying (after a morning/day training session) or sleeping (after a night session).

Sport. Socialise. Study. Sleep. The epitome of balance.

3. The Motivator

The Motivator gives us a burst of *motivation* and *determination*. They are upbeat, dynamic and inspiring. Those who feel drawn to this role are often focused and driven to *act* – they're likely using their Motivator traits to encourage *themselves* to succeed. Their positive energy is infectious, whether through conversation, shared activities, or simply being in their presence.

We can use their support when we're suffering from any form of *inaction*. It could be as simple as a productivity dip, or as complex as feeling overwhelmed by the thought of how much content we have left to cover and not knowing where to start. Whatever task we need to do, we can use their positivity to kick ourselves out of stagnation and into some form of action. Once we're moving again, we can apply the Motivational Fire Formula to *keep* building on our progress.

If we're in a bad mood, it may better to avoid the Motivator as we may find their support to be irritating and unhelpful. Instead, we should take time to understand the source of our bad mood (RUDMA framework – Principle 3) and attempt to manage it. It may also be useful to speak to someone playing the Listener role.

In my case, one of my closest friends played the Motivator role. He was an entrepreneur trying to balance his Cambridge studies with the business he was successfully running. When it came to motivation, his words didn't do the talking. His actions, lifestyle and the attitude with which he approached challenges did.

I can still hear his voice in my head sometimes, encouraging me to *stop talking* and *start doing*. This book probably wouldn't exist without his influence in my life.

4. The Mentor

The Mentor offers *solutions* and *advice* to the problems that we bring to them based on *their own experiences*. As such, the effectiveness of their advice is not *guaranteed* given that our personality and perspective may differ considerably from theirs. However, at the very least they give us *options* to consider when we're stuck. They may even inspire us to come up with new, authentic solutions to our problems.

The person we choose to play the role of the Mentor should have a *track-record of success*. Ideally, they'll have shared similar experiences to us (both academic and personal), which will allow them to give *effective*, *relatable* advice. Teachers, siblings or older students can all play the role of a Mentor.

Regardless of who we select, it's vital that we have *respect* for our Mentor.

Our ego doesn't like being told what we can do, should do or must do. If our Mentor is offering advice or solutions to our problems, we need to respect them enough to silence our ego and allow our mind to fully absorb the information being shared *without* judging ourselves or our Mentor.

We must not forget that *we* are ultimately responsible for the actions we take. If we follow our Mentor's advice and it yields an unsuccessful outcome, the fault doesn't lie with them. We made the *choice* to take their advice. We must own the decision we made by taking responsibility for the outcome, learning the appropriate lessons, and moving on (which may include looking for a different Mentor!).

In my case, my Mentor during my 3rd year was a student in the year above me who studied the same course. He'd achieved one of the top grades in his year group, fulfilling the criteria of having a track-record of success. I consulted him for advice about the best way to study each of the modules we were being examined upon. His input shaped my study plan, helping me to decide how much time I needed to allocate to each module.

To be completely honest, I didn't know him prior to starting my course. During the year, I didn't speak to him more than a handful of times – and yet I would have been unlikely to achieve my 1st Class grade if it wasn't for his input. Given that he had no reason whatsoever to help me, I'm incredibly grateful to him for the time and energy he gave without expecting anything in return.

5. The Coach

The Coach empowers us to identify and implement our *own* solutions to the challenges we're facing. They don't listen to us vent, nor do they offer us advice. Instead, they ask us the *right questions* to challenge us and guide our thoughts towards our own solutions. This probing can be uncomfortable, which is why it's often recommended that we should not coach or be coached by our family or close friends.

The Coach needs to be a *good listener* to understand our current situation. However, they also need to be assertive enough to direct us to come up with our own *options* to resolve the problem. Once we select our preferred option, they then ask the questions that guide us to create and execute our own plans.

The Coach empowers us to *take action quickly* in line with the study goals we've set ourselves. They help us to get *unstuck* when we're unsure of which direction to take. They help us to identify *obstacles* which might interfere with our plans and guide us to come up with ways in which we can overcome them. They also help us to identify the *limiting beliefs* which are holding us back from committing to our goals, exam-related or otherwise.

The Coach can play a highly impactful role in your ME Support Group, but they do require a greater *investment* of time (and potentially money) than the other roles in order to be effective. Some councillors and teachers have been trained as coaches, and may be willing to coach you, or teach you the basics to coach yourself. Some of your friends may also seem naturally attracted to the role of the Coach. In this case, there are plenty of resources on the Internet that can help you to get an idea of coaching-style questions to ask each other.

Finally, the most effective (albeit potentially expensive) solution may be to hire your own coach. Not only is it effective, but it saves you time and effort by accelerating the process of resolving your problems.

In my case, I attended a 2-day coaching seminar (run by The Coaching Academy) where my partner was extremely helpful in applying his coaching skills to my studying problems. Having recognised the power of coaching (and having enjoyed the process tremendously), I then self-coached using the skills I was learning through coaching courses and books.

I'll be honest here - it certainly wasn't as effective as seeking out a professional coach. However, it helped me to come up with solutions to my challenges and achieve my exam goals, as well as convincing me that it was a career path worth considering in the future – ultimately one which I ended up pursuing!

Even if you can't afford a coach, I highly recommend learning how to coach yourself using the resources available on the Internet, as well as those in this book. After all, the activities I've included in each Principle are 'coaching-style questions' to help you elicit the answers that will help you move closer to your Exam Success goals!

6. The Comforter

The Comforter has the simplest role of anyone in our ME Support Group. We all struggle with days where we're filled with doubt, fear and anxiety. The Comforter is the person who makes us feel safe, loved and untroubled. With just a few short words of reassurance and a warm hug, they leave us feeling *significantly* better than we were before.

I'll be honest; sometimes, it isn't enough. But on many occasions, it's *exactly* what we need. Don't underestimate the power of the Comforter. The role is not time-consuming and can be played by anyone we're close to – for example, our best friend, partner, sibling or parents.

In my case, a few short words with my father on the phone were all I needed. He was someone I considered an Executioner before I set appropriate boundaries to manage the pressure on myself. He didn't have the emotional capacity to listen to me vent, nor the ability to coach or mentor me. He couldn't motivate me with his words or actions. He couldn't offer a balanced perspective or reality check.

However, what he *did* say each time we talked was: "Don't worry about it. Do your best, as you always do. And don't forget – if you can't control it, f**k it!"

Cringeworthy? Maybe. Profane? Certainly.

Comforting?

More than anything in the world. (He also gave great hugs when I came home between university terms – never underestimate the power of a good hug.)

The key message of Principle 8 is this; none of us are ever *truly* alone. And nor should we *try* to be.

Becoming consumed by pride and fear is *easy*, no matter how much they *pretend* to represent strength. But *true strength* is *difficult*.

True strength is knowing that our self-worth and pride are *not tied* to the supporting cast that helps us achieve our goals. True strength is being able to recognise our problem, identify what the *right* support is, and use it to resolve the situation quickly and effectively. True strength is being able to *cut* the *wrong* people out of our life to ensure a state of optimal mental health and well-being.

Most importantly, true strength is being able to show *gratitude* to the *right* people who have helped us to achieve the things we have accomplished, and who have guided us to becoming the people that we are today.

In Summary:

- We should always follow the 5 Golden Rules when dealing with anyone in either of our support groups.

- We can create and use our Academic Support Group to maximise our subject-related learning.

- We should cut, block or set boundaries for the *wrong people* and the 6 Negative Roles they play in the context of exams.

- We should create an ME Support Group consisting of the *right people* who can play the 6 Positive Roles.

9. Final Words

I truly hope that this book has equipped you with the tools, mindset and perspective to succeed in achieving your ideal exam grades.

During the course of this book, we've learned how to *optimise our studying process* through the first 4 Principles of Exam Success:

1. **Time-Management**

2. **Study Tools & Techniques**

3. **Mind-Management**

4. **On-The-Day Performance**

And we've learned how to optimise our lifestyle through the final 4 Principles of Exam Success:

5. **Movement & Physical Activity**

6. **Nutrition & Hydration**

7. **Sleep**

8. **Support Group**

Remember - this isn't a one-time book.

Review the 8 Principles of Exam Success frequently to remind yourself of relevant tools. Make a note of the sections that you found most insightful or motivating and refer back to them as needed. Most importantly, actually *apply* the 8 Principles to balance your studying process with your lifestyle – don't just read them!

I'll end with this: When your exams are finally completed, I hope that you can look back and *smile* knowing that you performed at your *optimum* level throughout the study period, and that you gave yourself the best chance of achieving your *ideal grades* in the *least stressful* way possible.

In other words, I hope that you can look back and smile knowing that you successfully achieved Exam Success.

I sincerely wish you all the best on your journey towards Exam Success, and beyond it.

Keep growing. Keep striving. Keep shining.

10. About Kam: My Story

Dear Reader,

Throughout this book, you'll have read some of my personal anecdotes and experiences to supplement the content in each Principle. I hope that these have been useful for you.

This section is *different*.

It delves into my fears, insecurities and the obstacles I had to overcome to reach this point in my life.

It digs into the experiences that helped me to break away from the constraints of my personal demons and limiting beliefs, to excel academically, to begin my personal journey as a coach and speaker, to write this book, and to create the 'Own It' Philosophy.

It's 100% *authentic*, *raw* and *real*.

Of course, it can get boring reading about the experiences of someone you don't even know! I've tried my best to write this chapter in an amusing, captivating style – but don't let the tone of my writing take away from the authenticity of the message.

Because the truth is, I don't enjoy writing about these things, and I'm not *truly* comfortable sharing them.

But there's a reason why I'm doing it anyway…

It's my hope that by sharing my vulnerabilities with you, it inspires you in some way to confront and overcome your own. I hope that my experiences help you realise that it's absolutely possible to *get the best out of yourself while dealing with the worst of yourself*, whether in your exams, relationships, careers, and life in general.

Believe me, I'm not *gaining* anything from sharing my embarrassments, failures and petty problems!

But if it helps or inspires you in some small way, then I'll consider it 100% worthwhile.

Last warning. You don't have to read this section…

You're still here?

Then let's get on with it.

Part 1 – Afraid and Insecure

As a young boy, I allowed my identity to become defined by my accomplishments. Getting good grades, winning tennis matches, receiving praise from my family and friends...I craved that validation to believe that I was a 'successful' human being.

I'd worked hard to achieve 13 A* in my GCSE grades. GCSEs don't look deeply at any subject, so this suited me perfectly. I was just as good at writing essays as I was at solving Mathematics problems or speaking French. I knew how to plan. I knew how to work intelligently. I knew what examiners were looking for. And I performed well on-the-day.

I was playing tennis and basketball at club level. I had a good group of friends with similar interests. I had a loving family. We didn't have a nice car or a big house, but we had a good quality of life.

And yet, I was suffering.

Why?

Because I was afraid. Deeply afraid.

Afraid of failure. Afraid of being judged. Afraid of disappointing my family. Afraid of rejection – every girl I'd liked up to this point had 'friend-zoned me'. Insecure about my physical appearance – I was short and skinny. Frustrated by my lack of popularity – I was good at exams and, despite my best efforts, wasn't considered to be sporty or cool.

None of this should surprise you – we *all* have fears and insecurities.

To some extent, mine would drive me to push harder and accomplish more (as they do for many of us). And yet, they would also exhaust me, limit me and paralyse me. When they were triggered, I had no control over them.

When they were triggered, they *owned* me.

And I was constantly *living in fear* of them being triggered…

I came to realise that my relationship with *myself* was not sustainable. Sure, I would accomplish something and feel the satisfaction that came with it. But I was burning myself out. I was draining my mental and physical health. I was becoming volatile, and at times difficult to be around for my family and friends.

The truth is that I felt broken, and I didn't know how to fix myself.

Ironically, I compensated by letting the nurturing side of my character develop, taking solace in listening to my friends and supporting them through their problems…but still never resolving my own.

But you can't pour from an empty cup. Before you can give to others, you must fill your own cup first. And I was about to learn this the hard way…

Part 2 – The Path To 'Owning' Myself

It's been said that the Universe gives you what you *need*, not what you *want*.

I was 17 when I met *her*. I could tell immediately that this wasn't just an ordinary crush. I was completely taken by her. I can't remember what gave me the confidence to talk to her – possibly the fact that I *expected* to be rejected by someone as beautiful as her, so I had nothing to lose! – but we became friends. We would text each other and chat…but I was much too afraid of rejection to really ask her out. She was the kind of girl that you daydream about, but never tell. I guess I hoped that she'd realise how good a person I was and feel the same way about me…

It didn't happen. Instead, my daydreams got out of control and became all-consuming. My sports, my academics, my friends…none of it mattered in comparison to her. I felt intense joy each time we talked, yet at the same time feeling intense pain that I couldn't tell her how I felt.

I remember reading a quote by Oscar Wilde: "It is better to know and be disappointed, than to not know and always wonder".

It helped me to finally summon up the courage to tell her how I felt.

And she rejected me.

Brutally.

She told me how I was so smart, sporty, and kind…

…but how, despite all my positive traits, I was too *short* for her.

I remember the words echoing through my mind. I remember feeling my stomach churning, the slow build-up of anguish as one of my worst nightmares came to fruition.

Height. One of my biggest insecurities. One of the things people at school bullied me about. One of the things I was secretly petrified that girls would reject me for. One of the only things I couldn't change about myself. Now, the only thing between me and the girl I liked.

It hurt more than anything I'd experienced. I cried in pain, I cried in anger, I beat my pillow to shreds. I felt like the most worthless creature that ever lived.

I don't even remember the next two days. I was a zombie. A vegetable. I went through the motions on autopilot. I was alive – but I couldn't bring myself to *actually live*. I couldn't allow the pain I was suppressing to erupt while I was in school.

Coming back from school the second day, I went straight back to bed. I curled up and cried. Then, suddenly, the tears dried up, and I just stopped caring. Numbness. I didn't matter, she didn't matter, the world didn't matter...

I realised that what hurt the most was not that she'd *rejected* me, but that she'd rejected me over my *height*. The one thing I *couldn't control*. All she had done was showed me where one of my biggest insecurities lay dormant, brought it to the surface, and forced me to confront it.

I knew that I needed some sort of help to deal with this.

My father wasn't a tall man. I tried speaking to him about it. He didn't understand - and I don't blame him! At age 14, he'd left his home country to *escape a revolution*. He had bigger problems to deal with in his teenage years than girls and height issues!

I felt embarrassed bringing it up to him, and even more embarrassed hearing his response. I decided that no one would ever hear this story again. Social stigmas meant that I would be considered weak to talk about these things, and I felt weak enough as it was. Self-help books seemed too cliché, and besides, I was a bit too proud to admit to myself that I needed help.

But I knew that I had to make some changes.

I decided that my growth, my peace of mind, and how I perceived my reality was far more important than what I felt society would judge me for. After all, when I woke up in the morning, the only reflection staring back in the mirror was my own; not my parents, not my friends, and not my teachers.

And I knew that I needed to see my reflection smile.

I made a vow to myself that everything I *could* control, I *would* control. I would become so *successful* in so many areas of my life that, one day, she'd realise what a *mistake* she'd made.

(I laugh at this when I look back at it. Operating from a mentality of 'lacking' and 'compensating' just isn't sustainable – as I was soon to learn! But I'm grateful to her for teaching me these hard lessons.)

This mindset shift led me to push myself harder than I'd ever done before – academically, physically and mentally.

I was studying Maths, Chemistry, Physics and Further Maths. I was debating between Biology, French and English for the final spot, but Further Maths was only offered to high-achieving students at my school – and my ego liked the idea of being high-achieving!

Maths, Chemistry and Physics were fine. A-Levels were tougher than GCSEs, but the principles I'd used in terms of exam technique and studying didn't change too much.

But Further Maths was a completely different experience. I couldn't just rely on memorising *facts* or *patterns* to help me answer questions; I actually needed to *understand* the fundamentals behind the mathematical concepts we were covering.

I struggled immensely. I fell behind. I lost motivation. After my first year of A-Levels, I pulled my foot off the gas pedal.

I went for a Cambridge interview to study Chemical Engineering, fully expecting not to get in. I didn't stress about it. I smiled a lot. I was honestly just *grateful* for the *chance* to be interviewing at Cambridge! I made quite a few mistakes in my interview, but stayed relaxed, kept smiling and was able to correct my own mistakes.

Then I put the interview aside and returned to the horrible world of Further Maths.

We did a mock-exam in December for the FP2 module. On January 3rd, I returned after the Christmas holidays to find that I'd scored 28% in that test. I'd scored a U-grade – below a *fail* grade!

On January 6th, to my surprise, I received an offer from Cambridge. My family were ecstatic. I was overjoyed. We celebrated for nearly half an hour…before I read my offer in its entirety and realised that they *specifically* wanted an A* in Further Maths.

I remember my face dropping in dismay.

I needed to get a 90% average across three modules. And I'd just scored 28% in the mock-exam for one of those modules.

This was January 6th.

January 14th was one of my module exams for one of the other key Further Maths modules (Statistics 2) that would contribute to my grade.

And January 10th was my 18th birthday.

I realised that I had a choice. I could say: "Forget Cambridge; Imperial College and Loughborough are good enough!" and just aimed for the more realistic A or B-grade that I needed to meet my offer. And at the *same time*, potentially wonder for the rest of my life whether I could actually have gotten into Cambridge had I tried my hardest…

Or I could say: "I'm scared of failing, but I can still try my best – I'd rather know that Cambridge wasn't right for me despite my *best* effort, rather than be a coward and regret not even giving myself a chance".

In other words: "It is better to know and be disappointed, than to not know and always wonder."

It wouldn't be an easy path. But unlike growing taller, giving my best effort was *fully in my control*.

I revised like crazy during the next week. I even revised on my 18th birthday! And I was rewarded – I scored 100/100 on that S2 module.

I still struggled with the remaining Further Maths modules, but I stepped up my level of effort. I created a plan and worked as hard as I could in a healthy, balanced way during Easter and my study leave.

I sat my exams.

And by Results Day that summer, I knew that no matter the result, I had given it my all. I knew that I could be disappointed by that outcome, but that would have been *temporary*, whereas my *regret* at not trying at all would have been permanent.

I'm grateful that despite my very real fear of failure, my courage to give it my all was rewarded. I met my offer to study Chemical Engineering (via 1st Year Natural Sciences) at Cambridge University.

I thought I had it all figured out.

But as I was soon to learn, the journey to owning myself had just begun…

Part 3 – The Cambridge Struggles

I came to Cambridge *expecting* myself to be less intelligent and less academically capable than everyone else. I decided that I was going to play sports, have a social life and aim for the bare minimum pass grade in a year that didn't count towards my final grade.

And I absolutely achieved my goal.

I played for the Cambridge University Lawn Tennis Club Men's 2nd Team. I found myself in a long-term relationship with a beautiful, intelligent girl within 2 weeks of being in Cambridge. I made many friends, establishing myself as a slightly loud (and insecure) but generally friendly and good-hearted person.

And I *scraped* through academically. How bad did I do? Here's an extract from an email my Director of Studies sent me on 6th July 2012.

"...I advise you to think carefully about how your studies have gone this year and about what you need to do (and what help you might seek) to shift up a gear. If the Seconds were divided in Part IA you would have had a rather low 2.ii and your overall ranking in the university cohort was 558 out of 619 -- dangerously close to the bottom..."

Bare minimum pass grade.

As I said, I *absolutely* achieved my goal.

And I felt *horrible* about it.

I realised that I had been so *afraid* to face failure, that I had simply lowered my expectations and commitment levels instead of facing it with courage.

Why?

Because I was *petrified* by the thought that I may be nothing more than average even if I *had* given it my best! My ego refused to admit that others might be *better* than my best, and it preferred me to fail half-heartedly under the veil that I 'could have done more if I wanted to', than to fail giving it my authentic best.

Despite all of the progress and growth that I thought I had made in the years before coming to Cambridge, I realised that I had let my old insecurities get the better of me again.

I vowed to do things differently in my 2nd year. I was going to be studying the Chemical Engineering course that I had originally applied for, and I felt that *now* I was motivated to truly give my best, no matter what the outcome may be. My past best may not have been enough, but my current best could get better every single day. There was no excuse…

Except for one problem.

Over the summer, I did an internship at a Chemical Engineering company. It was a wonderful learning experience, challenging yet positive. And one lesson stood out more than the others…

Chemical Engineering was not for me.

Not the best thing to discover before you begin a Chemical Engineering course at Cambridge!

I tried to remind myself of the reasons why I had *applied* for the course in the first place. I remembered that I had chosen it for its *versatility*; the fact that it would allow me to keep my options open in pursuing a future career.

It was a powerful realisation. I realised that a good grade in my course would *still* open doors to prestigious careers, such as banking or management consulting. I found my motivation…

…and lost it immediately within a few months.

In applying to management consulting firms, I realised that my 'Cambridge degree' would not even guarantee me an *interview*, let alone a job! No summer internship was forthcoming. Every company I applied to rejected me. This burst an illusion in my naïve mind that a Cambridge degree translated to instant jobs. I still had two years to figure out a way to make it work… but that didn't stop me from worrying about it!

The course wasn't giving me any joy either. As I said earlier, Chemical Engineering was *not* for me.

I became disheartened, taking solace in my sports and spending time with my girlfriend (who was doing the same Chemical Engineering course). In fact, I began to over-compensate on my dissatisfaction with my course by doing *too much* sport and weight training. It was only a matter of time before the inevitable happened…

I woke up one morning to find that I couldn't move.

My lower back was in complete spasm. After an emergency physiotherapist appointment in London, I was told that my 'spine had begun to compress' because of genetic issues with the curvature of my spine that had been exacerbated by the direct pressure exerted by the weights I placed on my upper back when squatting.

No more tennis. No more basketball. No more gym.

No more coping mechanism for the pressures of reality.

No more being able to put socks on in the morning…

My girlfriend was my rock through this. She supported me not only through dealing with my injuries, but academically as well. She helped me with my coursework, revision and exam preparation.

Still, I knew that the Chemical Engineering course wasn't right for me. Thankfully, I discovered a 3rd year specialisation option to study Manufacturing Engineering, a course that combined engineering *and* business elements. I applied for the course and found out soon after that I had been accepted.

Meanwhile, my back improved slightly, and I returned to doing light exercise (including some light basketball which led me to injure my ankle the day before my exams, as mentioned in the book…)

Things were generally good.

I went into my exams feeling confident of achieving my 2.1 goal…

…and then spent 2 hours admiring the curtains in the exam hall during a *shockingly difficult* first exam.

I ended up *failing* that module (34% - damn you, Fluid Dynamics & Heat Transfer!). The other exams went well – but not well enough. My coursework grades were strong. They pulled my grade up – but not by enough.

My overall grade at the end was 59.8%.

0.2% away from my goal of a 2.1.

I'm somewhat embarrassed to admit this, but I cried upon finding out my results. Not because of the result itself, but because I had summoned the strength to set aside my fear of failing and *whole-heartedly* committed to achieving my goal.

And I had been so close…

So close to achieving the goal that I had emotionally and mentally invested so much in…and yet so far from it. This was the moment that I realised that *failure* was *subjective.*

I had passed the year. But I had failed to achieve my goals. To Cambridge, to my peers, to my parents, I had passed.

To myself, I had failed.

I was utterly disappointed. My confidence was shattered. I knew that my 3rd year was important, but I didn't know *yet* whether I would be able to muster up the strength to commit to my goal again given the very real chance of failure…

I tried to just relax and enjoy the summer…

And then my relationship ended.

2 years spent with the girl I was in love with.

Gone in an instant.

I thought I took it well. I believed that I had the self-awareness and maturity to move past this quickly and emerge stronger. I put on a brave face and said all the right things about how it was for the best, how it was amicable and mutual, how it had been a wonderful experience but our growth together had started to stagnate and so it was the right time to end things, how I respected her courage for ending it when I had been too afraid to do so, and so on…

But my body wasn't fooled by my mind's narrative. My back started to get *a lot* worse…

I returned to Cambridge for my 3rd year.

Same room. No girlfriend.

Haunted by memories every night I returned to my room after dinner.

Salt on the wound?

She was now in a relationship with the gentleman next door to me. (She was actually very considerate and asked me beforehand if I would be okay with it – of course, I said I was happy for her and wished them well.)

No sports. No coping mechanism for life. My back got progressively worse.

The new course? I was too consumed by my other issues to even *permit* myself to become interested in it.

Friends? It turned out that I'd lost most of them due to the time I'd devoted to my (now ex) girlfriend, during which I'd neglected them. I came back after a year and a half of absence, expecting to resume things as they were. Naive and arrogant of me. Lesson learned: *never take friendships for granted.*

Family? They were very supportive. We would have phone conversations nearly every evening. And yet, every single night when we talked, all I would feel was that I was a complete failure, that I'd disappointed them, and that I didn't deserve them. Our conversations were *bittersweet* – it was sweet to know that they cared and loved me; it was bitter in that I felt unworthy and undeserving of their time or love. In hindsight, I'm immensely grateful for them. They were the one thing that kept me from doing anything *really* stupid.

Here's the thing – I was aware enough to recognise the blessings still in my life. I had food, shelter and water. I was alive. I will never *pretend* that my challenges compare to those faced by others around the world.

Heck, as I wrote the first edition of this book, there were children in Aleppo, Syria, *dying* from injuries sustained because of bomb explosions at their schools.

It's a tragedy that there is so much suffering in the world.

But suffering is not prejudiced. *Everyone* suffers.

The reason for this is that the source of our suffering is *subjective.* We can *only* see things from the lens with which we view *our* reality. Of course, we can look to the world around us and *try* to understand how our suffering measures in comparison to the rest of the world, and how we *should* feel because of it.

But in the end, what causes us to suffer, and the extent to which we feel that suffering, is unique to us. It is relative *only* to our personal experiences and the unique way in which we have interpreted them.

Someone else can tell us that we're making a mountain out of a molehill. But it's irrelevant – if it *feels* like a mountain in our reality, it *is* a mountain.

And *we* are the only ones who can climb it and conquer it.

Sometimes that involves changing our lens of reality. Sometimes it just takes time and perspective for the mountain to reduce in size. Sometimes the mountain just gets bigger and bigger…

Regardless, either we conquer it, or it conquers us.

So, I admit it.

I would come back to my room, night after night, and feel sorry for myself and my suffering. I didn't drink alcohol. I didn't take drugs. I just wallowed in my suffering, feeling sorry for myself and the problems I was dealing with, frustrated at my inability to move beyond it, and releasing my emotions in the privacy of my room.

The last point is really important.

I didn't *internalise* my suffering – I would *release* it. I would cry *a lot*. I would write journal entries. I didn't tell anyone about these things. But in hindsight, I realise that these outlets for my emotions kept me from doing permanent damage to myself and my loved ones.

This went on for over a month before I finally snapped out of the cycle…

I was walking on the Churchill College fields on a cold, autumn afternoon as the sun was setting. I was tired, just as I had been throughout the past month – releasing emotions may be healing, but it's also exhausting.

Today, I was especially tired, and I found myself thinking less and less as I walked.

The thoughts about my experiences, suffering and anxieties stopped flowing through my mind for the first time in months, and I found myself becoming entranced by the rhythm of my steps. In the moments to come, I became aware of the feel of my feet with each step on the frosty grass. I heard the music of the few remaining tree leaves swaying with the late-autumn breeze. I looked up…and became mesmerised by the sunset.

And I began to smile.

It was a joy unlike any I had ever experienced, a joy that stemmed from feeling completely *peaceful,* from feeling completely *liberated,* from completely *surrendering* my ego-driven thoughts*,* from being completely immersed in the *present moment* and completely free of the pain from the past and worries of the future.

In that moment, I made a promise to myself.

I promised myself that, no matter how painful life gets, as long as there is still a sunset to see somewhere in this world, I'm *happy* and *blessed* to live another day.

After the sunset, I returned to my room with a new realisation that I wrote down in my journal: "Yes, things aren't great right now…but they are going to get better. Every day, little by little, things are going to get better. I am going to make them better."

My problems didn't magically disappear, but I had found a new level of self-awareness and self-expression to deal with them.

It all started with *taking back control.*

I began to use *poetry* as an outlet to express my emotions and experiences, using my command of language to *control* it. I started *walking* everywhere as a way of detaching from the hectic pace of Cambridge and controlling my own pace of life, knowing that if something was *important* to me, I would always be on time.

My back slowly recovered, and I began attending tennis training again (always on time!).

I even started attending lectures again (…not always on time!).

In fact, it was during my final project of that first term that I discovered something else about myself. I discovered why I could *never* leave Cambridge. I discovered why I could *never give up* on myself.

Somewhere deep within me was an *authentic* sense of *pride* and *defiance* that didn't care about anything outside of myself. It *refused* to back down from a challenge, refused to let me stay down when I fell, and refused to let me *settle* for anything *less than my best*.

I believe that we *all* have this if we look deep enough.

This was the final piece to my puzzle.

That winter break, I found my old study plans and decided to take them to another level. I created a 5-month study plan to give myself a chance to *truly* find out what I could achieve when I studied *my way*.

Not the "Cambridge way" – stressed out, anxious, and spending hour after hour in dark, musky libraries. *My way* – productive, relaxed, and balanced.

In doing it *my way*, I didn't know if I would succeed in achieving a good grade. However, I decided that I would rather face the disappointment and failure that *my way* wasn't good enough (and that I would have to improve it for the future), than to spend another year failing by doing it *someone else's way* because I was too afraid to try what felt right to me.

I began including daily *mindful walks* in my schedule. I added light exercise, which I built up as my back improved. I cut out the people who negatively affected my mental state, and found joy in spending time with the new friends I began to make.

More importantly, I learned to find peace in *solitude*. Up until this point, I was afraid of being *alone*, which was part of the reason why I had grown *dependent* on my past relationship. Now, I was forced to confront this demon…

I would walk alone to do my shopping, cook alone and eat alone. I would study alone, train alone and sleep alone. On a whim, I decided that I wanted to travel and see the world. Me – the boy who at one point was so disgusted by the idea of sharing a communal bathroom! Now, I felt ready to throw myself out of my comfort zone and embrace the uncertainty of the stretch zone.

I was ready to *evolve*.

I applied to a summer teaching scheme in China and was rejected. But then someone dropped out from the scheme and they needed another teacher – I immediately emailed them and was accepted!

Most importantly though, I began to *read* a lot more; in particular self-help books, philosophy books and books exploring spirituality.

It was through reading that I discovered life coaching – a book called 'Unlimited Power' by Anthony Robbins. It inspired me. It motivated me. It empowered me to take action.

I attended a 2-day Coaching Course one month before my exams (planned my revision around it, of course). And during these two days, I finally found what I had been searching for. I finally *realised* what I wanted to do with my life. I wanted to empower others to become the best-version of themselves, just as I was striving to do the same for myself.

I used this realisation to motivate me to keep studying, knowing that nothing would stop me from giving my best in these exams. The balance remained. The back improved. I returned to tennis. Filled with a new gratitude for the game, my mentality towards it had completely transformed. I found myself playing better than ever before…

And so, after two challenging years of sub-optimal performance (2.2's in both years), I managed to achieve a 1st class in my final year of undergraduate studies, and secured my spot for the Men's 2nd Team Lawn Tennis "Varsity" fixture against Oxford.

Following this, I went to China for 2 months. Lessons, adventures and wonderful experiences awaited me.

I came back and began a Masters in Manufacturing Engineering in my 4th year.

Not because I enjoyed the subject, but because I had fallen in love with Cambridge. It was where my life had transformed, and I felt truly grateful and privileged to be there.

I created my own small-scale performance coaching and fitness training business to gauge how realistic it could be to pursue as a career. I captained the Cambridge University Lawn Tennis Club Men's 2nd Team. I lived with two wonderful, supportive friends, and made many more. I conducted projects in three very different engineering firms – firmly reinforcing that it was most certainly *not* my career path in the immediate future.

I achieved a Masters with Merit and competed in my final Varsity tennis fixture.

But, as shown by the pages in this chapter so far, what I had truly gained went far beyond academic and sporting achievements…

With time, patience and strength, I had managed to take control of my fears and insecurities. I confronted them, I understood them, I soothed them, and I managed them.

I learned to own them.

I learned to *own myself* – until a new situation would come along and trigger existing fears or create new ones!

But as I realised, that simply couldn't be helped – just as life was dynamic and ever-changing, so too would I continuously evolve as a result of the new experiences I faced.

But I realised that it was my *choice* as to *how* I evolved.

I could resist and fight growth, desperately clinging to the familiar past, the self-pity and injustices of my life.

Or I could accept the new circumstances, adapt to them, and learn to *own* them.

And with each new situation that acted as a trigger, the self-awareness that I'd cultivated would allow me to regain control over my emotional state at a quicker rate each time. I could get to the source of the fear, understand how it impacted me, and most importantly, manage it to mitigate its harmful impact on myself and those around me.

I learned to reconfigure my mindset to allow me to perform at my 'best', while dealing effectively and proactively with my 'worst' in a sustainable way.

It was time to make a move into the 'real world', but I still hadn't decided whether to pursue my own coaching business, or to continue to build my foundations with a secure, well-paid city job...

Part 4 – The Consulting Chronicles

As mentioned, I had started doing performance coaching work at Cambridge University in the final year of my Masters. I worked with A-Level and university students to help them overcome stress and plan effectively in order to improve their performance and accomplish their goals.

I loved it.

It was far more fulfilling than academics (even more so than my sports!) – and my clients were achieving great results.

But I soon realised that I just wasn't *ready* to pursue this as a full-time career.

Being honest, this wasn't too much of a surprise. A 1st class Engineering degree from Cambridge meant that I had a chance for a 'stable' future with a 'well-paying' job, exactly what I had been brought up to believe was the most desired outcome from the educational process.

And it fit with my *own* values too. Two of my key values are security and purpose, and I wanted to build the financial foundations (security) for the family I one day wanted to support (one of my personal 'life purposes').

That...and I was also risk-averse, afraid of disappointing my family who had helped to support me in reaching this point, and still felt the need to prove to myself that I could 'make it' in the city.

My plan was to work for 10 years in what society deemed to be a 'prestigious' and 'elite' profession. After all, just as Cambridge had been the validation that I sought to prove that I had succeeded academically, my job would be the validation that I had succeeded professionally.

(Yes, here were my insecurities and approval issues rearing their ugly head again...)

Then, once I had a stable, successful career, I would start my own family. And then once I had the life experience and a healthy amount of money in the bank, I would become a coach.

The plan started well.

I managed to get a highly-coveted job as a strategy consultant with a prestigious, global management consulting firm. I approached it with no expectations, simply wanting to learn as much as I could while establishing myself as a high-potential individual.

Then came the staggering learning curve...

On the positive side, it was challenging and intellectually-stimulating work, and I was surrounded by talented, driven and intelligent people. The culture seemed so different from that of the management consulting firms that my friends were working for, and I really felt like I was in an atmosphere that cultivated ideas, inspired ambition and promoted self-development.

On the negative side, the hours were very long, and the work was not fulfilling in the way that coaching had been. I began longing for deep interactions with other people, knowing that all the time and energy that I was devoting to this job could be spent making a positive impact on the lives of others. I yearned for *purpose!*

The longer I let the thought percolate in my mind, the more I realised that the doubts I once had about making my coaching dreams happen (the business strategy and marketing aspects in particular) were rapidly disappearing.

The sheer amount of time and energy that I was willing to dedicate to a cause that *wasn't even mine...* imagine what would be possible if I redirected that same time and energy towards chasing my coaching dreams!

I let my thoughts flow for the next six weeks, planning and scheming despite the high demands of the job, and imagining the day that I left the strategy consulting world and began living my dream for myself...

And then, I decided to stop imagining, and start *doing.*

And here we are.

Part 5 – My Motivation As A Coach

I learned a lot from school, university and work. But for some reason, the *basic* tools needed to begin owning myself (such as self-awareness, mindfulness, values etc.) were never covered.

This struck me as ironic, because these organisations all seek optimal performance from their people (in exams for schools and universities, and in jobs for companies) – and the aforementioned tools were *exactly* the kind of catalyst that could facilitate this.

So, I made a decision to do what these institutions neglect to do.

And I decided to start with the people who felt the brunt of social, academic and professional pressures the most, the people whom I could relate to the most based on my *own* experiences...

Students.

Our generation of students faces both opportunities and challenges far different than any before us. Social media means that we have the potential to have tremendously large networks at a very early age, and the ever-changing job landscape means that we can pursue careers that our parents and grandparents could never even imagine!

This can be very positive – social networks can be a great asset as our generation of students enter professional careers, and having so many career choices means that we're more likely to find or create a career that we're passionate about.

But at this early age, without the tools to manage ourselves, our social network can be a tremendous source of angst. The pressures from perceived scrutiny and judgement is huge. Social trends emerge one day and die the next. Every move we make (or don't make) is subject to peer approval (or disapproval).

The end result is that, despite being more connected to others than ever before, we're more disconnected from ourselves as a consequence.

And though there are many jobs being created that didn't even exist before (people making their living playing computer games and streaming them online – try explaining that to your grandparents!), having *too much choice* can also be paralysing!

What if we choose the wrong career? What if we fail at it and all our friends find out? What if there's a better career around the corner? Would we really be happy doing this job? Would we be as happy as our friends?

These questions are very destructive; instead of taking advantage of the choices we have, we become overwhelmed by our options.

We need to remember that our careers are *not permanent*. We're free to grow and change our careers throughout our lives. In fact, one of the best ways to figure out which career choice would fulfil you is by doing a *job that you hate*!

Why? Because doing jobs that we're not happy with forces us to ask ourselves the question, "so, what do I *really* want?" – and gives us the motivation to chase after it!

There will always be a career option where your *aptitudes* (what you're good at) overlap with your *passions* (what you love). And if it doesn't exist yet – create it!

That's what I'm doing, anyway.

Over the last few years, I've seen too many students fall victim to the same fears and insecurities that I had. They remain stuck in these vicious cycles to the detriment of their health, well-being and performance. Worse still, it carries on into their professional lives, social lives and relationships, where they manifest in even more harmful ways.

But it doesn't have to be this way.

I want to show all students how to retake control of their own life. I want to show them that they *themselves* are their *only* judge - not the network of people around them. I want to show them how they can optimise their mindset to overcome the limits that constrain them, wherever their source. And most importantly, I want to show them how to translate this into sustainable high-performance in every area of their lives, while maintaining their health and well-being.

If you've finished 'The Ultimate Guide To Exam Success' and are now reading this, something may have just clicked…

In this book, I've offered suggestions, tools and techniques to achieve Exam Success, as this is something most students seek to do. Exams are a problem that you can relate to.

But in truth, most of the tools in this book reach *far beyond* exams! Whether we're reading about productivity skills, planning or prioritising; mindset management and motivation tools; mental & emotional support groups; or the improvements that we can make to optimise our lifestyle – they can *all* be applied *throughout our lives*!

Which is why I wrote this book.

Because more than anything, it's my greatest wish to be the person that I wanted and desperately needed to talk to all those years ago, but didn't feel worthy enough to even look for.

I truly hope that this book has been valuable for you. I wish you success not only in achieving your *Exam Success* goals, but also in learning to *embrace your potential, own your life* and *become the best-version of yourself.*

Keep growing. Keep striving. Keep shining.

With love and gratitude,

Kam

11. Appendices

Appendix 1: List Of All Activities Outlined In The Book

Principle 1

Activity 1.1: Think of 3 recent examples of procrastination that you've experienced. For each example, write down: the task you were meant to be doing, how you procrastinated, how you felt after procrastinating, and what the overall outcome of the task was. Which of the reasons for procrastination outlined above applied in each situation?

Activity 1.2: Write down where you currently prioritise exam preparation with respect to the other categories listed above. Is this something that you want to change in line with your exam goals?

Activity 1.3: Write down ANY 10 tasks you need to do in the next few days (study-related, leisure-related, home-related, social etc.) and assign them into Covey's 4 Quadrants of Time Management.

Activity 1.4: For the same 10 tasks that you wrote down for Activity 1.2, assign each task a letter corresponding to the ABCDE Rule.

Activity 1.5: Decide on the method that you want to use to create your plan. Using the 6 Laws of Study Planning and the 5-step process outlined above, create your own initial plan. If you don't know where to start, read the next section outlined 'Kam's Planning System' before creating your plan.

Principle 2

Activity 2.1: Are you more of a time-focused or task-focused worker? What can you do to prevent yourself from falling victim to the pitfalls of your dominant type?

Activity 2.2: Think about what your natural tendencies are for how you prefer to learn. Which other cognitive abilities should you develop to help you study more effectively? For each subject you study, which learning methods do you want to experiment with?

Activity 2.3: Of the 10 studying techniques described above, which ones would you like to integrate into your studying process? How can you begin implementing them?

Activity 2.4: Create your own personal workspace. Where will it be? What will you choose to have on your desk? What can you do to make a habit of only doing productive work at your workspace?

Activity 2.5: Reflect on how you use music when studying. Is the music you are listening to helping or hindering your studying? What can you change in order to improve your situation?

Activity 2.6: Write down your main sources of distraction. How can you manage them more effectively? How can you set measures in place to stop yourself from becoming easily distracted?

Activity 2.7: Reflect on your most productive study times during the day. Are these optimal to ensure that you are awake and focused when sitting your exams? If not, what can you do to change this?

Principle 3

Activity 3.1: Get a notepad or journal. Create a habit of writing in it as a method of managing your anxiety (or other mindset-related problem area), using the RUDMA framework to structure your journaling.

Activity 3.2: Recall a positive memory and practise associating with it. Notice how your emotional state is affected. When you're ready, dissociate from that same memory. Notice how your emotional state is affected. Practise entering an associated state when studying. Practise entering a dissociated state on any occasion when your stress response is triggered.

Activity 3.3: Make a list of 5-10 recent occasions which caused you to experience stress. Use the RUDMA Framework to run through each example. When you reach the 'Manage' stage, make a note of what actions you can take in the future to manage your stress response more effectively.

Activity 3.4: Identify 5 of your key 'towards and 'away-from' values. Rank them in order of which has the most influence over your decision-making.

Activity 3.5: Write down your value fulfilment conditions for each of your towards and away-from values. For each, identify whether it's empowering or disempowering. For any disempowering rules, write down a suitable empowering rule to replace it with.

Activity 3.6: Use Appendix 2 as an example to create your own 'strands' linking your values with the studying, revision or other tasks you need to complete.

Activity 3.7: For any goal you're striving to achieve, write down a list of the knowledge and resources you already possess to help you achieve your goal. Write down what knowledge and resources are *missing* – for each of these, make a note of how you can acquire them.

Activity 3.8: For any goal you're trying to achieve, write down the reasons which are stopping you from taking action, and what you can do to overcome them. Reinforce to yourself that taking action will motivate you to take *more* action. Make a commitment to start carrying out the action steps you've defined in your plan.

Activity 3.9: Make a list of all the expectations you've placed on yourself (and others have placed upon you) to achieve a goal. Go through each one using RUDMA, and make a choice to *downgrade* it from an expectation to a *hope*. If necessary, use the 'Manage' stage of RUDMA to confront and resolve the worst-case scenario if your expectations aren't met.

Activity 3.10: Decide on which of the above options you want to use to track your progress during your studies, and how exactly you'll track them. Think about any other progress tracking options you can add that would be useful to you.

Activity 3.11: List down 5-10 quick-wins you have made in the last few weeks – they can be as big or small as you like. From today onwards, make a commitment to write down *at least 3* Quick Wins *every single day* in your journal/diary/planner.

Activity 3.12: Over the next week (or longer), write down each occasion you catch yourself having a *limiting belief* or *thought*. Describe the thoughts and the situation that triggered it. Come up with an alternative thought or belief that creates a feeling of *freedom* and *expansiveness* instead of *tension* and *constriction*.

Activity 3.13: Address each of the limiting thoughts and beliefs you wrote down in Activity 3.12 in turn using the 8-Question Belief Transformation Process outlined above.

Activity 3.14: Begin applying the '…yet' technique to your own limiting beliefs as described in the above examples.

Activity 3.15: Make a note of at least 10 disempowering "should/ must/ have to/ need to" statements that you make. For each one, replace it with a more empowering version using "could/ would like to/ get to/ allow myself to/ it would be nice to". Write this new, empowering statement down and repeat it to yourself whenever you notice yourself thinking or using the old, disempowering statement.

Activity 3.16: Write down some of the negative identity statements in your self-dialogue. Beside each one, write down a rephrased statement in which that identity is phrased as a behaviour. Recite this to yourself daily until you no longer associate that behaviour with an identity.

Activity 3.17: How can you apply The Path Of Least Regret to help you in your studying? What feelings can you 'redefine' to trigger you to take positive action towards your exam preparation?

Activity 3.18: How can you incorporate mindfulness practices into your studying routine? Consider *when*, *where* and *how often* you will practise them in order to turn them into a habit.

Activity 3.19: Create 5 (or more) visualisations that you can use to aid you in your studies and during your examinations. Write down their exact description to aid you in this. Set aside 5 minutes, twice a day, to practise these.

Activity 3.20: Write down the affirmations that you want to include with your 5 (or more) visualisations. Write down 5 (or more) other affirmations that can aid you in your studies.

Principle 4

Activity 4.1: Which of the exam day tactics discussed above are you going to try? Make a note of what you will do and exactly how you'll do it.

Principle 5

Activity 5.1: Identify the days and times each week during which you are going to engage in physical activity. Which activity will you do? How long will you do each activity for? Think of 5 obstacles that might stop you keeping to your schedule, and consider methods by which you can overcome them.

Activity 5.2: Check Appendix 3 (and watch the YouTube video) – if the bodyweight circuit routine appeals to you, how will you implement it into your schedule?

Principle 6

Activity 6.1: Having looked through the 7 factors and the food list, what changes can you make to your diet to aid with studying? Which foods are you going to add? Which foods will you consume less or remove from your diet?

Activity 6.2: How will you ensure that you stay well-hydrated? Think about how you can implement regular water consumption into your study schedule.

Principle 7

Activity 7.1: Consider downloading the Sleep Cycle app (it's free!) and trying it out for a week. Make a note of any possible factors that influence the quality of your sleep. What can you change to improve the quality of your sleep?

Activity 7.2: If you have trouble sleeping, which of the sleeping techniques described above do you want to experiment with? Make a note of which nights you are going to try each of the techniques you selected.

Activity 7.3: Create your own quick, energising morning routine to try tomorrow morning. Use the ideas outlined above or come up with your own. Make a commitment to stick to this routine for one week, and note down how you feel after doing it every morning.

Principle 8

Activity 8.1: Consider your current academic support group as you read through the list below. Write down what you can do to ensure that you use them in the most effective way. Who else can you add to your academic support group?

Activity 8.2: If you are looking for a study partner or group, identify which of the above incentives fits most with yours. Use this to find your ideal study partner or group.

Activity 8.3: If you feel like you don't need a ME Support Group, which of the reasons above (if any) do you resonate most with for not needing one? If none, think about (and write down) what your personal reasons are.

Activity 8.4: As you read the descriptions of each *negative* role below, write down which roles some of the people around you embody, and think of what actions you can take to reduce their negative influence. More importantly, write down which roles *you* might have a tendency to play. Simply becoming aware of this can help you to address it and mitigate the negative effect you might have on others around you.

Activity 8.5: When reading the descriptions of each *positive* role below, write down which ones fit you most naturally, and which you would like to become better at. Think about who you can choose to play each role in your ME Support Group.

<u>Appendix 2: Motivational Fire - The Intention Sheet</u>

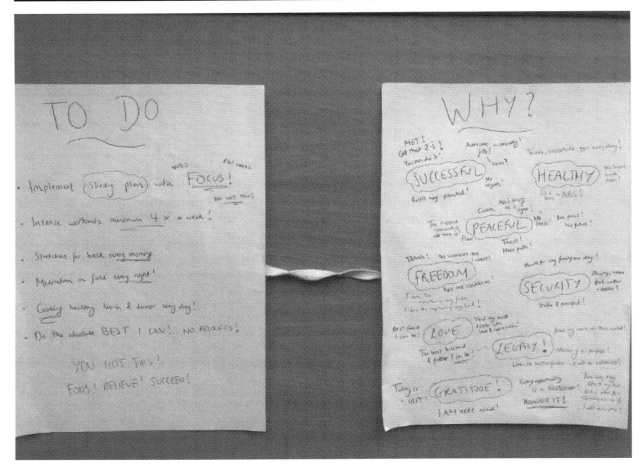

I created these two sheets during my 3rd year of Cambridge. I pinned them to the noticeboard above my desk, so that I could always look up and remember *why* I was doing the things on my '*To Do*' sheet.

In the context of the **Motivational Fire Formula**, this allowed me to focus the *heat* (Intention) needed to ignite my Motivational Fire.

In case the image is too small to read, I've written down my exact words below. Please forgive them if they're cryptic, or if they sound silly to you! I didn't intend for these words to be seen by *anyone*!

The first sheet is titled '**To Do**'. I've written 6 points below it:

1. Implement study plan with FOCUS (around this, I wrote 'notes', 'past papers' and 'you got this!').
2. Intense workouts minimum 4x a week.
3. Stretches for back every morning.
4. Meditation on field every night.
5. Cooking healthy lunch & dinner every day.
6. Do the absolute best I can! No regrets!

Below this, I wrote a short motivational message to myself: "You got this! Focus! Believe! Succeed!"

This sheet highlighted *what* I needed to be doing every single day in order to attain my goals.

My second sheet is my '*Why'* sheet. It contains all of the *values* driving me and what those words mean to me as an individual. I wrote down the values first in large writing. Around them, I wrote what fulfilling those values meant to me – in other words, I wrote down my *rules*.

On this sheet, I personally wrote:

- **SUCCESSFUL:**
    - MET! Get that 2.1! You can do it!
        - (Manufacturing Engineering Tripos, the name of my 3rd year Cambridge course)
    - Awesome job! Consulting? Coaching?
    - Fulfil my potential! No regrets!

- **HEALTHY:**
    - Tennis, basketball, gym every day!
    - No more back pain!
    - Fit + lean = ABS!

- **PEACEFUL:**
    - The present moment is all there is! Flow!
    - All is passing as right! Calm!
    - No past! No future! No stress!
    - Trust! Have faith!

- **FREEDOM:**
    - Travel!
    - Do whatever job I want!
    - No one controls me!
    - I am the master of my fate! I am the captain of my soul!

- **SECURITY:**
    - Provide for my family one day!
    - Always have food, water, shelter!
    - Stable & peaceful!

- **LOVE:**
    - Treat my parents and sister with love and appreciation!
    - Best friend I can be!
    - The best husband and father I can be!

- **LEGACY:**
    - Leave my mark on this world!
    - Meaning + Purpose!
    - When the lustre fades…I will be LEGEND!
        - A reference to a song called 'When The Lustre Fades' by Substantial.

- **GRATITUDE:**
  - Today is a GIFT!
  - Every opportunity is a BLESSING! HONOUR IT!
  - I AM HERE NOW!
  - Live every day like it's my last, but I plan for tomorrow as if I will never pass!
    - A reference to a song called 'Own Appeal' by Oddisee.

Let me clarify – at this stage, I hadn't heard of *values* or *rules* for fulfilling our values. All I wanted to write down was *why* I wanted to achieve my goals – in other words, *why* I was willing to carry out the actions on my *to-do* sheet every single day.

I attached a shoelace between the *'to-do'* sheet and the *'why'* sheet to form my *Intention Sheet*. The shoelace acted as a way for me to *visualise* the strand connecting what I was doing with why I was doing it.

Note that the *Intention Sheet* doesn't explicitly include the *realisation* component of the fire. In other words, it doesn't explain *how* to create my study plan, do my workouts, perform my back stretches, meditate and cook.

By this stage, I had already created my study plan and collected the knowledge needed for my workouts, back stretches, meditation practice and cooking. I already believed that my goals were realistic and within my potential to achieve. My *realisation* was already strong at this stage.

If this isn't the case for you, it may be worth creating a *Realisation Sheet* to make notes on *how* you are going to carry out each component on your *Intention Sheet*.

I hope that you find a way to adapt the idea of the Intention Sheet for your own purposes. It was a true game-changer for me.

Appendix 3: Kam's 'Efficient Study Training' Circuit

During my fourth and final year (my Master's degree year) at Cambridge, I combined two of my passions (fitness and personal training) and began running time-efficient, group fitness sessions for busy university students. These involved a series of bodyweight exercises being carried out as a 'circuit'.

"Wait a second, I'm new to all of this. What *is* a circuit?"

A circuit workout follows these steps:

- Exercise for a defined time period.
- Rest for a defined time period.
- Repeat the above for each exercise in the circuit, until all exercises are done.
- Take a longer rest.
- Begin the next circuit/ repeat the same circuit again…

"Okay, that makes sense. So, what's so special about these bodyweight circuits?"

Aside from providing all the benefits of physical activity outlined in <u>Principle 5</u>, bodyweight circuits are especially effective because:

1. They are perfect for anyone of any fitness level. You just need to push yourself to the best of *your* ability over the defined time period. The difficulty level of each exercise can also be modified to suit your current fitness and strength levels.

2. No gym membership or equipment is required. All you need is enough space to lie flat on your stomach and jump!

3. Easy to get your friends involved and train together as a group.

4. Bursts of intense exercise over a short duration of time (rarely more than 25 minutes) elevate your heart rate and leave you feeling energised and focused.

5. You don't need to waste time thinking about what exercise to do next and how long you need to do it for – all you need is a stopwatch and printout of the exercises.

6. Circuits help to build a good foundation of both strength and cardiovascular fitness. A well-constructed circuit works most major muscle groups of the body, as well as developing both your aerobic and anaerobic capacity.

7. When carried out at a moderate-to-high intensity, circuits are *efficient* with respect to the number of calories burned per minute spent exercising – great if you're trying to avoid putting on body fat during exams!

8. Easy to gauge your own progress. In just a few weeks, you'll notice that you can do more repetitions of each exercise within the defined time. You'll also notice yourself feeling stronger, less tired and more energised once the circuit is finished.

"Oh, wow! That sounds pretty awesome. Are there any negatives to it?"

No more than any other form of physical activity.

You'll probably feel sweaty and out-of-breath when it's done. But by the time you catch your breath and take a shower, you'll feel even more energised than before.

It can also be difficult to motivate yourself to push yourself during the workouts – we all have some days where we just don't feel our best! At these times, just remember that *any* physical activity is *better* than *no* physical activity! Even carrying out a circuit at low intensity is better than not doing it at all.

Aside from that, some bodyweight exercises are considered to be 'high-impact exercises' which exert greater force on your body. It may be worth consulting a physician or doctor if you have had prior (or current) injuries, joint problems or other health conditions.

"Alright, it sounds a bit intense…but I think I'm ready to give it a shot. What bodyweight exercises are involved in these circuit routines?"

There are 8 different bodyweight exercises used in my circuits, each of which has 4 difficulty levels:

- Beginner (A)
- Intermediate (B)
- Advanced (C)
- Insane (D)

All of the exercises are written down below. Please check my YouTube video for instructions on each exercise, and to ensure that the exercises are being carried out with the correct form. You can view it on YouTube by searching 'Bodyweight Exercise Circuit Workouts – Kam Taj'.

1. **Running:**

    A. Jogging (on-the-spot)
    B. Sprints (on-the-spot)
    C. Heel-flicks (on-the-spot)
    D. High-knee sprints (on-the-spot)

2. **Push-Ups:**

    A. Push-up (with knees and toes on the ground)
    B. Push-up (with only knees on the ground)
    C. Push-up (standard)
    D. Clapping Push-up (or any other challenging push-up variation)

3. **Squats:**

    A. Squat (thighs parallel to the ground)
    B. Deep Squat (thighs below parallel)
    C. Squat Jacks
    D. Squat Jumps

4. **Mountain Climbers:**

    A. Mountain Climbers
    B. Mountain Climbers (with leg to opposite elbow)

    C. In & Out Jumps (central)

    D. In & Out Jumps (central-left-right)

5. **Burpees:**

    A. Beginner Burpee (one leg at a time, no jump)

    B. Intermediate Burpee (no jump)

    C. Burpee (standard)

    D. Burpee (with star jump, or single-leg alternating)

6. **Lunges:**

    A. Forward Lunges (alternate legs)

    B. Reverse Lunges (alternate legs)

    C. Side Lunges (alternate legs)

    D. Split Lunge Jumps

7. **Plank:**

    A. Plank (standard)

    B. Plank (with alternating leg & arm raise)

    C. Plank (with 'Spiderman-legs')

    D. Plank-to-push-up

8. **Floor Core:**

    A. Sit-up

    B. Sit-up (elbow-to-opposite leg)

    C. 'Crunchy Frog'

    D. 'Crunchy Frog' (with rotation)

"Awesome! Just checked out the YouTube video (and subscribed!) – I think I'm finally ready to do these exercises as a circuit! What are the circuits that you've created?"

Each of my circuits is 4 minutes long. There are 2 time-patterns to follow:

1. **'Tabata' format:** 20-seconds exercise, 10-seconds rest (8 exercises total)
2. **'Beast' format:** 40-seconds exercise, 20-seconds rest (4 exercises total)

Once the circuit is complete, rest for 1 minute. Repeat the circuit for the desired time-duration – for example, 4 circuits will take a total of 20 minutes (4 x 4-minute circuits, 4 x 1-minute rests).

I also recommend doing some light jogging and dynamic stretching for at least 1 minute to warm-up *and* cool-down.

Kam's Morning Energiser Circuit

I like to start my day with a 4-minute Tabata as soon as I wake up. I start with a 1-minute light warm-up, and then pick my 4 favourite exercises of the 8 listed above. In my case, that includes push-ups (2), squat jumps (3), burpees (5) and the Spiderman plank (7). Over 4 minutes, I repeat them in this order: 23572357.

You can do the same using your 4 favourite exercises, or using all 8 different exercises. You can even change the exercises each day, for example doing 12341234 on Mondays and 56785678 on Tuesdays.

Kam's Tabata Booster Circuit

I use my Tabata Booster when I want to elevate my heart rate, break a sweat and de-stress, but don't have time for a full workout. After a quick warm-up, I do 4 Tabata circuits (20 minutes in total, including rests):

- Tabata 1: 12341234
- Tabata 2: 56785678
- Tabata 3: 12341234
- Tabata 4: 56785678

I've chosen the order of exercises quite carefully. For example, I avoid putting push-ups (2) and mountain climbers (4) together as I find it fatiguing on my shoulders. I also avoid putting squat jumps (3) and split lunge jumps (6) together as they're both very taxing on the quadriceps (thigh). On the other hand, I intentionally put the plank (7) and floor core (8) exercises together to really hit the abdominal muscles. They're also slightly less intense than burpees (5) and split lunge jumps (6), allowing me to catch my breath!

Play around with the order and see what works best for you. If 20 minutes feels like too long, start with just 10 minutes (2 Tabata Circuits).

Kam's Beast Burner Circuit

The 20-second exercise, 10-second rest format of Tabata circuits allows for a short recovery after each exercise. If I'm feeling particularly energetic or in need of something more challenging, I switch to the 40-second exercise, 20-second rest format, with a 1-minute rest at the end of each 4-minute circuit. After a 1-minute warm-up, my 20-minute workout includes:

- Beast 1: 1234
- Beast 2: 5678
- Beast 3: 1234
- Beast 4: 5678

Sustaining an exercise with good form over double the time is a sure way to challenge yourself and gauge your fitness levels. Give it a go once you're comfortable with the Tabata Booster workout.

"Wow! I'll definitely create a short energising workout for myself in the morning. Maybe I'll do my first 10-minute Tabata Booster on Wednesday. Actually, how often should we do these workouts?"

How often you do these workouts depends on three main factors:

1. **Your current fitness level** – if you're not used to physical activity, these workouts can be fatiguing. A single, energising 4-minute circuit can be done every day at low intensity. For the Tabata Booster, start with once or twice a week. Write it down in your planner and create a *habit* of doing the workout.

2. **The amount of physical activity in your routine** – if you're playing sport or going to the gym 3-4 times a week, then the Tabata Booster is by no means necessary. It's still worth getting into a habit of doing a single 4-minute Tabata circuit in the morning just to boost your energy.

3. **The *intensity* with which you do these circuits** – if you're working to your maximum ability, try not to do the Tabata Booster more than 4 times a week. High intensity exercise can be taxing on the central nervous system (CNS), which takes up to 48 hours to recover. For the 4-minute Morning Energiser, alternate between higher and lower intensity days. Remember – *any* physical activity is *better* than *no* physical activity, but *too much* physical activity can be harmful too!

All done! A couple of awesome circuits to boost your energy, improve your fitness and put you on the path towards Exam Success.

If you have any questions about these workouts, please don't hesitate to contact me. Message me on Facebook or Instagram (@kamtajcoaching) or email me at contact@kamtaj.com.

PS: If you're finding it annoying to constantly check the stopwatch during your Tabata circuits, check out 'TabataSongs.com'. They make songs that tell you exactly when to start and stop exercising – Tabata Electric Guitar and Tabata Success Stories are two of my favourites!

Appendix 4: Glycaemic Load of Common Foods

To understand the effect a food has on blood sugar, we need to understand how quickly the food causes an increase in blood glucose, and how much it increases it by.

The glycaemic index (GI) of a food is a number that indicates the effect a food has on a person's blood glucose levels after 2 hours of consuming the food. Foods low on the glycaemic index (GI) scale tend to release glucose slowly and steadily. Foods high on the glycaemic index release glucose rapidly.

The glycaemic index range is defined as follows:

- High GI – 70 or more
- Medium GI – 56 to 69
- Low GI – 55 or below

However, for the purposes of Exam Success, we need to identify which foods are most likely to increase blood glucose in larger quantities, and are therefore more likely to lead to a sugar crash as the glucose is taken up by bodily cells. This means we need to account for *how much* food is actually being consumed at any one time.

This is done by taking the Glycaemic Index (GI) value of any carbohydrate-containing food, multiplying it by the grams of carbohydrate per standard serving of the food, and then dividing it by 100. This gives us the Glycaemic Load (GL) of the food.

The glycaemic load range is defined as follows:

- High GL – 20 or more
- Medium GL – 11 to 19
- Low GL – 0 to 10

Below are a list of common foods and their GL per serving, taken from a 2015 article published in Harvard Health Publications, containing data from the December 2008 issue of Diabetes Care, Vol. 31.

Beans & Nuts	Glycaemic Index (Pure Glucose = 100)	Serving Size (grams)	Glycaemic Load per Serving
Baked beans	40	150	6
Black-eyed peas	50	150	15
Black beans	30	150	7
Chickpeas, canned in brine	42	150	9
Kidney beans, average	34	150	9
Lentils	28	150	5
Soy beans, average	15	150	1
Cashews, salted	22	50	3
Peanuts	13	50	1

Vegetables	Glycaemic Index (Pure Glucose = 100)	Serving Size (grams)	Glycaemic Load per Serving
Green peas	54	80	4
Carrots, average	39	80	2
Parsnips	52	80	4
Boiled white potato	82	150	21
Boiled sweet potato	46	150	11

Fruits	Glycaemic Index (Pure Glucose = 100)	Serving Size (grams)	Glycaemic Load per Serving
Apple, average	36	120	5
Banana, raw, average	48	120	11
Dates, dried, average	42	60	18
Grapefruit	25	120	3
Grapes, black	59	120	11
Oranges, raw, average	45	120	5
Peach, average	42	120	5
Peach (canned in syrup)	52	120	9
Pear, raw, average	38	120	4
Pear (canned in pear juice)	44	120	5
Prunes, pitted	29	60	10
Raisins	64	60	28
Watermelon	72	120	4

Pasta & Noodles	Glycaemic Index (Pure Glucose = 100)	Serving Size (grams)	Glycaemic Load per Serving
Fettuccini	32	180	15
Macaroni, average	50	180	24
Spaghetti (white), boiled, average	46	180	22
Spaghetti, whole-grain, boiled	42	180	17

Bakery Products & Breads	Glycaemic Index (Pure Glucose = 100)	Serving Size (grams)	Glycaemic Load per Serving
Sponge cake, plain	46	63	17
Bagel, white, frozen	72	70	25
Baguette, white, plain	95	30	14
Hamburger bun	61	30	9
White wheat flour bread, average	75	30	11
Whole wheat bread, average	69	30	9
Pita bread, white	68	30	10
Corn tortilla	52	50	12
Wheat tortilla	30	50	8

Grains	Glycaemic Index (Pure Glucose = 100)	Serving Size (grams)	Glycaemic Load per Serving
Sweet corn on the cob	48	60	14
Couscous	65	150	9
Quinoa	53	150	13
White rice, boiled	72	150	29
Quick cooking white basmati rice	63	150	26
Brown rice, steamed	50	150	16

Snack Foods	Glycaemic Index (Pure Glucose = 100)	Serving Size (grams)	Glycaemic Load per Serving
Corn chips, plain, salted	42	50	11
M&M's (peanut)	33	30	6
Microwave popcorn, plain, average	65	20	7
Potato chips, average	56	50	12
Snickers Bar (average)	51	60	18
Hummus	6	30	0
Honey (average)	61	25	12
Chicken Nuggets (frozen, reheated)	46	100	7
Pizza (plain baked dough, with tomato sauce)	80	100	22

Dairy Products And Alternatives	Glycaemic Index (Pure Glucose = 100)	Serving Size (grams)	Glycaemic Load per Serving
Milk, full-fat, average	31	250mL	4
Milk, skim, average	31	250mL	4
Ice Cream, regular, average	62	50	8
Reduced-fat yogurt with fruit, average	33	200	11

Breakfast Cereals And Related Products	Glycaemic Index (Pure Glucose = 100)	Serving Size (grams)	Glycaemic Load per Serving
Muesli, average	56	30	10
Oatmeal, average	55	250	13
Instant oatmeal,	79	250	21
Puffed wheat cereal	80	30	17
Cornflakes, average	81	30	20
Coco Pops, average	77	30	20
All-Bran, average	44	30	9
Special K (US Formula)	69	30	14

Beverages	Glycaemic Index (Pure Glucose = 100)	Serving Size (grams)	Glycaemic Load per Serving
Coca Cola, US Formula	63	250mL	16
Fanta (Orange)	68	250mL	23
Lucozade (Original)	95	250mL	40
Gatorade (Orange, US Formula)	89	250mL	13
Apple Juice, unsweetened	41	250mL	12
Cranberry Juice (Ocean Spray)	68	250mL	24
Orange Juice (unsweetened, average)	50	250mL	12
Tomato juice, canned, no sugar	38	250mL	4

References

Principle 1:

1. Wahl, M.J.A; Pychyl, T.A; Bennett, S.H. (2010). *I forgive myself, now I can study: How self-forgiveness for procrastinating can reduce future procrastination.* Available: https://www.sciencedirect.com/science/article/pii/S0191886910000474. Last accessed 22/05/2018.

2. Rubinstein, J. S., Meyer, D. E. & Evans, J. E. (2001). Executive Control of Cognitive Processes in Task Switching. *Journal of Experimental Psychology: Human Perception and Performance, 27*, 763-797.

3. Uncapher, M.R; Thieu, M.K; Wagner, A.D. (2015). *Media multitasking and memory: Differences in working memory and long-term memory.* Available: https://link.springer.com/article/10.3758%2Fs13423-015-0907-3. Last accessed 22/05/2018.

4. Cszikszentmihaly, M. (1990). *Flow: The Psychology Of Optimal Experience.* Available: https://www.researchgate.net/publication/224927532_Flow_The_Psychology_of_Optimal_Experience. Last accessed 22/05/2018.

5. Morin, A. (2017). *Want to Stop Procrastinating? Try the 10-Minute Rule and Get More Done.* Available: https://www.inc.com/amy-morin/want-to-stop-procrastinating-try-the-10-minute-rule.html. Last accessed 22/05/2018.

6. Wallner, E. (2016). *THE 80–20 RULE APPLIED TO LEARNING.* Available: http://www.edukwest.com/80-20-rule-learning/. Last accessed 22/05/2018.

7. Lally et al. (2009). *How are habits formed: Modelling habit formation in the real world.* Available: https://onlinelibrary.wiley.com/doi/abs/10.1002/ejsp.674. Last accessed 22/05/2018.

Principle 2:

1. Pashler, H., McDaniel, M., Rohrer, D., & Bjork, R. (2008). Learning styles concepts and evidence. *Psychological Science in the Public Interest, 9.*

2. Massa, L & Mayer, R. (2006). *Testing the ATI hypothesis: Should multimedia instruction accommodate verbalizer-visualizer cognitive style?.* Available: http://www.sciencedirect.com/science/article/pii/S1041608006000331. Last accessed 24th Jun 2017.

3. Cassidy, S. (2004). *Leaning Styles: An overview of theories, models and measures.* Available: http://www.acdowd-designs.com/sfsu_860_11/LS_OverView.pdf. Last accessed 24th Jun 2017.

4. An, D., & Carr, M., Learning styles theory fails to explain learning and achievement: Recommendations for alternative approaches. *Personality and Individual Differences* (2017), Available: http://dx.doi.org/10.1016/j.paid.2017.04.050. Last accessed 21st May 2017

5. Meyer, R. E., & Anderson, R. B. (1992). The instructive animation: Helping students build connections between words and pictures in multimedia learning. *Journal of Educational Psychology, 4.*

6. Mangen, A & Velay, J. (2010). *Digitizing Literacy: Reflections on the Haptics of Writing.* Available: https://www.intechopen.com/books/advances-in-haptics/digitizing-literacy-reflections-on-the-haptics-of-writing. Last accessed 24th Jun 2017.

7. Mueller, P & Oppenheimer, D. (2014). *The Pen Is Mightier Than The Keyboard: Advantages of Longhand Over Laptop Note Taking.* Available: http://journals.sagepub.com/doi/abs/10.1177/0956797614524581. Last accessed 24th Jun 2017.

8. Cirillo Company. (.). *Pomodoro Technique.* Available: http://cirillocompany.de/pages/pomodoro-technique. Last accessed 22nd Dec 2016.

9. Chen et al. (2017). *Strategic Resource Use for Learning: A Self-Administered Intervention That Guides Self-Reflection on Effective Resource Use Enhances Academic Performance.* Available: http://journals.sagepub.com/doi/10.1177/0956797617696456. Last accessed 24th Jun 2017.

10. Larsen et al. (2013). *Comparative effects of test-enhanced learning and self-explanation on long-term retention..* Available: https://www.ncbi.nlm.nih.gov/pubmed/23746156. Last accessed 22nd Dec 2016.

11. Cepeda et al. (2006). *Distributed Practice in Verbal Recall Tasks: A Review and Quantitative Synthesis.* Available: http://www.evullab.org/pdf/CepedaPashlerVulWixtedRohrer-PB-2006.pdf. Last accessed 22nd Dec 2016.

12. Taylor & Rohrer. (2010). *The Effects of Interleaved Practice.* Available: http://uweb.cas.usf.edu/~drohrer/pdfs/Taylor&Rohrer2010ACP.pdf. Last accessed 22nd Dec 2016.

13. AcademicTips. (.). *Association, Imagination & Location.* Available: http://www.academictips.org/memory/assimloc.html. Last accessed 22nd Dec 2016.

14. Dolegui. (2013). *The Impact of Listening to Music on Cognitive Performance.* Available: http://www.inquiriesjournal.com/articles/762/2/the-impact-of-listening-to-music-on-cognitive-performance. Last accessed 22nd Dec 2016.

Principle 3:

1.   WebMD. (-). *Anxiety & Panic Disorders Health Center.* Available: http://www.webmd.com/anxiety-panic/. Last accessed 2nd Jan 2017.

2.   Kramer, A.D.I; Guillory, J.E; Hancock, J.T. (2014). *Experimental evidence of massive-scale emotional contagion through social networks.* Available: http://www.pnas.org/content/111/24/8788. Last accessed 22/05/2018.

3.   Sagioglou, S & Greitemeyer, T. (2014). *Facebook's emotional consequences: Why Facebook causes a decrease in mood and why people still use it.* Available: https://www.sciencedirect.com/science/article/pii/S0747563214001241. Last accessed 22/05/2018.

4.   Parkin, S. (2018). *Has Dopamine Got Us Hooked On Tech?.* Available: https://www.theguardian.com/technology/2018/mar/04/has-dopamine-got-us-hooked-on-tech-facebook-apps-addiction. Last accessed 22/05/2018.

5.   Higgins, ES. (2009). *Do ADHD drugs take a toll on the brain?.* Available: https://www.amphetamines.org/adhd/drugsbrain.html. Last accessed 2nd Jan 2017.

6.   Lieberman et al. (2007). *Putting Feelings Into Words: Affect Labeling Disrupts Amygdala Activity in Response to Affective Stimuli.* Available: http://www.scn.ucla.edu/pdf/AL(2007).pdf. Last accessed 22/05/2018

7.   Harvard Health Publishing. (2011). *Understanding The Stress Response.* Available: https://www.health.harvard.edu/staying-healthy/understanding-the-stress-response. Last accessed 22/05/2018.

8.   Helsen, K. (2013). *OBSERVATIONAL LEARNING AND PAIN-RELATED FEAR.* Available: https://biblio.ugent.be/publication/3258527/file/4336361.pdf. Last accessed 22/05/2018.

9.   Toni-Lee Sterley, Dinara Baimoukhametova, Tamás Füzesi, Agnieszka A. Zurek, Nuria Daviu, Neilen P. Rasiah, David Rosenegger, Jaideep S. Bains. **Social transmission and buffering of synaptic changes after stress.** *Nature Neuroscience,* 2018; DOI: 10.1038/s41593-017-0044-6

10. O'Connor, J. (2001). Chapter 8: Emotional State. In: *The NLP Workbook.* London: Harper Collins. 74-76.

11. Gray, R.M & Liotta, R.F. (2012). *PTSD: Extinction, Reconsolidation, and the Visual-Kinesthetic Dissociation Protocol.* Available: https://www.researchgate.net/profile/Richard_Gray3/publication/258194224_PTSD_Extinction_Reconsolidation_and_the_Visual-Kinesthetic_Dissociation_Protocol/links/00b4952176ada330aa000000.pdf. Last accessed 22/05/2018.

12. O'Connor, J. (2001). Chapter 8: Emotional State. In: *The NLP Workbook.* London: Harper Collins. 79-83.

13. Salleh, M.R. (2008). *Life Event, Stress & Illness.* Available: https://www.ncbi.nlm.nih.gov/pmc/articles/PMC3341916/. Last accessed 22/05/2018.

14. Keller et al. (2012). *Does the Perception that Stress Affects Health Matter? The Association with Health and Mortality.* Available: https://www.ncbi.nlm.nih.gov/pmc/articles/PMC3374921/. Last accessed 22/05/2018.

15. Jamieson, J.P; Nock, M.K; Mendes, W.B. (2012). *Mind over matter: reappraising arousal improves cardiovascular and cognitive responses to stress.* Available: https://www.ncbi.nlm.nih.gov/pubmed/21942377. Last accessed 22/05/2018.

16. Anthony Robbins. (2013). Taking Control - The Master System (Part 2). In: *Re-Awaken The Giant Within*. Robbins Research International. 45-57.

17. Anthony Robbins. (2013). Taking Control - The Master System (Part 2). In: *Re-Awaken The Giant Within*. Robbins Research International. 58-70.

18. Amabile, T & Kramer, S.J. (2011). *The Power Of Small Wins*. Available: https://hbr.org/2011/05/the-power-of-small-wins. Last accessed 22/05/2018.

19. Lally et al. (2009). *How are habits formed: Modelling habit formation in the real world*. Available: https://onlinelibrary.wiley.com/doi/abs/10.1002/ejsp.674. Last accessed 22/05/2018.

20. Hill, A.P & Curran, T. (2015). *Multidimensional Perfectionism and Burnout*. Available: http://journals.sagepub.com/doi/abs/10.1177/1088868315596286?journalCode=psra. Last accessed 22/05/2018.

21. Flaxman and Flook. (2009). *Brief Summary of Mindfulness Research*. Available: http://marc.ucla.edu/workfiles/pdfs/MARC-mindfulness-research-summary.pdf. Last accessed 2nd Jan 2017.

22. Mindful Staff. (2016). *Jon Kabat-Zinn: Defining Mindfulness*. Available: http://www.mindful.org/jon-kabat-zinn-defining-mindfulness/. Last accessed 2nd Jan 2017.

23. Loder V. (2014). *The Power of Vision - What Entrepreneurs Can Learn From Olympic Athletes*. Available: http://www.forbes.com/sites/vanessaloder/2014/07/23/the-power-of-vision-what-entrepreneurs-can-learn-from-olympic-athletes/#5be2a7e7afdf. Last accessed 2nd Jan 2017.

24. V Plessinger, A. (2009). The effects of Mental Imagery on Athletic performance. Research paper at 2027 Washington D.C. The World Bank

Principle 4:

1. Chaddock, Hillman et al. (2010). *Basal ganglia volume is associated with aerobic fitness in preadolescent children*. Available: https://www.ncbi.nlm.nih.gov/pubmed/20693803. Last accessed 2nd Jan 2017.

2. Onyper et al. (2011). *Cognitive Advantages of Chewing Gum*. Available: https://web.stlawu.edu/sites/default/files/resource/Onyper,%20Carr,%20Farrar,%20and%20Floyd%20(2011).pdf. Last accessed 3rd Jan 2017.

3. Russo, M, Santarelli, D & O'Rourke, D. (2017). The Science Of Slow Deep Breathing. Available: https://www.ncbi.nlm.nih.gov/pmc/articles/PMC5709795/. Last accessed 3rd Jan 2017.

4. Eckberg, D. L. (2003). The human respiratory gate. The Journal of Physiology, 548(Pt 2), 339.

Principle 5:

1. Hogan et al. (2013). *Exercise Holds Immediate Benefits for Affect and Cognition in Younger and Older Adults*. Available: https://www.ncbi.nlm.nih.gov/pmc/articles/PMC3768113/. Last accessed 2nd Jan 2015.

2. Van Dongen et al. (2016). *Physical Exercise Performed Four Hours after Learning Improves Memory Retention and Increases Hippocampal Pattern Similarity during Retrieval*. Available: https://www.ncbi.nlm.nih.gov/pubmed/27321998. Last accessed 2nd Jan 2017.

3. Erickson et al. (2010). *Exercise training increases size of hippocampus and improves memory*. Available: http://www.pnas.org/content/108/7/3017.abstract. Last accessed 2nd Jan 2017.

4. Treadway et al. (2012). *Dopaminergic Mechanisms of Individual Differences in Human Effort-Based Decision-Making*. Available: http://www.jneurosci.org/content/32/18/6170. Last accessed 2nd Jan 2017.

5. España et al. (2016). *Norepinephrine at the nexus of arousal, motivation and relapse*. Available: www.sciencedirect.com/science/article/pii/S0006899316000032. Last accessed 2nd Jan 2017.

6.   Weicker & Struder. (2001). *Influence of exercise on serotonergic neuromodulation in the brain.* Available: http://link.springer.com/article/10.1007/s007260170064. Last accessed 2nd Jan 2017.

7.   Stoppler MC. (2014). *Endorphins: Natural Pain and Stress Fighters.* Available: http://www.medicinenet.com/script/main/art.asp?articlekey=55001&page=2. Last accessed 2nd Jan 2017.

8.   Mahoney, S. (2011). *Exercise & Cortisol Levels.* Available: http://www.livestrong.com/article/86687-exercise-cortisol-levels/. Last accessed 2nd Jan 2017.

9.   Chaddock, Hillman et al. (2010). *Basal ganglia volume is associated with aerobic fitness in preadolescent children.* Available: https://www.ncbi.nlm.nih.gov/pubmed/20693803. Last accessed 2nd Jan 2017.

10.   Clark, S. (2015). *High-Intensity Interval Training Is An Effective Fitness Trend, But It is Not For Everyone.* Available: http://www.medicaldaily.com/high-intensity-interval-training-effective-fitness-trend-its-not-everyone-336448. Last accessed 2nd Jan 2017.

Principle 6:

1.   Dhillon et al. (2016). *The Effects of Increased Protein Intake on Fullness: A Meta-Analysis and Its Limitations.* Available: http://www.andjrnl.org/article/S2212-2672(16)00042-3/abstract. Last accessed 3rd Jan 2017.

2.   Maljaars et al. (2009). *Effect of fat saturation on satiety, hormone release, and food intake.* Available: http://ajcn.nutrition.org/content/89/4/1019.full. Last accessed 3rd Jan 2017.

3.   Blundell, J. E. & Burley, V. J. (1987) Satiation, satiety and the action of fibre on food intake. *Int. J. Obes.* 11:9-25.

4.   Major et al. (2008). *Multivitamin and dietary supplements, body weight and appetite: results from a cross-sectional and a randomised double-blind placebo-controlled study..* Available: https://www.ncbi.nlm.nih.gov/pubmed/17977472. Last accessed 3rd Jan 2017.

5.   Hughes, DA. (1999). *Effects of dietary antioxidants on the immune function of middle-aged adults.* Available: https://www.ncbi.nlm.nih.gov/pubmed/10343344. Last accessed 3rd Jan 2017.

6.   Serafini et al. (2010). *Flavonoids as anti-inflammatory agents.* Available: https://www.ncbi.nlm.nih.gov/pubmed/20569521. Last accessed 3rd Jan 2017.

7.   Owen et al. (2008). *The combined effects of L-theanine and caffeine on cognitive performance and mood.* Available: https://tryjubi.com/wp-content/uploads/2016/01/L-theanine-and-caffeine-paper.pdf. Last accessed 3rd Jan 2017.

8.   Evert, D.L., and Oscar-Berman, M. Alcohol-related cognitive impairments: An overview of how alcoholism may affect the workings of the brain. Alcohol Health Res World 19(2):89-96, 1995.

9.   Diet Doctor. (2016). *Low-Carb Side Effects & How To Cure Them.* Available: https://www.dietdoctor.com/low-carb/side-effects. Last accessed 3rd Jan 2017.

10.   (2015) *What Happens When You Overeat.* Available: http://nickyforlife.com/what-happens-when-you-overeat/. Last accessed 3rd Jan 2017.

11.   Afaghi A. (2007). *High-glycemic-index carbohydrate meals shorten sleep onset.* Available: http://ajcn.nutrition.org/content/85/2/426.full. Last accessed 3rd Jan 2017.

12.   Franke et al. (2008). *Postprandial walking but not consumption of alcohol digestifs or espresso accelerates gastric emptying in healthy volunteers.* Available: https://www.ncbi.nlm.nih.gov/pubmed/18392240. Last accessed 3rd Jan 2017.

13.   Armstrong et al. (2012). *Mild dehydration affects mood in healthy young women.* Available: https://www.ncbi.nlm.nih.gov/pubmed/22190027. Last accessed 3rd Jan 2017.

14.   Adan, A. (2012). *Cognitive Performance and Dehydration.* Available: https://www.ncbi.nlm.nih.gov/pubmed/22855911. Last accessed 3rd Jan 2017.

15.   Kempton et al. (2011). *Dehydration affects brain structure and function in healthy adolescents.* Available: https://www.ncbi.nlm.nih.gov/pubmed/20336685. Last accessed 3rd Jan 2017.

16. Popkin et al. (2010). *Water, Hydration and Health.* Available: https://www.ncbi.nlm.nih.gov/pmc/articles/PMC2908954/. Last accessed 3rd Jan 2017.

17. Crain, E. (-). *11 Reasons You are Always Hungry.* Available: http://www.health.com/health/gallery/0,,20920951,00.html#you-re-dehydrated-. Last accessed 3rd Jan 2017.

18. Doheny K. (2016). *The Surprising Link Between Dehydration and Obesity.* Available: http://www.health.com/nutrition/drink-water-stay-slimmer. Last accessed 3rd Jan 2017.

19. Blau et al. (2004). *Water-deprivation headache: a new headache with two variants.* Available: https://www.ncbi.nlm.nih.gov/pubmed/14979888. Last accessed 3rd Jan 2017.

20. Sellgren K. (2012). *Drinking water improves exam grades, research suggests.* Available: http://www.bbc.co.uk/news/education-17741653. Last accessed 3rd Jan 2017.

Principle 7:

1. Ferrie et al. (2011). *Change in Sleep Duration and Cognitive Function: Findings from the Whitehall II Study.* Available: https://www.ncbi.nlm.nih.gov/pmc/articles/PMC3079935/. Last accessed 5th Jan 2017.

2. Alhola and Polo-Kantola. (2007). *Sleep deprivation: Impact on cognitive performance.* Available: https://www.ncbi.nlm.nih.gov/pmc/articles/PMC2656292/. Last accessed 5th Jan 2017..

3. Baert et al. (2014). *On the relationship between sleep quality and academic achievement.* Available: https://papers.ssrn.com/sol3/papers.cfm?abstract_id=2450423. Last accessed 5th Jan 2017.

4. National Sleep Foundation. (/). *Sleep Drive And Your Body Clock.* Available: https://sleepfoundation.org/sleep-topics/sleep-drive-and-your-body-clock. Last accessed 5th Jan 2017.

5. Sleepdex. (/). *Stages of Sleep.* Available: http://www.sleepdex.org/stages.htm. Last accessed 5th Jan 2017.

6. Division of Sleep Medicine, Harvard Medical School. (2007). *Sleep, Learning and Memory.* Available: http://healthysleep.med.harvard.edu/healthy/matters/benefits-of-sleep/learning-memory. Last accessed 5th Jan 2017.

7. National Sleep Foundation. (2015). *National Sleep Foundation Recommends New Sleep Times.* Available: https://sleepfoundation.org/press-release/national-sleep-foundation-recommends-new-sleep-times. Last accessed 5th Jan 2017.

8. Kronholm et al. (2009). *Self-reported sleep duration and cognitive functioning in a general population.* Available: https://www.researchgate.net/publication/26791423_Self-reported_sleep_duration_and_cognitive_functioning_in_a_general_population. Last accessed 5th Jan 2017.

9. Mann D. (2013). Alcohol and a Good Night's Sleep Don't Mix. Available: http://www.webmd.com/sleep-disorders/news/20130118/alcohol-sleep#1. Last accessed 5th Jan 2017.

10. Broomfield & Espie. (2003). *Initial Insomnia And Paradoxical Intention: An Experimental Investigation Of Putative Mechanisms Using Subjective And Actigraphic Measurement Of Sleep.* Available: https://www.cambridge.org/core/journals/behavioural-and-cognitive-psychotherapy/article/div-classtitleinitial-insomnia-and-paradoxical-intention-an-experimental-investigation-of-putative-mechanisms-us. Last accessed 5th Jan 2017.

11. Axe, J. (2016). *Get More Tryptophan for Better Sleep, Moods & Fewer Headaches.* Available: https://draxe.com/tryptophan/. Last accessed 5th Jan 2017.

12. Medical News Today. (2009). *Sleep / Sleep Disorders / Insomnia: Studies Suggest Calcium And Magnesium Effective.* Available: http://www.medicalnewstoday.com/releases/163169.php. Last accessed 5th Jan 2017.

13. Abbasi et al. (2012). *The effect of magnesium supplementation on primary insomnia in elderly: A double-blind placebo-controlled clinical trial..* Available: https://www.ncbi.nlm.nih.gov/pubmed/23853635. Last accessed 5th Jan 2017.

14. Drake et al. (2013). *Caffeine Effects on Sleep Taken 0, 3, or 6 Hours before Going to Bed.* Available: https://www.researchgate.net/publication/26791423_Self-reported_sleep_duration_and_cognitive_functioning_in_a_general_population. Last accessed 5th Jan 2017.

15. Schwartz S. (2015). *15 Science-Backed Ways To Fall Asleep Faster.* Available: http://www.huffingtonpost.com/entry/15-ways-to-fall-asleep-faster_us_55dde3e7e4b04ae497054470. Last accessed 5th Jan 2017.

16. Weil A. (2015). *3 Breathing Exercises.* Available: http://www.drweil.com/health-wellness/body-mind-spirit/stress-anxiety/breathing-three-exercises/. Last accessed 5th Jan 2017.

17. Lipman F. (2010). *Sleep Tips: Top 10 Sleep Mistakes And Their Solutions.* Available: https://www.bewell.com/blog/sleep-tips-top-10-sleep-mistakes-and-their-solutions/. Last accessed 5th Jan 2017.

18. Pinola, M. (2013). *How Long to Nap for the Biggest Brain Benefits.* Available: http://lifehacker.com/how-long-to-nap-for-the-biggest-brain-benefits-1251546669. Last accessed 5th Jan 2017.

19. Lovato & Lack. (2010). *The effects of napping on cognitive functioning.* Available: https://www.ncbi.nlm.nih.gov/pubmed/21075238. Last accessed 5th Jan 2017.

Principle 8: None.

Acknowledgements

To my family and close friends for supporting me on my journey – past, present and future. To the close friends, students and teachers who have helped with the content, proof-reading and final editing of the book. And to my younger self, who desperately wanted a book like this to help him during his struggles and promised that he would write one in the future so that others wouldn't have to suffer those same adversities. I am grateful for each and every one of you.

Thank you for inspiring me.

Kam

About UniAdmissions

UniAdmissions is an educational consultancy that specialises in supporting **applications to Medical School and to Oxbridge**.

Every year, we work with hundreds of applicants and schools across the UK. With over 50 books in press and a team of **500 Expert Tutors**, its easy to see why our students are **three times as likely to get into Oxbridge and Medical School**.

Contact us now to book a one-to-one session with Kam - www.uniadmissions.co.uk

Get in touch with Kam via his website – www.kamtaj.com – or via social media (@kamtajcoaching)

Your Free Book

Thanks for purchasing this Ultimate Guide Book. Readers like you have the power to make or break a book – hopefully you found this one useful and informative. If you have time, *UniAdmissions* would love to hear about your experiences with this book.

As thanks for your time we'll send you another ebook from our Ultimate Guide series absolutely FREE!

How to Redeem Your Free Ebook in 3 Easy Steps

1) Find the book you have either on your Amazon purchase history or your email receipt to help find the book on Amazon.

2) On the product page at the Customer Reviews area, click on 'Write a customer review'

Write your review and post it! Copy the review page or take a screen shot of the review you have left.

3) Head over to www.uniadmissions.co.uk/free-book and select your chosen free ebook! You can choose from:
- ✓ The Ultimate ECAA Guide
- ✓ The Ultimate BMAT Guide
- ✓ The Ultimate UKCAT Guide
- ✓ The Ultimate TSA Guide
- ✓ The Ultimate LNAT Guide
- ✓ The Ultimate NSAA Guide
- ✓ The Ultimate ECAA Guide
- ✓ The Ultimate ENGAA Guide
- ✓ The Ultimate Medical School Personal Statement Guide
- ✓ The Ultimate Medical School Interview Guide
- ✓ The Ultimate Dental School Application Guide
- ✓ The Ultimate HSPSAA Guide
- ✓ The Ultimate Oxbridge Interview Guide
- ✓ The Ultimate UCAS Personal Statement Guide

Your ebook will then be emailed to you – it's as simple as that!

Alternatively, you can buy all the above titles at **www.uniadmissions.co.uk/our-books**

BMAT Online Course

If you're looking to improve your BMAT score in a short space of time, our **BMAT Online Course** is perfect for you. The BMAT Online Course offers all the content of a traditional course in a single easy-to-use online package- available instantly after checkout. The online videos are just like the classroom course, ready to watch and re-watch at home or on the go and all with our expert Oxbridge tuition and advice.

You'll get full access to all of our BMAT resources including:

✓ Copy of our acclaimed book "The Ultimate BMAT Guide"
✓ Full access to extensive BMAT online resources including:
✓ 10 hours of BMAT on-demand lectures
✓ 8 complete mock papers
✓ 800 practice questions
✓ Fully worked solutions for all BMAT past papers since 2003
✓ Ongoing Tutor Support until Test date – never be alone again.

The course is normally £99 but you can get **£ 20 off** by using the code "*UAONLINE20*" at checkout.

https://www.uniadmissions.co.uk/product/bmat-online-course/

£20 VOUCHER:
UAONLINE20

Medical Online Interview Course

If you've got an upcoming interview for medical school but unable to attend our intensive interview course– this is the perfect **Medical Interview Online Course** for you. The Online Course has:

✓ 40 medical interview on-demand videos covering Oxbridge and MMI-style questions.
✓ Copy of the book "The Ultimate Medical Interview Guide."
✓ Over 150 past interview questions and answers.
✓ Ongoing Tutor Support until your interview – never be alone again

The online course is normally £99 but you can get £20 off by using the code *"UAONLINE20"* at checkout.

https://www.uniadmissions.co.uk/product/online-medical-interview-course/

£20 VOUCHER:
UAONLINE20

<u>UKCAT Online Course</u>

If you're looking to improve your UKCAT score in a short space of time, our **UKCAT Online Course** is perfect for you. The UKCAT Online Course offers all the content of a traditional course in a single easy-to-use online package-available instantly after checkout. The online videos are just like the classroom course, ready to watch and re-watch at home or on the go and all with our expert Oxbridge tuition and advice.

You'll get full access to all of our UKCAT resources including:

✓ Copy of our acclaimed book "The Ultimate UKCAT Guide"
✓ Full access to extensive UKCAT online resources including:
✓ 10 hours of UKCAT on-demand lectures
✓ 6 complete mock papers
✓ 1250 practice questions
✓ Fully worked solutions for all UKCAT past papers since 2003
✓ Ongoing Tutor Support until Test date – never be alone again.

The course is normally £99 but you can get **£ 20 off** by using the code "*UAONLINE20*" at checkout.

https://www.uniadmissions.co.uk/product/ukcat-online-course/

£20 VOUCHER:
UAONLINE20

TSA Online Course

If you're looking to improve your TSA score in a short space of time, our **TSA Online Course** is perfect for you. The TSA Online Course offers all the content of a traditional course in a single easy-to-use online package- available instantly after checkout. The online videos are just like the classroom course, ready to watch and re-watch at home or on the go and all with our expert Oxbridge tuition and advice.

You'll get full access to all of our TSA resources including:

✓ Copy of our acclaimed book "The Ultimate TSA Guide"
✓ Full access to extensive TSA online resources including:
✓ 20 hours of TSA on-demand lectures
✓ 6 complete mock papers
✓ 300 practice questions
✓ Fully worked solutions for all TSA past papers since 2008
✓ Ongoing Tutor Support until Test date – never be alone again.

The course is normally £99 but you can get **£ 20 off** by using the code *"UAONLINE20"* at checkout.

https://www.uniadmissions.co.uk/product/tsa-online-course/

£20 VOUCHER: UAONLINE20

NSAA Online Course

If you're looking to improve your NSAA score in a short space of time, our **NSAA Online course** is perfect for you. The NSAA Online Course offers all the content of a traditional course in a single easy-to-use online package – available instantly after checkout. The online videos are just like the classroom course, ready to watch and re-watch at home or on the go and all with our expert Oxbridge tuition and advice.

You'll get full access to all of our NSAA resources including:

- ✓ Copy of our acclaimed book "The Ultimate NSAA Guide"
- ✓ Full access to extensive NSAA online resources including:
- ✓ 2 Full Mock Papers
- ✓ Full worked solutions for all NSAA past papers
- ✓ 600 practice questions
- ✓ 6 hours online on-demand lecture series
- ✓ Ongoing Tutor Support until Test date – never be alone again.

The course is normally £99 but you can get **£ 20 off** by using the code *"UAONLINE20"* at checkout.

https://www.uniadmissions.co.uk/product/nsaa-online-course/

£20 VOUCHER:
UAONLINE20

ECAA Online Course

If you're looking to improve your ECAA score in a short space of time, our **ECAA Online Course** is perfect for you. The ECAA Online Course offers all the content of a traditional course in a single easy-to-use online package- available instantly after checkout. The online videos are just like the classroom course, ready to watch and re-watch at home or on the go and all with our expert Oxbridge tuition and advice.

You'll get full access to all of our ECAA resources including:

✓ Copy of our acclaimed book "The Ultimate ECAA Guide"
✓ Full access to extensive ECAA online resources including:
✓ 2 complete mock papers
✓ 400 practice questions
✓ 5 hours online on-demand lecture series
✓ Past Paper Worked Solutions
✓ Ongoing Tutor Support until Test date – never be alone again.

The course is normally £99 but you can get £20 off by using the code "*UAONLINE20*" at checkout.

https://www.uniadmissions.co.uk/product/ecaa-online-course

ENGAA Online Course

If you're looking to improve your ENGAA score in a short space of time, our **ENGAA Online Course** is perfect for you. The ENGAA Online Course offers all the content of a traditional course in a single easy-to-use online package- available instantly after checkout. The online videos are just like the classroom course, ready to watch and re-watch at home or on the go and all with our expert Oxbridge tuition and advice.

You'll get full access to all of our ENGAA resources including:

- ✓ Copy of our acclaimed book "The Ultimate ENGAA Guide"
- ✓ Full access to extensive ENGAA online resources including:
- ✓ 2 complete mock papers
- ✓ 400 practice questions
- ✓ Fully worked solutions for all ENGAA past papers
- ✓ 4 hours of online on-demand lecture series
- ✓ Ongoing Tutor Support until Test date – never be alone again.

The course is normally £99 but you can get **£ 20 off** by using the code "*UAONLINE20*" at checkout.

https://www.uniadmissions.co.uk/product/engaa-online-course/

£20 VOUCHER:
UAONLINE20

LNAT Online Course

If you're looking to improve your LNAT score in a short space of time, our **LNAT Online Course** is perfect for you. The LNAT Online Course offers all the content of a traditional course in a single easy-to-use online package- available instantly after checkout. The online videos are just like the classroom course, ready to watch and re-watch at home or on the go and all with our expert Oxbridge tuition and advice.

You'll get full access to all our LNAT resources including:

- ✓ Copy of our acclaimed book "The Ultimate LNAT Guide"
- ✓ Full access to extensive LNAT online resources including:
- ✓ 4 complete mock papers
- ✓ 400 practice questions
- ✓ 10 hours Online on-demand lecture series
- ✓ Ongoing Tutor Support until Test date – never be alone again.

The course is normally £99 but you can get **£ 20 off** by using the code "*UAONLINE20*" at checkout.

https://www.uniadmissions.co.uk/product/lnat-online-course/

£20 VOUCHER:

UAONLINE20

Made in the USA
Middletown, DE
03 September 2019